SKILL AND CONSENT

Contemporary Studies in the Labour Process

Edited by
Andrew Sturdy, David Knights
and Hugh Willmott

London and New York

First published 1992
by Routledge
11 New Fetter Lane, London EC4P 4EE

Simultaneously published in the USA and Canada
by Routledge
a division of Routledge, Chapman and Hall, Inc.
29 West 35th Street, New York, NY 10001

Typeset in Garamond by Witwell Ltd, Southport.
Printed and bound in Great Britain by
Biddles Ltd, Guildford and King's Lynn

British Library Cataloguing in Publication Data
A catalogue record for this book is available from the British Library.

ISBN 0-415-08585-3
0-415-08671-X pbk

Library of Congress Cataloging-in-Publication Data
Skill, and consent : contemporary studies in the labour process /
edited by Andrew Sturdy, David Knights, and Hugh Willmott.
p.   cm. — (Organization and eemployment studies series)
Includes bibliographical references and index.
ISBN 0-415-0867-X
1. Industrial relations.   2. Industrial sociology.   3. Personnal
management.   4. Quality of work life.   5. Skilled labor.   6. Labor
discipline.   I. Sturdy, Andrew.   II. Knights, David.
iii. Willmott Hugh.   IV. Series.
HD6961.S55   1992
331—dc20
92-8731
CIP

CONTENTS

CONTENTS

NOTES ON THE
CONTRIBUTORS

Peter Ackers is a Lecturer in the Business School at the University of Loughborough. He has published articles on paternalism, employee involvement and workplace industrial relations and has an interest in labour history and union leadership.

Ava Baron is Professor of Sociology at Rider College in Lawrenceville, New Jersey, USA. She has written on gender and work in printing, sewing and the legal profession and on labour legislation and women's work. She is editor of *Work Engendered: Toward a New History of American Labor* (Cornell University Press, 1991) and is completing her book 'Men's Work and the Woman Question: Gender and Work in the Printing Industry, 1830–1920.'

Jack Baroudi is Associate Professor and Undergraduate Director of Information Systems at New York University's Stern School of Business. His current research interests focus on the careers and management of information systems personnel. Professor Baroudi's articles have appeared in various journals, including *Communications of the ACM, MIS Quarterly,* the *Journal of MIS*, and *OFFICE: Technology and People*. He is currently an associate editor of *MIS Quarterly* and *Management Science*.

John Black is a Principal Lecturer in Industrial Relations and Human Resource Management at Wolverhampton Business School, Wolverhampton Polytechnic. He has published a variety of articles in the area of management strategy. His latest publication, with Peter Ackers, is on Employee Involvement in the US car industry. Currently he is editing a UK–Soviet comparative text on the nature and development of the modern business organization.

David Knights is a Reader in Organizational Analysis in the School of Management at the University of Manchester Institute of Science and Technology. He has conducted research and published in the following areas: industrial relations, equal opportunity, labour process, management strategy, the management of information technology and regulation in financial services. His current research is on Financial Services in the Single European Market and on inter-organizational relations and the use and development of IT. He is co-author of *Managing the Multi-Racial Workforce* and *Managing to Discriminate* and co-editor of a number of books on the labour process.

Mick Marchington is a Senior Lecturer in Employee Relations at the Manchester School of Management, UMIST. He has conducted research on employee participation, workplace industrial relations and the management of employee relations. He is the author of a number of articles and books, including *Changing Patterns of Employee Relations*, and is currently co-editing a series of books on management, work and organizations.

Michael Rosen is a New York City real estate developer, property owner and construction contractor occasionally impersonating a social theoretician and semi-professional academic. Previous to his current work, he was a full-time and thoroughly professional academic and social theoretician occasionally impersonating a stockbroker, ad-man, illicit drug world voyeur and finally, for the money and glory, a real estate industry mogul. His current academic work – written for free – spins in the chaotic interstices of symbolic social constructivism, critical theory and postmodernism.

Ron Sakolsky is on the Government and Public Policy Faculty at Sangamon State University, USA. Recently, he was a Visiting Faculty Member in the Political Economy and Social Change programme at The Evergreen State College. He is currently on the editorial board of the *Workers Democracy* magazine, a member of the editorial collective for *Cultural Democracy* and a national board member of the Alliance for Cultural Democracy.

Andrew Sturdy is a Research Fellow in the School of Management at the University of Manchester, Institute of Science and Technology, and an Honorary Fellow at Bristol Business School, Bristol Polytechnic. His recent research has been on information technology management and consultancy in the financial services sector. He has published a number of articles on gender and new technology and edited a book, *Managing Information Technology in Insurance.*

Alan Warde is Lecturer in Sociology at Lancaster University. His research interests include industrial restructuring, divisions of labour, consumption, urban sociology and political sociology. He has recently published a jointly authored book, P. Bagguley *et al.*, *Restructuring: Place Class and Gender.*

Hugh Wilmott is Senior Lecturer in the School of Management at the University of Manchester Institute of Science and Technology. His recent research has been on the ESRC-funded studies of accounting regulation and the strategic development of the personnel specialism. He has published in a wide range of social science, management and accounting journals, and is co-editor of a number of books on the labour process.

Michael Yarrow is Associate Professor of Sociology at Ithaca College, New York. The major focus of his research has been the labour process in underground mining, the development of the control system for mine labour, and the class/gender consciousness of miners. It is based on field observation and over 200 interviews with more than 100 miners and their family members between 1978 and 1991 in southern West Virginia, western Virginia and Eastern Kentucky. He has written numerous articles on coal miners, technology and the labour process and the civil rights campaign in Mississippi in 1964.

ACKNOWLEDGEMENTS

With the exception of the introduction, all the following chapters were originally presented at the annual UMIST-Aston Labour Process Conferences. The contributions by Baron and Warde were subsequently published elsewhere and are reproduced here in a revised form with the kind permission of The University of Michigan Press, Ann Arbor, Michigan and The British Sociological Association, London respectively.

INTRODUCTION
Skill and consent in the labour process
Andrew Sturdy, David Knights and Hugh Willmott

This volume is one of a series bringing together papers originally delivered at the annual UMIST-Aston Labour Process conferences. Previous collections have explored a variety of themes within the labour process debate, such as the redesign of jobs, the positions of women and non-manual labour, the use of new technology and the development of labour process theory (Knights *et al.*, 1985; Knights and Willmott, 1986a; 1986b; 1987; 1990; Smith *et al.*, 1991). This volume focuses on the analytically distinct concepts of skill and consent in the labour process. Through a range of commentaries reflecting the development and diversity of contemporary labour process literature, it highlights the interrelationship between skill and consent and their historical and social construction in capitalist societies.

Ever since its revival in Braverman's (1974) *Labour and Monopoly Capital*, labour process theory has been characterized as being concerned principally with the progressive erosion of workers' skills through management control, and with the resistance of labour to such deskilling (Wood, 1982). Yet the exercise of *skill* and labour's cooperation or *consent* in the production of surplus value are central and continuing features of labour processes (Burawoy, 1979; Littler, 1982). Labour cooperation and the deployment of new or tacit skills, for example, are as much a condition of the reproduction of capital (Burawoy, 1979; Cressey and MacInnes, 1980; Manwaring and Wood, 1985) as of any collective resistance to the demands of management. Equally, managerial skill and cooperation cannot be ignored in an analysis of the labour process (Knights and Willmott, 1986b).

Moreover, skill and consent are integrally related to issues of gender and subjectivity in the labour process (Phillips and Taylor, 1980; Pollert, 1981; Cockburn, 1983; Knights, 1990; Willmott, 1990) and to a broader politics of production (Strinati, 1990; Burawoy, 1985;

1

Thompson, 1990). Finally, skill and consent have become important in the critical interpenetration between labour process analysis and the apparently countervailing paradigm associated with flexible specialization (Wood, 1989; Thompson, 1989; Pollert, 1988). The latter is characterized as portraying the development of a polyvalent or multiskilled (cf. deskilled) workforce and collaborative employee relations (cf. worker resistance).

This introductory chapter is divided into four sections. Firstly, we seek to clarify the concepts of skill and consent. Secondly, their interrelationship is elaborated by selectively exploring theoretical developments in contemporary labour process literature. This theme is continued in the third section, where issues of gender relations and subjectivity are addressed in an attempt to account for workers' use of skill and consent in exercising control. Finally, resumés of the remaining chapters are provided, indicating their contributions to continuing debates.

SKILL AND CONSENT

The transformation of the raw materials of nature into useful products was, for Marx, a creative process. Under the capitalist labour system, however, the creative skill of labour is subjected to, and often degraded by, the demand to secure the private accumulation of surplus value (Marx, 1976:293). However, Marx also recognized the tension generated by the need to deskill (cheapen) labour, on the one hand, and the demand for multiskilled and flexible workers (1976: 618, quoted in Littler, 1982), on the other. But in predicting that the homogenization and socialization (i.e. interdependence) of labour would contribute to the development of revolutionary class conscious-ness, resulting in the overthrow of the capitalist system, Marx underestimated the degree to which the tension between deskilling and flexibility could be managed.

Consent

As Burawoy has shown, opportunities for maximizing bonuses, or 'making-out', as the workforce labelled it, can provide workers with an adaption to, or mental escape from, the deprivation of monotonous work (1979:224). Not only are capitalist production relations actively reproduced, but, as workers get 'lost' in the 'game', hierarchical conflict is diffused. It is either laterally diverted in competition and conflict with fellow workers, expressed within the rules of the game, or tolerated by management in return for overall worker consent (cf.Gouldner, 1954).[1]

Burawoy's notion of consent has been subjected to some critical questioning (see Thompson, 1983; Knights and Collinson, 1985; Joyce, 1987; Littler 1982 and 1990; Edwards, 1990). Concern has been expressed about the level of agreement or acceptance of rules implied by the term. Given that income can only be enhanced through achieving bonus output targets, it has been argued that compliance might be a more appropriate concept (Knights and Collinson, 1985; Thompson, 1983). Edwards, for example, suggests that Burawoy overemphasizes the necessity for there to be an element of active consent or 'choice' beyond compliance to 'formal' rules (e.g. bonus schemes) to secure surplus value. Nevertheless, a problem remains as to what consent should be taken to include. For example, does the term incorporate all forms of cooperation ? Careerism could be related to compliance in a generic sense (Etzioni, 1975), in that the internal labour market is a definite means of securing self-discipline and control. By contrast, where workers are indifferent and distance themselves mentally from their work activities (Palm, 1977; Sennett and Cobb, 1973; Knights and Roberts, 1982), their relation to management control is more clearly a form of compliance. But this form of compliance may, through adaptation, develop into acceptance (Thompson, 1989). Equally, does consent refer to all forms of adaptation, such as those where there is an avoidance of work effort rather than an apparent commitment to it? Overall, as Edwards notes, 'consent. . .cannot be reduced to a single measure. The analytical task is to explore its nature and constituent parts' (1990:141). This is equally the case, if not more so, with the concept of skill, to which we now turn.

Skill

Skill is one of the most frequently debated issues in labour process literature (e.g. Cutler, 1978; Zimbalist, 1979; Wood, 1982; 1989; Cockburn, 1983; Knights et al, 1985). Skill is often conceptually divided into objective (technical) and subjective (social) components, although the distinction is by no means straight forward (Rolfe, 1985). The objective view is more closely related to the commonsense approach of neoclassical economists and psychologists, who measure skill as an acquired capability, property or capital resource possessed by individuals. In contrast, the identification of 'subjective', 'tacit' (Manwaring and Wood, 1985) or 'gendered' (Davis and Rosser, 1986) skills indicates a problem with the 'objective' conception of skill. Many skills may be realizable or 'objective' yet remain indeterminate and/or unacknowledged, since they are acquired through the process of job or life experience. They typically pass unrecognized and unrewarded, yet they are of vital importance, exposing the limits of direct management control and highlighting the irremediable dependence of capital upon labour (Cressey and MacInnes, 1980).

It is useful to distinguish between two forms of a social construction theory of skill (Littler, 1982:9–10). The 'strong' version holds that the skill label does not depend on job content but on the control of supply through employers' or workers' entry barriers. In the 'weak' form, most jobs have significant skill but this is recognized and rewarded as 'skilled' only to the extent of the capacity of workers to define it as skill – a capacity which is derived from their 'strategic position in the production process' and collective organization (1982:9–10). It is clear, then, that skill cannot be treated simply as an objective set of human capabilities. Rather, the reality of skill is socially constructed and contested by capital and labour and by men and women. As with the concept of consent, a concrete, invariant definition is neither useful nor possible. We now situate a discussion of skill and consent in labour process literature, firstly in relation to the structure of capitalist relations of production and secondly, to gender and subjectivity.

SKILL AND CONSENT - INTERCONNECTIONS AND THEORETICAL DEVELOPMENTS

As noted earlier, Braverman's deskilling thesis has been the focus of sustained criticism, documented at length elsewhere (Wood, 1982 and 1989; Attewell, 1987; Knights and Willmott, 1990; Thompson, 1989). Criticisms range from the presentation of particularistic (firm, sector and culture) and broad countervailing evidence, to accounts of constraining, intervening and counter tendencies to deskilling. Critics have also drawn attention to factors which condition processes of (de)skilling, such as labour markets, product markets and other mechanisms in the circuit of capital through which profit is realized (Kelly, 1985).[2] In *The Nature of Work* (1989), Thompson concludes that unqualified reference to deskilling as the major tendency in the development of the capitalist labour process is now untenable. Rather, 'a more adequate analysis has to specify the conditions under which deskilling or *other* means of securing surplus value are likely to be the strategy or outcome' (1989:218, original emphasis; cf.1983:118).

Braverman has also been criticized for the, albeit intentional, neglect of worker consciousness and action (1974:27), of resistance (Friedman, 1977; Edwards, 1979; Zimbalist, 1979) and what Burawoy termed the 'manufacture of consent' (1979; 1981). In fact, Braverman specifically addresses the issue of the 'habituation' of the worker to subordination, but theorizes it in terms of economic dependence or compliance (1974:chapter 6) which grows out of 'the destruction of all other ways of living' (ibid:151). There is no place for active incorporation of the kind described by Burawoy (1979), where consent is produced through interdependence, or by rendering power invisible to workers and incorporating them into the company. In criticizing Braverman's account of deskilling, Buroway notes how he:

> missed the equally important parallel tendency toward the expansion of choices within those ever narrower limits [of discretion]. It is [this]. . .that constitutes a basis of consent and allows the degradation of work to pursue its course without continuing crisis.
>
> (1979:94)

Like Edwards (1979), Burawoy suggests a historical trend towards internalized or invisible control – hegemony in the factory through job enrichment and rotation schemes, for example (1979:94). These forms of 'delegated' (Katz, 1968) 'controlled' (Coriot, 1980) or 'responsible' (Friedman, 1977) automony 'represent managements' attempts to invade the spaces workers created under the preexisting regime and mobilize consent for increased productivity', (Burawoy, 1983:603, quoted in Littler, 1990; see also Rosen and Baroudi, and Sakolsky in this volume).

The impact of Friedman's work on the labour process debate rests principally on his explicit recognition that surplus value need *not* be secured through a strategy of 'direct control' and deskilling. Under monopoly capitalism especially, other labour control strategies may be chosen that are conditioned both by labour resistance and product and labour market competition. In particular, he distinguishes strategies of 'responsible autonomy' from those of 'direct control' (Friedman, 1977, cf. 1990). The deskilling, machine-pacing and/or strict hierarchical supervision of direct control is associated with labour compliance and resistance. By contrast, responsible autonomy

5

is associated with worker consent, achieved through the provision of maintenance of greater levels of individual job discretion (control) and responsibility and related means of eliciting workers' identification with their organization (e.g. through career hierarchies and job security). The control of labour is pursued by handing back some job control to workers, in anticipation of their being coopted (1977:106). Capital must control labour while also drawing on or eliciting its cooperation in securing surplus value – the 'control-engage' dilemma (Thompson, 1989:238, cf. Cressey and MacInnes, 1980) However, the manipulative nature of responsible autonomy also gives rise to contradictions (Friedman,1977:108) as workers exploit their autonomy in ways that are unintended by and /or are undesirable for management.

Through historical and political analysis, Burawoy (1985) attempts to incorporate the labour process and point of production into a wider analytical schema. Specifically he introduces the typological concept of the 'factory regime' (see also Warde, in this volume): the political and ideological apparatuses that regulate production relations and class interests. Broadly speaking, 'despotic' regimes, associated with coercive, direct control and market instability are superseded by the rules and expanded 'choices' of 'hegemonic' regimes in monopoly capitalism. This shift is grounded in the increasing role of the state in the reproduction of labour power (e.g. welfare systems). The subsequent development of 'hegemonic despotism' is associated with the increased mobility of capital and global accumulation dynamics.

Criticism of this work is not dissimilar to that provoked by Burawoy's earlier work (see Thompson, 1983; Knights and Collinson, 1985). His continued attention to increasing hegemony and consent has been criticized for its neglect of the significance and persistence of resistance (Thompson, 1989 and 1990; Littler, 1990; cf. Sturdy in this volume). Equally there are objections to his marginalizing of the influence of 'external' factors such as culture, race and gender and of social institutions (e.g. school, media, family) in conditioning the organization of the labour process, especially of core workers (Knights and Willmott, 1990). Other contributions to the debate have highlighted the interpenetration of 'internal' and 'external' factors, especially of gender, and have sought to account more adequately for individual subjects' susceptibility to discipline but also their exercise of power through skill and control (Knights, 1990; Knights and Sturdy, 1990). Before discussing such literature, this section concludes with a brief review of the debate concerning flexible specialization.

Debate over the contestation and qualified provision of job autonomy (the discretionary content of 'skill') and its exercise by labour as
cooperation or consent has been partially informed or reinforced by
the emergence of the 'flexibility debate' (see Marchington and Ackers
and Black, both in this volume) stimulated by the work of Piore and
Sabel (1984) in particular. Contra Braverman, historical developments in work organization are seen to result in a recombination of
conception and execution (skill) and in collaborative employee relations characterized by employee involvement schemes (Piore and
Sabel, 1984:278; cf.Hyman, 1988). Broadly speaking, alongside the
impact of Japanization, American quality of work life programmes
and the 'flexible firm' model of Atkinson (1984), the customization of
production and the use of an adaptability in new manufacturing
technology have, it is argued, undermined an assumption of deskilling
and conflictual capital labour relations.

These arguments have been subjected to considerable critical
attention. (Pollert, 1988; Wood, 1989: chapter 1). Flexibility, it has
been argued, coexists with, rather than replaces, Taylorist methods of
work organization (Bergrenn, 1989). Apparently harmonious
employee relations are regarded as a fragile product of manipulative
schemes in which control is maintained and obscured by 'responsible
autonomy' strategies and the blandishments of corporate culture
(Thompson, 1989; Hyman, 1988; Rosen and Baroudi, in this volume).
A number of these criticisms echo those directed earlier at
Braverman's work, such as the unproblematic treatment of skill and
craft labour, particularly in relation to gender, to which we now turn
(Liff, 1986; Walby, 1989; Jenson, 1989; Bergrenn, 1989).

THE QUESTION OF GENDER AND SUBJECTIVITY
IN THE ANALYSIS OF SKILL AND CONSENT

There are a number of studies that explore how workers are prepared
ideologically, in the school, the family, and in other socio-political
contexts, for paid employment and how this preparation is often
subsequently reinforced and reproduced both at, and beyond, the
workplace (Sennett and Cobb, 1973; Sharpe, 1976; Willis, 1977;
Pollert, 1981; Cockburn, 1983; Pearson, 1986; Cunnisson, 1986). The
development of distinctions and segregations around gender within
the labour process are well documented (Cockburn, 1983; 1986;
Knights and Willmott, 1986a; Collinson *et al.*, 1990) but these are not
independent of class differences (see Willis, 1977). Working-class

men may learn to value 'hard' (manual) work, as middle-class men may readily become attached to the competitive demands of career and business success. Women's preparation for paid employment tends to be conditioned by the expectation that they will also be primarily responsible for domestic labour. Their 'grooming for marriage' (see Pollert, 1981) and for caring responsibilities informs a sexual competition for the attention of men and a variable commitment to prolonged paid work. Both men and women are prepared for certain distinct types of work which condition a gender-based solidarity with their peers.

These generalized conditions are not without internal and mutual contradictions, such as between competition and solidarity and resistance and 'hard work' (see Yarrow, in this volume). However, the preoccupation with dominant (male, inspired) 'feminine' and 'masculine' identities informs the choice and allocation of jobs, and shapes the nature of skill and consent for both men (Knights and Collinson, 1985; 1987) and women (Pollert, 1981). With regard to consent, Pollert has shown how, despite being critical of management and men generally, the women factory workers of her study would tend to collude with or draw upon patriarchal stereotypes, because of their disadvantaged position in the home and workplace. Similarly Thompson highlights how management exploit women's 'traditional' attributes of 'natural' skills (see below) – passivity, sentimentality and 'niceness', which connect to experience beyond the workplace (1989:197). Equally, both Yarrow and Baron (in this volume) show how men's 'natural' strength is exploited to intensify their labour.

The concern with adopting gender (and class) identities can, like other consenting practices, be seen as a defensive way of coping with subordination that provides a sense of self-worth. For example, blocked hierarchical mobility for women may encourage their preoccupation with the prospect of marriage or 'something different' that informs a workplace culture around romance and 'external' activities (Pollert, 1981; Westwood, 1984) thereby reproducing job segregation and gendered subordination (Pollert, 1981; Collinson et al., 1990). It is through this patriarchal ideology that specific skills and job differences, along with the symbolic and material values ascribed to them, come to be seen as gendered or 'natural'.

Management's exploitation of gendered skills serves not only to secure worker consent. The low value given to women's work because of an assumed natural suitability (e.g. dexterity) and lesser material need for it ('pin money') may be used to further cheapen deskilled labour, such as in the feminization of clerical work (Phillips and Taylor, 1980; cf. Knights and Sturdy, 1987). Phillips and Taylor argue that skill is a gendered category, constructed by male employers and in the related struggles of male workers to retain their own, relatively powerful position (1980). While the authors do not suggest that skill is totally subjectified, they have been criticized for understating the material differences between men's and women's work (see Jenson, 1989; West, 1990). This material basis of male power in their overestimation or defence of skill is a focus of attention for Cockburn (1981, 1983). The 'tangible factors' in skill, such as men's acquisition of bodily advantage, are 'made to matter'. For example, she shows how the physical units of work and the form of technology are political in their design – built by men and for men (1981). However, such factors are not fixed but are adaptable - variable over time and in relation to technology – and are selectively overstated in the collective defence of skill. Cockburn uses the case of UK print compositors' resistance to innovation, showing that this was not so much a fight against technology as an effort to retain workplace control and class position together with their identities both as craft/print workers and as men. Their resistance was a 'fight for virility' (Phillips, 1983:102) (see also Baron, in this volume).

The work of gender theorists (e.g. Liff, 1986; Walby, 1986; 1989) explores the ways in which ideologies of patriarchy and capitalism interpenetrate with gender issues as well as skill and consent. Some, such as in the case of Cockburn cited above, also highlight the theoretical importance of subjectivity to labour process analysis. Constrained by a structuralist tradition in Marxism, subjectivity has been either neglected or inadequately conceptualized in labour process literature (Knights, 1990; Willmott, 1990; and Sturdy and Sakolsky, both in this volume). The full range of labour actions and orientations have been accounted for by reference to the 'control-engage' dilemma (Manwaring and Wood, 1985; Edwards, 1986). While this formulation addresses the problem of explaining the coexistence of conflict and cooperation such as in practices of consent, the relationship between structure and action is rather deterministic. Both management and labour are constrained or even 'compelled' (Thompson and Bannon, 1985:98-9) by the structure of capitalism to secure and advance their respective control over the labour process.

It has been suggested that a more adequate analysis would need to take fuller account of human susceptibility to consensual control through ideology and self-discipline or consent. More specifically, it would need to account for individuals' defence of: workplace routines or 'choices' (Burawoy, 1979); 'self expression and skill' (Cressey and MacInnes, 1980) and securing 'self' in social identity (Knights and Willmott, 1983; 1985) – for example, through gender distinctiveness such as the elevation of masculinity associated with particular crafts and skills (Cockburn, 1981) or manual work (Willis, 1977; Knights and Collinson , 1987; and Yarrow and Baron in this volume). Several authors have sought to develop such an approach by developing and combining insights from Marx and other labour process writers with those of, for example, Foucault, Giddens and Berger and Luckmann (e.g. Knights, 1990; Willmott, 1990; Doorewaard, 1988; Sakolsky, in this volume). For example in contrast to Burawoy's (1979) account wherein an essential (humanist) interest in 'choice' is assumed, Willmott argues that we are constituted to know, expect and value *choosing* as part of our identity. However, these processes are obscured by subjects in 'fetishizing' or seeking to secure a 'solid' sense of self or identity (see also Sturdy, in this volume).

ADVANCING THE DEBATE

The following chapters further demonstrate the interconnections between skill and consent (and resistance) and highlight their socially/historically constructed nature. Together, they draw on a diversity of empirical themes and theoretical perspectives, reflecting not so much a core theory but an exploration of new directions and foci of analysis that are broadly sympathetic to recent developments in labour process theory. The eight chapters are organized as pairs in the following way. The first two chapters (Yarrow and Baron) explore the complex interrelationships between gender, skill and class consciousness through rich historical studies of the US mining and printing industries. The second pair (Warde and Sturdy) each critically develop Burawoy's main contributions to the debate on consent (1985 and 1979, respectively). Warde highlights the import-ance of geographical location and labour markets in an account of factory regimes in Lancaster. Sturdy's account of a form of consent practised by UK insurance clerks challenges a persistent stereotyping of white-collar workers in labour process literature and develops a more adequate account of subjectivity. The next two chapters (March-ington, and Ackers and Black) examine the developing economic and industrial relations climate of the UK in recent years. Marchington systematically explores the concept of consent, before focusing on the relationship between product market competition and employee involvement initiatives. Ackers and Black's study documents manufacturing shop stewards' complex and often ambivalent orientations to similar schemes during the years of the Thatcher government. The final pair of chapters (Rosen and Baroudi, and Sakolsky) focus on how power and control are rendered invisible, particularly in relation to the use of new technologies in the labour process. Rosen and Baroudi chart the historical development of new control forms with information technologies, while Sakolsky applies a Foucouldian analysis to account for disciplinary power and consent. A more detailed resumé of each chapter is set out below.

Chapter 1

Michael Yarrow explores aspects of labour skill and consent as they inform the historical development of class consciousness among Appalachian coal miners in the USA. From an analysis of social relations in both production and the wider mining community, attention is focused on the harmonies and discords between gender and class elements in workers' consciousness. For example, the male miners' sense of tough independence and resistance is shown to limit solidarity with both fellow miners and women, and to lead to a preference for tough paternalistic union leaders and government. A strong sense of male bonding is shown sometimes to reinforce class solidarity, while at other times solidarity is impeded – for example in the collaboration with (male) management to exclude women.

The complex process of developing consciousness is illuminated through a comparison of three historical periods: the 'hand-loading era' (1880–1930), when both men and women shared an experience of subordination to the paternalistic coal lords in coal-camp communities; a period of relative prosperity and militancy during the 1970s coal 'boomlet'; and the converse experience in the rationalization of the 1980s. Changes in consciousness are tied, in a non-deterministic manner, to changes in material conditions, sources of information about them and available interpretations. A strong link is suggested between the experience of power in the labour process and a 'social imagination' that may counter 'dominant ideologies'. Conversely, the heightened subordination of the 1980s is associated with a redefinition of masculinity, from 'facing up to the boss' to being a 'hard worker'. Many changes are documented, yet Yarrow also

11

observes an 'amazing continuity in consciousness', which he attributes
to basic continuities in capitalist social relations.

Chapter 2

Ava Baron rejects the familiar distinction between capitalism and
patriarchy, emphasizing, like Yarrow in the previous chapter, how
gender is embedded into class and, thus, should be integral to labour
process analysis. Her study complements that of Yarrow in charting
the historical construction of a masculine gender/class identity.
Moreover a similar redefinition of masculinity is documented as
resulting from a process of struggle. Male workers' efforts to preserve
a skilled status and to exclude women led them to redefine their
competence and identity in terms of endurance and speed (hard
workers) which 'heightened demands on them as men and as
workers'. This gendered form of consent was not only socially
constructed but politically contested.

Echoing the work of Cockburn (1981, 1983), deskilling is shown to
represent a crisis of masculinity – demasculinization – as well as one
of class position. Indeed, there are also empirical parallels with
Cockburn's study of the UK printing industry. Baron provides a
detailed analysis of the contested introduction of new technology (the
linotype machine) to the work of print compositors in the USA
between 1850 and 1920. However, the study presents both an implicit
and explicit challenge to Cockburn's dual system (capitalism–patriarchy) analysis. Gender, it is argued, is over-simplified in such an
approach, by assuming a static or monolithic set of gender interests.
Rather, male power, its limitations and its variations among different
groups, needs to be questioned. Accordingly, the chapter emphasizes
how the meanings of gender equality and difference are historically
produced through class struggle, and not based on pre-capitalist
ideology or fixed interests.

Chapter 3

Alan Warde critically develops Burawoy's *Politics of Production* or,
more specifically, his concept of the 'factory regime', in a local
historical study of the industrial and political quiescence of
manufacturing labour in Lancaster in the twentieth century.
Recognizing the theoretical contribution of Burawoy's work in seeking to interconnect power relations in the workplace and beyond,

Warde highlights and subsequently addresses a number of weaknesses. In particular, he exposes a neglect of the significance of local labour market conditions for industrial discipline. More generally, that of the local or spatial aspects of the politics of production are claimed to result in an underestimation of the range and complexity of factory regimes.

In accounting for the quiescence of the semi-skilled and unskilled workers of Lancaster, Warde rejects the notions of paternalism and deference that were deployed in Martin and Fryer's earlier study of the region (1973). Rather, conditions of dependence are seen to rest on a geographically isolated labour market and a small number of major employers. Moreover, the two principal local employers collaborated to exploit their dominance over labour with regard to wage levels, union recognition and the internal labour market. The latter is seen as having been particularly important in maintaining worker dependence, in that only young workers were taken on, with the expectation of a 'job for life'. Each employer agreed not to take on the other's former employees – an arrangement with parallels in Japan and the UK clearing banks, until recently. Thus, the internal labour market is highlighted as an 'exclusionary device', rather than simply as a progressive provision of benefits tying workers to specific companies.

Chapter 4

Andrew Sturdy also critically draws on Burawoy's earlier work (1979) in addressing two concerns: the inadequate treatment of human subjectivity and the neglect of clerical forms of consent in labour process literature. The fixed concept of human nature that is either latent or distorted in the capitalist labour process is rejected in favour of a concept of existential insecurity, whereby identity is variable in form – a condition and consequence of structure. This is applied to a clerical setting where a concern with control structures and class location in labour process literature has led to the portrayal of workers as existing at one of two poles. They have been seen as different to manual labour because of 'privileged' conditions and status, or equivalent to them but only in terms of militancy and compliance. Clerical consent has been neglected, other than by reference to traditional notions of privilege.

The chapter documents a consenting practice that is equivalent to Burawoy's 'making out'. A concern with the completion of allocated

13

tasks – 'shifting work' – is shown to coexist with resistance and thereby to reflect a compliant orientation. Control structures impose an individual accountability on staff. However, such activity assumes an apparently self-disciplinary or even compulsive form – workers are anxious to complete their work, to relieve the experience of subordination. This tension of conflict and self-disciplinary cooperation (consent) is explored by conceiving of controls as both existentially enabling and constraining. 'Shifting' is identified as a form of mental escape *into*, rather than, *from* work (completion). Workers actively 'engage in', as well as resist and resent, control structures, all in an attempt to secure a sense of identity (or competence) and individual control – of existential security. The chapter shows that both conflict and cooperation in the labour process reflect less the distortion of human subjectivity, than its constitution.

Chapter 5

Mick Marchington draws on a range of literature, as well as original research, to establish a conceptual famework for the analysis of worker consent or cooperation. This analysis is then applied in the development of a systematic model of the links between forms of product market competition and the production of consent. Initially, three key characteristics of consent are identified, each associated with a different 'principal source' (worker, joint union-management and management). Firstly, the technical and attitudinal elements of tacit skills are explored in relation to product quality and consent. Three sub-categories of consent are described: 'getting back', 'getting by' and 'getting on'. The first two of these refer to the familiar adaptations of workers in using tacit skills to resist or acquiesce to management goals. The third form refers to their use in a more active commitment to 'doing a good job' founded on instrumentalism, socialization and/or securing identity. Interestingly, the consenting practice described in Sturdy's contribution reflected all three of the sub-categories.

The second characteristic or area of consent is that of representative participation or what Burawoy (1979) refers to as the 'internal state'. The author points to the persistence of arrangements for workplace union organization in the 1980s, despite membership and legislative changes, and raises questions about employers' desire and ability to transform this situation. The third area is concerned with management's direct employee involvement (EI) and communications schemes aimed at securing worker commitment. The recent increase in such initiatives is explored before raising a number of practical and theoretical problems with them and with 'team briefing' in particular. Nevertheless their effectiveness is not wholly dismissed. Finally, analysis of consent and EI in particular is integrated with a model for analysing product markets in terms of their potential power over the organization. The concepts of monopoly (competitive pressure) and monopsony (customer/demand pressure) are deployed to assess the experience of market power. Broadly speaking, managerial discretion over employee relations practices is reduced the greater the market power, although the connection is by no means straight forward. Indeed, it is also shown how management use competitive pressure as an ideological tool to elicit consent and justify actions.

Chapter 6

Peter Ackers and John Black also examine changes in UK workplace industrial relations in the 1980s, but focus on documenting the orientations of shop stewards in two medium-sized West Midlands manufacturing companies. They reject the persistent and popular stereotype of stewards as militants or 'wreckers', and the theoretical portrayal in some labour process literature of the capital–labour relation as necessarily antagonistic. Rather, by attempting to let the actors speak for themselves, the authors argue that stewards are more informed and sympathetic towards management than is generally recognized. They are often 'industrially constructive', reflecting a consciousness of interdependence, rather than one derived solely or even primarily from structured conflict. Ackers and Black reveal shop stewards' strong positive expectations of management to modernize, provide leadership and be open in communications. In addition, complexities are revealed by separating their views on management in general from those towards its different hierarchical levels. In the latter case, changes in management's knowledge of, and visibility on, the shop floor were especially significant. Changes occurring through the introduction of new EI intitiatives, such as team briefings and quality circles, were examined. Generally, where a union role was maintained in such schemes, which in most cases it was, they were often greeted positively by stewards as evidence of management's dynamism. Indeed, the study goes some way in supporting Marchington's claim in the previous chapter that unions are maintaining an active role in industrial relations on the shop floor. The complex, yet frequently cooperative, orientations of shop stewards clearly facilitate such continuity.

Chapter 7

Michael Rosen and Jack Baroudi adopt a rather different approach in examining emerging management practices which are directed at securing greater worker cooperation. The authors locate these efforts within a broader historical schema that charts changes in the forms of management control. Three broad types of control are identified: simple/hierarchical, bureaucratic and post-bureaucratic. A dominative or direct mode of control, with a focus on output, is superseded by two hegemonic modes whereby control becomes increasingly unobtrusive or invisible to the worker, as its focus shifts from workers' behaviour to the formation of their ideas. The latter, *ideational* mode, they argue, renders the strict division of labour, Taylorist deskilling and explicit rational legal rules characteristic of bureaucratic forms potentially redundant. Control is increasingly internalized, through corporate culture for example, and facilitated particularly, by the increasing use of, and dependence upon, information technology.

Information technology is seen as central to post-bureaucratic control forms, but not in a deterministic sense nor, necessarily, as a specific intention of management. Firstly, and echoing Burawoy's (1978) earlier critique of Braverman's (1974) deskilling thesis, technology may be used to limit choices in tasks and yet increase the perception of discretion. For example, with control 'built-in' to the system, decentralization of processing becomes an illusion. Secondly, through ideologies of efficiency and inevitability, the social nature of technology is obscured and technical-rational control becomes more pervasive yet less obtrusive and, thereby, less contested. Thirdly, increased control is reflected in achieving the reputed efficiencies of the technology. It is 'as much a product of such deployment as its impetus'. In short, both ideational control and, relatedly, advanced technologies are shown to facilitate the expansion of hegemonic control in the labour process.

Chapter 8

Ron Sakolsky shares a similar empirical focus to Rosen and Baroudi in his account of power in the labour process, particularly with regard to the use of computer-based technologies. However, he is concerned principally with exploring the application of Foucault's theory of disciplinary power to the labour process in relation to Marxist analysis. Sympathetic to both approaches, points of convergence and divergence are identified. For example, power for Foucault has a capillary, rather than downwards, dynamic; it is productive as well as repressive; and it is located within capitalism, rather than derived from it. Accordingly, an 'ascending' analysis of power, of its multiple technologies, is required. This approach, it is argued, has links with anarchism, in that it seeks to challenge and reveal power and those who would seize it. Overall, Foucaudian and Marxist insights are seen as complementary, revealing different dimensions of the labour process and thus providing a deeper analysis.

Sakolsky explores the concept of 'panopticism', which Foucault identified with disciplinary societies and institutions such as the prison and the contemporaneous emergence of the factory system. This 'enlightenment' solution to disciplinary problems achieved its effect – docile subjects – through a combination of 'hierarchical surveillance' and 'normalizing judgement'. The former is illustrated in relation to the functions of management and their use of computer technology in the labour process – the 'information panopticon'. Such disciplinary power is understood to act on human bodies, as is clear in the regulation of work rhythms through Taylorist techniques and mechanization. While recognizing the concomitant and necessary resistance to power, consideration of 'non-repressive' forms of power provides further insight into worker cooperation with management. Here, 'normalizing judgement' is shown to be involved in workers' consenting practices or games, participatory management schemes such as quality circles and, more widely, the de-bureaucratization of organizations, discussed in the previous chapter. Here, individual personality characteristics are substituted for formal rules. In each case, discipline shifts from physical movements of the body towards the psyche – self-regulation, which is to be distinguished from self-management.

In this introduction we have sought to clarify the concepts of skill and consent in the labour process, to chart their theoretical development and introduce the contributions in this volume. Rather than portray the concepts as distinct themes, their interconnectedness has been highlighted. The so-called 'control–engage' dilemma illustrates this by showing how the historical negotiation of particular control forms or typologies of management control can be simultaneously associated with levels of skill and forms of labour cooperation where the power of the capitalist is rendered more or less invisible. More specifically, the autonomy or control component of skill conditions the exercise of 'choice' by labour in both consent and resistance. This relation is especially evident in technological change processes, such as that associated with flexible specialization. The interpenetration of skill and consent was further elaborated in our discussion of gender relations and subjectivity. Attention to the gendered nature of skill and consent has revealed the importance of power relations that extend beyond, yet also inform, those of the labour process. In the exercise and manipulation of skill and consenting practices, skill is shown to be politically contested, not only between management and labour but between men and women and other labour divisions. By introducing subjectivity into the analysis, both skill and consent can be seen as expressions of (a gendered) identity whereby, for example, deskilling may be experienced as a threat to that sense of self. Whether explicitly gendered in form or not, individuals' exercise and defence of control through skill and consenting practices can be accounted for by their interest in securing identity within capitalist production relations. The following chapters explore, and provide new insight into, many of the above issues through their analysis of historical and contemporary developments in the labour process.

NOTES

1 Burawoy's (1979) initial analysis of consent in the labour process extended beyond workplace 'games' towards broader historical processes whereby workers are increasingly consistituted as individuals and there is a coordination of interests and redistribution of conflict between capital and labour. In particular, he cites the role of the internal labour market and its associated competitive individualism, and of the 'internal state' where industrial conflict is institutionalized and workers are constituted as 'industrial citizens' with limited rights and benefits. By constituting lives as a set of constrained choices in which workers participate, capitalist production relations become objects of consent, while also being fetishized (ibid:93 and 193).

2 It is also worth recording that a number of authors (Attewell, 1987; Armstrong, 1988; Willmott, 1990) have noted Braverman's recognition of the uneven pace and qualified limits of deskilling (1974:171–2).

REFERENCES

Armstrong, P. (1982) 'If it's Only Women it Doesn't Matter so Much', in West, J. (ed.) *Work, Women and the Labour Market* (London: RKP).

Armstrong, P. (1988) 'Braverman and New Technology: A comment on some Recent British Empirical Work on the Labour Process', in Hyman R. and Streek W. (eds) *Trade Unions, Technology and Industrial Democracy* (Oxford: Blackwell).

Atkinson, J. (1984) 'Manpower Strategies for Flexible Organisations', *Personnel Management*, August, pp.25–31.

Attewell, P. (1987) 'The Deskilling Controversy', in *Work and Occupations* 14(3): 323–46.

Baldamus, W. (1961) *Efficiency and Effort: An Analysis of Industrial Administration* (London: Tavistock).

Bergrenn, C. (1989) ' "New Production Concepts" in Final Assembly: the Swedish Experience', in Wood S. (ed.) *The Transformation of Work* (London: Unwin Hyman).

Braverman, H. (1974) *Labour and Monopoly Capital: The Degradation of Work in the Twentieth Century* (New York: Monthly Preview Press).

Burawoy, M. (1978) 'Towards a Marxist theory of the Labour Process: Braverman and Beyond', *Politics and Society* 8(4): 247–312.

Burawoy, M. (1979) *Manufacturing Consent* (Chicago: University of Chicago Press).

Burawoy, M. (1981) 'Terrains of Contest – Factory and State Under Capitalism and Socialism', *Socialist Review* 11(4): 83–124.

Burawoy, M. (1983) 'Between the Labour Process and the State: Changing face of Factory Regimes under Advanced Capitalism' *American Sociological Review* 48: 587–605.

Burawoy, M. (1985) *The Politics of Production* (London: Verso).

Burrell, G. (1990) 'Fragmented Labours' in Knights, D. and Willmott, H. (eds) *Labour Process Theory* (London: Macmillan).

Cockburn, C. (1981) 'The Material of Male Power' *Feminist Review* 9.

Cockburn, C. (1983) *Brothers: Male Dominance and Technological Change* (London: Pluto).

Cockburn, C. (1986) *The Machinery of Dominance* (London: Pluto).

Collinson, D. and Knights, D. (1986) ' "Men Only": Theories and Practices of Job Segregation' in Knights, D. and Willmott, H. (eds) *Gender and the Labour Process* (Aldershot: Gower) pp. 140–78.

Collinson, D., Knights, D. and Collinson, M. (1990) *Managing to Discriminate* (London: Routledge).

Coombs, R. (1985) 'Automation, Management Strategies and Labour Process Change' in Knights, D. *et al.* (eds) *Job Redesign* (Aldershot: Gower).

Coriot, B. (1980) 'The Restructuring of the Assembly Line: A New Economy of Time and Control', *Capital and Class* 11.

Cressey, P. and MacInnes, J. (1980) 'Voting for Ford: Industrial Democracy and the Control of Labour', *Capital and Class* 11.

Cunnison, S. (1986) 'Gender, Consent and Exploitation among Sheltered Housing Wardens', in Purcell *et al.* (eds) *The Changing Experience of Employment* (London: Macmillan).

Cutler, T. (1978) 'The Romance of "Labour" ', *Ecomomy and Society* 7(1): 74–95.

Davis, C. and Rosser, J. (1986) 'Gendered Jobs in the Health Service', in

Knights, D. and Willmott, H. (eds) *Gender and the Labour Process* (Aldershot: Gower).

Doorewaard, H. (1988) 'Hegemonic Power', UMIST/Aston Labour Process Conference Paper, Aston.

Edwards, P. K. (1986) *Conflict at Work: A Materialist Analysis of Workplace Relations* (Oxford: Blackwell).

Edwards, P. K. (1990) 'Understanding Conflict in the Labour Process: The Logic and Autonomy of Struggle', in Knights, D. and Willmott, H. (eds) *Labour Process Theory* (London: Macmillan).

Edwards, R. (1979) *Contested Terrain* (London: Heinemann).

Elger, A. (1979) 'Valorisation and Deskilling: A Critique of Braverman', *Capital and Class* 7, Spring: 58–99.

Etzioni, A. (1975) *Complex Organizations* (New York: The Free Press).

Fox, A. (1974) *Beyond Contract: Work, Power and Trust Relations* (London: Faber and Faber).

Friedman, A. L. (1977) *Industry and Labour* (London: Macmillan).

Friedman, A. L. (1990a) 'Managerial Strategies, Activities, Techniques and Technology: Towards a Complex Theory of the Labour Process' in Knights, D. and Willmott, H. (eds) *Labour Process Theory* (London: Macmillan).

Friedman, A. L. (1990b) 'Strawmania and Beyond: The Development of Labour Process and Analysis and Critique', UMIST/Aston Labour Process Conference Paper, Aston.

Friedman, G. (1961) *The Anatomy of Work* (London: Heinemann).

Gouldner, A. (1954) *Patterns of Industrial Bureaucracy* (London: RKP).

Grossman, R. (1979) 'Women's Place in the Integrated Circuit', *Radical America* 14(1).

Hales, M. (1980) *Living Thinkwork: Where Do Labour Processes Come From?* (London: CSE Books).

Hobsbawm, E. J. (1964) *Labouring Men* (London: Weidenfeld and Nicolson).

Hyman, R. (1988) 'Flexible Specialisation: Miracle or Myth' in Hyman, R. and Streek, W. (eds) *Trade Unions, Technology and Industrial Democracy* (Oxford: Blackwell).

Jaques, E. (1961) *Equitable Payment* (London: Heinemann).

Jenson, J. (1989) 'The Talents of Women, the Skills of Men: Flexible Specialization and Women', in Wood, S. (ed.) *The Transformation of Work?* (London: Unwin Hyman).

Joyce, R. (ed.) (1987) *The Historical Meanings of Work* (London: Cambridge University Press).

Katz, F. E. (1968) 'Integrative and Adaptive uses of Autonomy: Worker Autonomy in Factories' in Salaman, G. and Thompson, K. (eds) (1983) *People and Organisations* (Milton Keynes: Open University Press).

Kelly, J. (1985) 'Management's Redesign of Work: Labour Process, Labour Markets and Product Markets', in Knights, D. *et al.* (eds) *Job Redesign* (Aldershot: Gower).

Knights, D. (1990) 'Subjectivity, Power and the Labour Process' in Knights, D. and Willmott, H. (eds) *Labour Process Theory* (London: Macmillan).

Knights, D. and Collinson, D. (1985) 'Redesigning Work on the Shopfloor –

A Question of Control or Consent?' in Knights, D. *et al.* (eds) *Job Redesign* (Aldershot: Gower).

Knights, D. and Collinson, D. (1987) 'Disciplining the Shopfloor: A comparison of the Disciplinary effects of Managerial Psychology and Financial Accounting' *Accounting Organisations and Society* 12(5): 457–77.

Knights, D. and Roberts, J. (1982) 'The Power of Organisation or the Organisation of Power?' *Organisation Studies* 3(1): 47–63.

Knights, D. and Sturdy, A.J. (1987) 'Women's Work in Insurance: I.T. and the Reproduction of Gendered Segregation in Insurance', in Davidson, M. J. and Cooper, C. L. (eds) *Women and I.T.* (Chichester: Wiley).

Knights, D. and Sturdy, A. J. (1990) 'New Technology and the Self-Disciplined Worker in the Insurance Industry', in Varcoe, I. *et al.* (eds) *Deciphering Science and Technology* (London: Macmillan).

Knights, D. and Willmott, H. (1983) 'Dualism and Domination: An Analysis of Marxian, Weberian and Existentialist Perspectives' *Australian and New Zealand Journal of Sociology* 19(1): 33–49.

Knights, D. and Willmott, H. (1985) 'Power and Identity in Theory and Practice' *Sociological Review* 33(1): 22–46.

Knights, D. and Willmott, H. (eds) (1986a) *Gender and the Labour Process* (Aldershot: Gower).

Knights, D. and Willmott, H. (eds) (1986b) *Managing the Labour Process* (Aldershot: Gower).

Knights, D. and Willmott, H. (eds) (1987) *New Technology and the Labour Process* (London: Macmillan).

Knights, D. and Willmott, H. (eds) (1990) *Labour Process Theory* (London: Macmillan).

Knights, D., Willmott, H. and Collinson, D. (eds) *Job Redesign* (Aldershot: Gower).

Kraft, P. (1990) 'Determining Technology: Why I Don't Like Skill and Why You Shouldn't Either', UMIST/Aston Labour Process Conference Paper, Aston.

Lee, D. J. (1981) 'Skill, Craft and Class: A Theoretical Critique and a Critical Case', *Sociology* 15(1): 56–78.

Liff, S. (1986) 'Technical Change and Occupational Sex Typing', in Knights, D. and Willmott, H. (eds) *Gender and the Labour Process* (Aldershot: Gower).

Littler, C. R. (1982) *The Development of the Labour Process in Capitalist Societies* (London: Heinemann).

Littler, C. R. (1990) 'The Labour Process Debate: A Theoretical Review 1974–1988', in Knights, D. and Willmott, H. (eds) *Labour Process Theory* (London: Macmillan).

Manwaring, T. and Wood, S. (1985) 'The Ghost in the Labour Process', in Knights *et al.* (eds) *Job Redesign* (Aldershot: Gower).

Martin, R. and Fryer, R. H. (1973) *Redundancy and Paternalist Capitalism: A Study in the Sociology of Work* (London: G.A. Unwin).

Marx, K. (1975) *Early Writings* (Harmondsworth: Penguin).

Marx, K. (1976) *Capital*, Vol 1, (Harmondsworth: Penguin).

Nichols, T. and Benyon, H. (1977) *Living with Capitalism* (London: RKP).

Palm, G. (1977) *The Flight from Work* (London: Cambridge University Press).

Pearson, R. (1986) 'Female Workers in the First and Third Worlds: The "Greening" of Women's Labour', in Purcell, K. *et al.* (eds) *The Changing Experience of Employment* (London: Macmillan).

Penn, R. (1982) 'Skilled Manual Workers in the Labour Process, 1856-1964', in Wood, S. (ed.) *The Degradation of Work?* (London: Hutchinson).

Phillips, A. (1983) 'Review of Brothers' *Feminist Review* 15: 101–4.

Phillips, B. and Taylor, A. (1980) 'Sex and Skill: Notes Towards a Feminist Economics' *Feminist Review* 6: 79–88.

Piore, M. J. and Sabel, C. F. (1984) *The Second Industrial Divide: Possibilities for Prosperity* (New York: Basic Books).

Pollert, A. (1981) *Girls, Wives, Factory Lives* (London: Macmillan).

Pollert, A. (1988) 'Dismantling Flexibility' *Capital and Class* 34: 42–75.

Rolfe, H. (1985) 'Skill, Deskilling and New Technology in the Non-Manual Labour Process', UMIST/Aston Labour Process Conference Paper, Manchester.

Sennett, R. and Cobb, J. (1973) *The Hidden Injuries of Class* (New York: Vintage).

Sharpe, S. (1976) *Just Like a Girl: How Girls Learn to be Women* (Harmondsworth: Penguin).

Smith, C., Knights, D. and Willmott, H. (eds) (1991) *The Non-Manual Labour Process* (London: Macmillan).

Strinati, D. (1990) 'A Ghost in the Machine?: The State and the Labour Process in Theory and Practice' in Knights, D. and Willmott, H. (eds) *Labour Process Theory* (London: Macmillan).

Sturdy, A. J. (1990) 'Clerical Consent: An Analysis of Social Relations in Insurance Work' PhD Thesis, UMIST, Manchester.

Tepperman, J. (1976) 'Organizing Office Workers' *Radical America* 10: 2–20.

Thompson, P. and Bannon, E. (1985) *Working the System: The Shopfloor and New Technology* (London: Pluto).

Thompson, P. (1983) *The Nature of Work* (London: Macmillan)

Thompson, P. (1989) *The Nature of Work* (2nd ed.) (London: Macmillan).

Thompson, P. (1990) 'Crawling from the Wreckage: The Labour Process and the Politics of Production', Knights, D. and Willmott, H. (eds) *Labour Process Theory* (London: Macmillan).

Walby, S. (1986) *Patriarchy at Work* (Cambridge: Polity).

Walby, S. (1989) 'Theorising Patriarchy', *Sociology* 23(2): 213–34.

West, J. (1990) 'Gender and the Labour Process: A Reassessment' in Knights, D. and Willmott, K. (eds) *Labour Process Theory* (London: Macmillan).

Westwood, S. (1984) *All Day Everyday: Family Factory and Women's Lives*, (London: Pluto).

Willis, P. (1977) *Learning to Labour* (Farnborough: Saxon House).

Willmott, H. (1990) 'Subjectivity and the Dialectics of Praxis: Opening up the core of Labour Process Analysis', in Knights, D. and Willmott, H. (eds) *Labour Process Theory* (London: Macmillan).

Wood, S. (1982) *The Degradation of Work? Skill, Deskilling and the Labour Process* (London: Hutchinson).

Wood, S. (ed.) (1989) *The Transformation of Work?* (London: Unwin Hyman).

Zimbalist, A. (1979) (ed.) *Case Studies on the Labour Process* (New York: Monthly Review Press).

1

CLASS AND GENDER

In the developing consciousness of Appalachian coal-miners*

Michael Yarrow

This is a singular time to be writing about working class consciousness. Apologists for Western capitalism have greeted the crumbling of the Eastern bloc planned economies as a vindication of the capitalist system *in toto* in spite of or maybe because of the serious economic crisis affecting the nations of the capitalist heartland, and the increasing income polarization in those nations. In an increasingly globalized economy, the working class of the US, Britain and other countries is being asked to subsidize the competitive position of domestic capital with lower real wages and deteriorating working conditions, while major employers in reality operate globally. One important element in the future of capitalism and the fortunes of the Western working class in how well workers understand and respond to their positions. Studies which furnish subtle understandings of the complexities of workers' consciousness and actions in the increasingly globalized context will be helpful.

The term 'class consciousness' has often been used in Marxist theory to mean the full realization by a class of its postition in the class system and of the actions it must take to revolutionize the system so as to advance its interests. The problem with this use of the term is that it often carries with it the assumption of an unconscious or falsely conscious working class, up to the revolutionary moment when material conditions arouse the class like a slap in the face (Jacoby, 1978). This Lukacsian essentialist conceptualization either ignores the role of subjectivity in the historical process, except in extraordinary times, or views subordinate classes as hopelessly bewil-

* Research for this chapter was supported by a sabbatical leave and released time from Ithaca College, an Appalachian Studies Fellowship and a James Still Fellowship. I am grateful for the help of Ruth Yarrow, who conducted some of the interviews and made numerous editiorial and analytical suggestions.

dered. Instead of scrutinizing the complex interplay of developing context, consciousness and action, it treats the development of class consciousness and class struggle as essentially inexplicable (Gintis, 1980). Understanding workers' subjectivity necessitates scrutiny of all the major factors affecting it. Workers lives under Western capitalism are structured by patriarchal as well as capitalist logic (Goldberg, 1981; Cockburn, 1983; Westwood, 1985; Yarrow, 1986; Hart, 1989). In the past decade a number of authors have demonstrated convincingly that workers' consciousness is profoundly influenced by gender as well as class relations (Willis, 1977; 1979; Goldberg, 1981; Cockburn, 1983; Westwood, 1985; Knights and Collinson, 1985; Hart, 1989). This chapter will explore the interrelationships of class and gender in the developing consciousness of male Appalachian coalminers during three dramatically different conjunctures.

There are two prominent theories about the development of class consciousness. The incremental theory asserts that class consciousness is developed by the working class as a whole, or by its members individually, through a series of incremental stages. The stages are derived from an *a priori* logic of cognitive development; for instance, consciousness of class conflict logically presumes consciousness of classes (Morris and Murphy, 1966). These stages are suggested not only as ideal typical models of the cognitive development of consciousness but as 'the trajectory most often followed' (Ollman, 1972:8). Michael Mann describes four stages, arguing that Marxism provides a theory of escalation from the first to the fourth stage 'as the worker links his own experience to an analysis of wider structures and then to alternative structures' (1973:13). Whether implicit or explicit, most of the incrementalist theories assume that the development is irreversible. Understanding, once learned, cannot be lost. These theories can be described as schematic, neatly rationalistic, additive and unidimensional.

In response to the inability of these theories to explain 'explosions of consciousness' such as the French uprising of 1968, Perry Anderson (1968) and Mann (1973) developed a dual consciousness oscillation theory. They suggest that the class consciousness of the pre-revolutionary working class typically involves two contradictory elements: a conservative acceptance of the dominant ideology, and an oppositional consciousness which may vary from latent rejection of a few specific elements of the dominant ideology to a fairly well-developed oppositional consciousness. According to the model, at any given time one element is typically dominant, the other latent. V.L. Allen (n.d.)

suggests that the working class develops the oppositional conscious-ness by discarding elements of the dominant ideology which are not helpful to their understanding and dealing with the world. Since people have the most urgent need for correct interpretations in matters of subsistence, it is in this sphere that oppostional conscious-ness will be most developed.

This model explains explosions of radical class consciousness and deradicalization as shifts in which consciousness is dominant, rather than the creation overnight of entirely new belief systems. What causes such shifts in which element is dominant? Perry Anderson writes: 'the context determines the consciousness' (1968:4).

According to this theory, class consciousness will oscillate with changing structural conditions. Shifts in consciousness are expected to change the structure of consciousness by leading to the further development of the contradictory elements and perhaps a change in relative importance. The worker who returns to the *status quo ante* after a strike or rebellion is expected to have an altered consciousness, but to be still under the sway of dominant ideology. For this model the development of class consciousness involves explosions and reversals, not slow incremental progress.[1]

Most theorizing about class consciousness approaches it from an epistemological problematic – as a problem of knowing what the society is really like (Eyerman, 1982). Even the Frankfurt School of Freudian-Marxists, who stress the emotional realm in their attempts to explain why Germans supported Hitler, saw specific emotional states as impeding the rational analysis of class interest (see Adorno *et al.*, 1950; Ollman, 1972 and Eyerman, 1982). Lockwood (1975) views working-class consciousness as deriving primarily from what workers see in their immediate workplace and community; Parkin (1972) stresses the impact of the dominant ideology on workers' images of society, Westergaard (1975) emphasizes that macro-level developments can also affect how workers see the world. The question concerning consciousness therefore becomes: under what conditions does the working class perceive and understand society the way Marxists or sociologists do?

The notion of class consciousness, in its Marxist version, grew out of a different problematic, one of working-class revolution. When viewed from this problematic of collective action, conditions are viewed as setting the terrain, or posing the problems for action, rather than as providing a landscape to view. Moreover, from this engaged perspective, it seems clear that the rationalist bias of the epistemological approach to class consciousness is misplaced. To act collectively against the powerful requires not only good analysis but appropriate emotions. I will assert that the gender consciousness of male miners can be shown to have affected their class consciousness in important emotional as well as cognitive ways.

Other reviewers have found previous research on class consciousness wanting both in terms of conceptualization and research methodology (Blackburn and Mann, 1975; Westergaard, 1975; Marshall, 1983; Brook and Finn, n.d.; Fantasia, 1988, Hart, 1989). The typlogies of workers' consciousness developed by Lockwood (1975), Goldthorpe, *et al.*, (1988), Parkin (1972), Mann (1970, 1973), Ollman (1972), and Anderson (1968) have been criticized as being ahistorical, divorced from context, unconsciously masculinist with a passive subject and as exhibiting little sense of how macro material factors affect consciousness and of the intricate dialectic between consciousness and action. Methodological critiques have concluded that survey research is unable to reveal the complexity and contradictions of workers' consciousness or the ways in which it is developed in various structural conditions and is engaged as they act (Blackburn and Mann, 1975; Yarrow, 1982; Marshall, 1983; Fantasia, 1988). Survey methodology is also critiqued as being individualist and thus inappropriate for the study of collective consciousness (Yarrow, 1982; Vanneman and Cannon, 1987; Fantasia, 1988).[2]

This study will attempt to avoid many of the shortcomings of previous research. Firstly, it will compare the incremental and dual consciousness oscillation models with the developments in male Appalachian coal-miners' consciousness during three different periods spanning most of the twentieth century: – the non-unionized hand-loading era up to the 1930s, the coal boom of the 1970s, and the coal employment crisis in the 1980s. The results of this comparison, I will argue, suggest powerful and complex effects of the changing material and ideological context as well as consistencies attributable in part to commitment to a gendered and classed identity and perspective. Secondly, previous studies of the effects of gender consciousness on consciousness of class of male workers stress the ways in which gender blocks class consciousness (Willis, 1979; Cockburn, 1983; Knights and Collinson, 1985; Ollman, 1986). I will argue that, at least for the coal-miners I studied, the effects are mixed. Miners seem to have adapted the received definition of manliness to meet their class needs. As a result, miners' gender consciousness in some ways enhances their class consciousness while also inhibiting it. Many theorists of class consciousness apparently assume that consciousness of any other structure of inequality distracts from consciousness of class, this belief seeming to be based on an assumption that these other factors cause perceptual confusion. I think this assumption must be explored empirically.

Thirdly, methodologically this study attempts to probe miners' consciousness of their situation through conversations about their work, their union, their employers, their families, women miners, the role of the government and the class system. I have also attempted to explore the relationship between consciousness and action, by observing respondents in various situations.[3]

The terrain on which Appalachian coal-miners lead their lives and develop their understandings and survival strategies has changed fundamentally several times in this century. To contextualize the consciousness of miners in the three periods explored in this chapter it is necessary to trace these developments and then describe the social relations of production and in the mining communities at the three times to be considered in detail. I will then trace how male Appalachian miners' consciousness changes from one period to the next.

MACROSTRUCTURAL DEVELOPMENT OF THE COAL INDUSTRY

Although endowed with rich coal deposits, ready access to timber postponed the United States' conversion to coal until the nineteenth century. The most rapid expansion in coal production was the nearly sixfold increase between 1890 and 1918 which was accompanied by a threefold increase in workforce (Nyden, 1974:969–71). After the First World War production fluctuated with the business cycle, until the expansion arising from the Second World War, which was followed by the post-war erosion of erstwhile coal markets by oil and natural gas. During the 1980s, utility demand for cheap steam coal pushed another significant increase in demand, which then came to be threatened by clean air regulations (Chapman, 1983).

The organization of property in an industry powerfully affects the class experience of its workers. Around the turn of the century, with the eager backing of eastern investors, many coal operators rushed into business, making the industry more competitive than most (Gordon, 1990). The coal industry has become increasingly concentrated in the last few decades, with oil, mineral and large conglomerate corporations buying up the major coal companies. Yet it is still less concentrated than many other industries (Chapman, 1983). Hyper-competition and demand sensitivity to the businesss cycle led to periodic overproduction crises which brought destruction of capital and hardship to mining families. The precariousness of the small operators necessitated a preoccupation with costs, since labour represented 70 per cent of costs, operators fought vehemently against wage, benefit and safety improvements (Gordon, 1990). Since southern operators had higher transportation costs to ship their coal to the industrial and population centers, they fought unionization even more grimly than northern operators (Gordon, 1990; Baretz, 1955).

From the mine wars of the teens and twenties, to the violent resistance to organizing efforts in non-union mines in the 1980s, union strength has been hard-won. During the 1920s fluctuating demand, anti-union Republican administrations in Washington and an all-out employer offensive rolled back the union to its Illinois strongholds. Then, with the help of the pro-labour Roosevelt administration and the desperate depression conditions, the coal-fields were reunionized in a matter of months during 1933 (Baretz, 1955). Since coal is an important fuel for the economy, when a high proportion of production is unionized, miners possess the power to shut down the economy. This has led to a sense of power among unionized miners and an extraordinary amount of state involvement in managing the industry's labour relations. During the New Deal and Second World War, United Mine Workers of America (UMWA) president John L. Lewis was able to use that federal involvement to make substantial gains in wages, pensions and health care (Baretz, 1955).

The introduction of technology has taken a different trajectory in the United States than in Europe. The industry was converted to mechanized loading in the 1930s and to continuous mining in the room and pillar system in the 1950s and 1960s. It was not until the 1980s that mechanized longwall production accounted for a significant portion of underground production; in Europe this technology has been used for decades (Coal Data, 1985). Highly productive surface mining has gradually grown to account for over 60 per cent of total production in the past three decades. The increasingly productive technology for both underground and surface mining has sent waves of redundant miners out of the coal fields to seek work elsewhere. In the 1950s and 1960s the labour force was reduced by three-quarters, causing a mass exodus from Appalachia to the urban industrial regions of the North East and Midwest. Fearing the total supplanting of coal by oil, Lewis promoted company consolidation and mechanization, even making loans from the UMWA-owned bank for operators to mechanize (Hume, 1971). He also delivered labour peace by avoiding contract strikes and disciplining unauthorized strikes (Nyden, 1974).

The gender relations of the Appalachian coal fields are distinctive. Until the 1930s young boys were used for light mining jobs. Between then and the 1970s coal employers hired men exclusively for all but office work. Coal-mining has also been socially constructed by miners as 'men's work'. In the 1970s women took legal action to gain mining jobs and by the late 1970s several thousand women had gained entry into this bastion of 'men's work'. The mass lay-offs of the 1980s resulted in the expulsion of the women miners, who tended to be the last hired and first fired. Although the mines are still considered by most male miners and their wives to be a male domain, there has been a grudging acceptance of women who work hard.

In the one-industry coal fields of central Appalachia miners have typically been the sole family breadwinners. Relatively few miners' wives have entered the wage labour force. This pattern provides the economic context for the traditional patriarchal family form and a culture in which there is considerable support for the notion of complementary male breadwinner and female homemaker roles. However, this pattern is disrupted by the periodic crises and injuries which expel miners from the mines. A value is placed on flexibility in achieving survival in hard times.

THE HANDLOADING ERA (1880–1930)

Coal development reached the mountains of central Appalachia when railroad spurs were built up the narrow valleys at the turn of the century. The economy of the region before the arrival of the coal industry was subsistence agriculture combined with hunting and gathering. Coal brought industrial plants, new industrial towns and Black and European immigrant workers to supplement the indigenous population. Since in the coal regions the seams underlay everything, operators and speculators sought to buy up all the land. To guarantee the supply of labour, the operators prevented the entry of other industries into the region. Thus in the Appalachian coalfields the population came to be dependent on coal and during this period, without the countervailing power of the miners' union, coal was king.

After various attempts at organizing miners, the UMWA was

formed in 1890. It had considerable success in the next two decades in organizing miners in the central competitive fields, from western Pennsylvania to Illinois. The southern fields of West Virginia, Virginia and eastern Kentucky were just being developed during this period. The union which was led by socialists, was successful in the decade to 1920 in organizing the fields of central West Virginia. In the 1920s the UMWA's new president, Lewis, was unable to maintain membership in competition with the non-union operators during a period of slack demand and liquidated the socialist district leadership in West Virginia and elsewhere.

Social relations of production

During the 'handloading' era (up to the 1930s), large mines were laid out with a central main-line entry tunnel connecting scores of 'rooms', tunnels branching off it at right angles every 80 feet or so (Dix, 1977). These rooms were occupied on a long-term basis by coal loaders working individually or with partners. They used their own hand tools to pick, blast, and shovel the coal from the face at the end of their rooms into small trolleys which they then pushed out to the main-line tunnel. The full trolleys were picked up and replaced with empties by mules, and later by small locomotives (ibid: 8–14). In this individualized labour process, the only need for coordination was in the delivery and retrieval of trolleys with the coal loader's production pace; this did not work very smoothly. One study in 1923 found that loaders spent 23 per cent of an eight-hour day waiting for trolleys (ibid.).

The coal loaders were paid by the ton, after deductions had been made for any rock found in the coal. With this piece-rate system, the mine owner bought the miner's intention to mine coal. Given this control built into the terms of the labour exchange, supervision could be minimal. Mines with hundreds of coal loaders spread over miles of tunnels typically had one mine foreman who might make the rounds at most once a day. Tonnage payment was an efficient means of control, not only because it required little supervision but because it forced the miners to absorb the inefficiences of the system (e.g. loaders were not paid for work that did not produce coal, such as cleaning up the rock after a cave-in, or for the time spent waiting for empty cars).

To increase their profit at stable prices, operators had to reduce the rate of payment, which tended to provoke resistance. The operators, therefore, often resorted to indirect means, such as docking pay excessively for rock in the coal, or by shortweighting coal (Dix, 1977). The miners' response to these widespread violations of the terms of the labour exchange was to organize and demand union checkweighmen. Also, tonnage pay required renegotiating with the introduction of any new machinery, which provided unionized miners with a means to resist redundancy-creating mechanization (Dix, 1988). Thus, tonnage pay as a control mechanism had its limitations.

Operators augmented their control repertoire by mobilizing aspects of patriarchal domination. In the mines the foreman used his power to assign rooms and trolleys to reward productivity and loyalty; the good 'sons' got preference. Competition for trolleys and for the productive, safe and dry rooms could become heated. Operators also attempted to adapt the pre-existent conception of manliness to meet their needs for a productive and tractable workforce. They appealed to valued male traits of physical prowess, mastery, competitiveness and toughness to get production. The structure of the labour process, with its stress on individual production lent itself to this appeal.

Social relations in the coal camp

Unsuccessful in controlling the labour process, the early operators extended their control to the miners' lives outside the mines. Coal camps, constructed by the mining companies in mountain valleys were run as paternalistic fiefdoms in which the operator owned the housing, schools, stores and churches, and hired doctors, storekeepers, school teachers, preachers and guards. The miners were paid in scrip, redeemable at the company store. During the frequent lay-offs, operators often gave their miners credit, resulting in debt bondage. Operators typically lived in the camps or a nearby town and ran the mine operations and camp personally, giving special treatment to loyal workers. Those who challenged the system of control were fired, evicted, and blacklisted from mines in the region (Corbin, 1981). Authorities beyond the coal camp were generally beholden to the operators. For example, in Logan County, West Virginia, Sheriff Don Chafin was paid a royalty for every non-union ton mined in the county (Nyden, 1974:34). The frequently violent labour struggles during this period were touched by lay-offs, wage cuts, abuses in the camps and union organizing drives. Often miners, supported by outside socialist or syndicalist labour organizers, confronted not only company guards but sheriffs' deputies, state militias and the National Guard (Lee, 1969). Although the sexual division of spheres was unquestioned, wives joined their husbands in fighting the operators during strikes, even though the formal agent of struggle was the male union. They were united with their husbands in confronting the oppression of the coal camps, and by grievances about the economic insecurity caused by lay-offs and injuries and eviction from company housing.

The coal operators reinforced a patriarchal family structure. Excluded from the one industry in the region, women could augment family income by gardening and taking in laundry and boarders, but they were economically dependent on their husbands. Operators promoted the patriarchal family by giving preference to family men in hiring and lay-offs (Corbin, 1981). The economic responsibility of the 'good provider' father role forced miners to be dependent 'sons' of the operators. Operators stressed family responsibility and required child-like loyalty.

THE 1970s COAL BOOMLET

In the 1970s, rising oil prices and electricity consumption led to a short-lived coal boom. Coal prices for West Virginia's deep coal rose by 720 per cent between 1968 and 1981 (*Coal Facts*, 1985). The price increase made profitable operation of the less productive mines in central Appalachia's thin seams; expanded operations attracted a new generation of miners to the high-paying jobs with health care and pensions. With strong demand for mine labour the UMWA was able to achieve a relatively high wage and benefits package and a strong position *vis-à-vis* management at the mine site. The Appalachian coalfields experienced one of the most militant rank-and-file mobilizations in the post-war American labour movement. Rank-and-file miners, their wives, pensioners and widows organized to get black lung compensation and new tougher mining health and safety laws, to depose an undemocratic union president and to democratize the miners' union. In the four years prior to 1978, rank-and-file miners, in opposition to their union leadership, participated in a wave of wildcat strikes, a number extending across the entire eastern coal-fields. In the first eight months of 1977 the man days lost to strikes as a percentage of available work days was 6,076 per cent of the rate for all industries. (BCOA, 1977). In 1977–8 miners conducted a 111-day strike. They turned down two proposed contracts negotiated by the union leadership and ignored a back-to-work injunction imposed by President Carter under the Taft-Hartley Law. They received support from other unions, farmers' associations and citizens' groups from as far away as New England, Georgia and California, but finally settled for a contract in which they lost the union health card, their attempt to equalize pensions and to regain the right to strike during the term of a contract of work.

Social relations of production

Mechanization has resulted in higher productivity, but since the miner still controls the speed and direction of the machines, it has not resulted in significant loss of power or skill (Seltzer, 1977; Yarrow, 1979). Specialization occurred as each miner's job was defined by the machine he operated, but with frequent job changing, miners' skills have not been fragmented. Also, management is still hindered in its efforts at surveillance of labour because most of the workforce works away from management's view most of the time. Mechanization and the increasingly cooperative nature of the labour process make attribution of production to individual miners impossible, so payment by the ton has been converted to hourly pay. With this change in the terms of the labour contract, management has lost a powerful work incentive, but has gained flexibility in introducing new technologies and speed-ups.

Although the production workforce has been concentrated in a smaller area with the level of supervision increasing twelvefold from 1890 to 1969 (Seltzer, 1977:57), miners have been able to retain considerable control of the labour process by applying power resources marshalled through group unity. Several aspects of the work seem to foster unity. First, the relatively small workforce in a mine allows miners to know their workmates. The time miners spend in the bathhouse dressing for work and showering after the shift, their often long rides to work locations in the mine, rest breaks and machine breakdown breathers throughout the day provide ample time to communicate with their mates without being overheard by management.

Second, the work necessitates cooperation among miners. Members of the crew must anticipate each other's actions to avoid bottlenecks in production and must help out when a mate runs into trouble. High production is a collective achievement; so is safety. Operating huge machines in tight, dark, explosive surroundings requires watching out for your 'buddies'. Typically miners collectively socialize a new recruit to work safely and think about his 'buddies' (Vaught and Smith, 1980;

Yarrow, 1979). Miners attempt to keep masculine traits of competitiveness and bravado in check to avoid their potential for divisiveness and danger. Common struggles against the foreman and the miners' willingness to strike locally to prevent disciplinary action against a mate also reinforce solidarity.

Foremen appeal to the male values of competition, physical strength and courage. They encourage competition between sections and shifts in tons of coal mined. Cautious miners may be ridiculed as unmanly. During the 1970s, workers were successful in countering most of the operators' attempts to mobilize patriarchal principles of control.

Miners and mine management have tended to react with hostility as a male group to the coming of women to the mines. Their definition of mining as 'men's work' and of men as being stronger, tougher, more skilled with machinery, dirtier and braver than women, convinces them that women cannot do the work. Both groups seem to fear the degradation of the status of their occupation if women can do it. Male miners are apprehensive about the possible disruption of their brotherhood but have typically made accommodations in order to maintain the unity of the crew.

Social relations in the mining community

The 1970s residential pattern can be thought of as representing a giant step towards the pattern typical of the urban working class. In some important ways, however, the 'occupational community' ballooned without bursting. Miners were dispersed geographically, but still maintained neighbourhood, peer and kin ties with other miners. Although the union secured for miners protection from many earlier abuses, land and employment monopolization still resulted in a concentration of power in the coal and land companies. The cultural isolation of the Appalachian coalfields was pierced by mainstream culture purveying the dominant ideology, but the mining subculture remained strong, as reflected in shared institutions, norms, and language. This subculture was still useful as a culture of struggle and resistance, providing miners with a framework and counter values with which to debunk at least some aspects of the invading culture (Johnson, 1976; Branscome, 1978; Lewis et al., 1978). Miners inhabited a bicultural milieu in which many elements of the two cultures were contradictory (Yarrow, 1982).

Some observers have argued that the social cohesion of the mining communities changed from a family-centred structure, in which kin networks were the foundation of all social relations, to a peer group society in which same-age, same-sex groups were dominant (Lewis, 1970). Although the evidence on this point is far from conclusive, and the family continued to be an important institution, there may have been a trend toward a greater importance of peer groups, especially among young male miners.

THE 1980s COAL EMPLOYMENT CRISIS

During the 1980s millions of Americans had to make major adjustments in their strategies for living as whole industries went into long-term decline. Estimates are that 2.3 million manufacturing jobs were lost during the early 1980s with one-third of the remaining jobs in that sector in jeopardy by 1985 (Swinney and Metzgar, 1986:101). One of the industries to decline most rapidly was metallurgical coal-mining. With the dismantling of the American steel and manufacturing industries and increasing competition on the international market, demand and price plummeted. This was followed by massive lay-offs.

Coal companies sought to defend profits in various ways. Mechanization was introduced rapidly, leading to the loss of many jobs. The companies pushed for deregulation of mine safety and environmental protection, subleased their coal properties to small non-union operators, who take the risks and pay a royalty on the coal they mine, introduced production bonuses, threatened lay-offs to induce miners to work faster (productivity doubled in the period since 1977) and fought to deunionize their workforce by closing union mines while opening non-union mines. The total coal mine labour force nationwide shrank from approximately 250,000 in 1978 to 150,000 in 1985 (*Coal Data*, 1985). United Mine Worker union membership fell from 160,000 in 1978 to slightly over 70,000 in roughly the same period (UMWA Executive Board Member). A sizeable proportion of the job loss was in the metallurgical coalfields of southern West Virginia and western Virginia. Production from UMWA mines shrank from 80 per cent of the total in 1960, to 30 per cent by 1990, reducing the union's power in the industry (Yarrow, 1982; Gordon, 1990). In these and other ways coal companies have coerced mining families and communities to achieve higher profits in the name of making the industry competitive.

Social relations of production

The social relations of production in underground mining have been increasingly differentiated in the crisis. In the highly unionized fields of southern West Virginia, more non-union operators have begun to operate. The technology of the labour process varies from a new wave of more mechanized technology, to small operators reverting to antiquated equipment. Productivity has doubled, partly because of mechanization but also because the massive lay-offs make those miners still in employment 'job scared'.

The large companies have rapidly introduced longwall mining. In this system coal is sheared from a 600-foot face directly on to a conveyor belt. The roof is supported by huge hydraulic jacks which can be advanced along with the shearer and conveyor, while the roof is left to fall behind. This system appears to extend managerial control in a number of ways. It mines more coal than a continuous mining section with the same size crew, thus attacking the miners' power in numbers. The crew is more closely coordinated, working on a rather disjointed machine, even though it is dispersed over a larger area. Although the foreman cannot see the whole crew, and movement along the face is impeded by the conveyor and a tangle of hydraulic hoses, it is obvious if anyone falls behind, and the foreman can quickly investigate the source of the problem. On the other hand, since the longwall operation is sensitive, requiring close coordination not only of the crew but also with the haulage workforce, workers have opportunities to slow down or sabotage the process. The close coordination of the labour process seems to foster a unified work crew.

In the small non-union operations, often with precarious capitalization, miners can be summarily fired and blacklisted. Also, insistance on miners' prerogatives might bankrupt the operator. In this context the operators are reasserting paternalistic control. Their claim to a harmony of interests with their employees, their 'sons', has increased plausibility. Production bonuses underscore operator benevolence.

It appears from my own observations and from the testimony of miners in small and non-union mines that the safety regulations for which miners fought and sometimes died are often honoured only in the breech. As one miner pointed out, every regulation was written because of a fatality. Not insisting on safety, in order to keep a job, is done with bitter resignation. Miners are unable to enjoy as boisterous and aggressive an underground brotherhood as during the 1970s although many of the forms and values have remained.

Social relations in the minining communities

The unemployment of two-thirds of metallurgical coal miners means hard times for those who have jobs, for those laid off and for their families and communities. Because the coal industry has gone through hard times before, its people have developed survival strategies but they have not been able to alter the hard economic facts.

Unemployment tends to cause strains and sometimes breaks in families. One wife told of the strain that comes from grown children moving in with their parents and living off their pension and black lung compensation when the children's unemployment benefits run out. Another miner's wife stressed that the strains had been too great for many families in her coal county:

> 'You see depression, you see aggravation, you see alcoholism, you see drug abuse, you see battered wives, you see mistreated children, you see abandoned children. I'm talking about the whole county' (MW180 19.1.87).

Yet considering the extent of the crisis and the relative lack of other well-paying employment in the coal region, it is amazing how well miners' families have weathered the storm. Since the unemployment is massive, blame is fixed outside the family. The whole family must learn to cut expenses. Miners, their wives and older children may take on odd jobs. The division of labour for housework sometimes changes. Working together to make ends meet brings many families together. Since mining families are shaped by a subculture forged in hard times, there is a value placed on flexibility in developing survival strategies.

Some miners have been forced to leave their families to seek work outside the region. Since the jobs they find tend to be low wage, non-union jobs in Virginia and North Carolina, and since many miners have mortgages on homes they cannot sell, the exodus has been delayed and smaller than might have been expected. Older miners who own their homes are often able to stay, eking out a living on compensation or public assistance.

Faced with unemployment of the breadwinner, the unit of economic struggle becomes the extended family, rather than the union. The union has been unable to stop the job haemorrhage or to provide much assistance to its laid-off members. Parents, spouses and other relatives are often there in the emergency. They remember their own hard times and typically can give without disapproval. This shift in survival strategy attenuates the practice of union solidarity.

The strain has also tested mine communities. With such widespread unemployment, people are locking their doors for the first time. It also means a destruction of the economic future for the region's young people, many of whom turn to the military as a way out. Others find temporary escape in drugs and alcohol. In one remote coal camp, residents complained that since miners who left could not sell their houses, they rented them to 'low lifes', long-term welfare clients who did not keep them up. Yet in this same community there remained a strong practice of mutual assistance among mine families.

THE DEVELOPING CONSCIOUSNESS OF APPALACHIAN MINERS

I will describe the melding of class and gender elements in the consciousness of central Appalachian coal-miners during the hand-loading era in the first decades of the twentieth century, tracing how that consciousness has changed with the boom of the 1970s and the crisis of the 1980s. I will then analyse the harmonies and conflicts between the class and gender elements in this consciousness.

The coal-camp era

The hand-loading labour process, in which individual miners accomplished production using their own tools with a minimum of supervision, fostered the claim for craft autonomy. This assertive independent stance *vis-à-vis* supervision was incorporated into the conception of manliness. Although this 'manly bearing toward the boss' was common among craftsmen, it seems to have been particularly well developed among miners (Green, 1978). A study of labour relations in coal in 1925 dubbed it the 'miner's freedom' (Goodrich, 1925). In addition to deriving pride from their craft, miners typically prided themselves in their capacity for hard work under arduous conditions. The connotation of not being ready for the next delivery of coal trolleys was that you could not keep up with 'good' miners (Brophy, 1964).

The competitiveness of this self-concept made miners susceptible to management division of labour but since they could only defend their craft autonomy collectively, they resisted the competitiveness.

They conceived of manliness as including fair dealing with workmates. They demanded the 'square turn' – equal distribution of coal trolleys – and condemned miners who stole coal or otherwise tried to take unfair advantage of their workmates. The collective defence of miners' autonomy led to an appreciation of the close relationship between the individual rights of workers and collective action (Brophy, 1964).

Although miners responded to this experience of labour in terms of masculine meanings, the terms of the labour exchange focused attention on the rate of exploitation. Miners were aware of the discrepancy between the price the operator got for a ton of coal and the wage they were paid for it (Brophy, 1964). Miners responded to widespread operator cheating on the tonnage pay by distrusting the operators and demanding union representation and a union checkweighman.

The craft consciousness which was fostered by the hand-loading labour process was pushed into a particularly bitter class conflict consciousness by contradictions in the operators' system of control. The assertive self-confidence of their craftsman identity was affronted by the smothering paternalism of the coal camp, in which they were treated as children. They responded by asserting their rights as free men and citizens. Miners were also confronted by the contradiction between their breadwinner role in their families and their total dependency on the operator. They demanded a family wage, rather than settling for the operator's determination of their worth. Being able to support one's family and being free from capital's control beyond the workplace were thus additional components of the concept of manliness which were charged with class content.

Competitive success came to the operator who kept labour costs down. There were instances of forced unpaid overtime and periodic lay-offs due to overproduction. Miners made unproductive by injury were often fired. This experience contradicted the claims of benevolent operator paternalism. This contradiction between patriarchal ideology and capitalist reality seems to have produced a bitter sense of antagonistic class relation for many miners of that period. For instance, Ed Kelly wrote in his unpublished manuscript, *The Life of a Coal Miner*:

> Coal companies have ruled with an iron hand like that of a dictator. . .Coal companies would come back to their old discarded machinery year after year and take depreciation on it to

avoid paying tax, but they never mentioned about paying any depreciation on the disabled miners who had met their fate while operating the machinery in the mine to make the coal companies the huge profits they enjoyed. If a miner became disabled to work, they didn't want him around any longer, and no one knows that any better than I do, because they did it to me.

(p.110)

This understanding of conflicting interests leads logically to a perception of the necessity of resisting the abuse. 'Everything that a miner has got from an operator, he has had to fight for it' (M145 7/78). The bitter struggles for union recognition reinforced their sense of capital–labour conflict and the role of the state as the protector of capital. The union was seen as the agency by which miners fought to abolish the near absolute power of the operators. As Herbert Hensley, who started working in the mines in 1918, stated:

'So I'd say the union was the best thing that ever happened to the coal-miners in West Virginia. It has to be to take them from being down-trodden in some ways, especially in some mines, until they could act like independent people and citizens' (Interview, Dec 9, 1973 Charleston, West Virginia in James Morrow Library, Marshall University, Huntington, W.V.).

With this common perception of the role of the union in delivering miners from slavery comes an understandable loyalty to the union. They see their role in keeping the union strong in their commitment to the oath of brotherhood they took upon joining it. Although the union freed them from coal-camp paternalism, they seemed comfortable with the paternalistic leadership of John L. Lewis and Tony Boyle, who ruled the union from 1920 to 1973. Their sympathy with Lewis's declaration that miners were not ready for democracy seems to have reflected the effects of limited education and coal-camp isolation on their confidence when operating in the sphere beyond the mine and camp. They appreciated Lewis's toughness in dealing with the operators and even in dealing with the union membership.

This loyalty also extended to the national Democratic Party of Roosevelt. The New Deal not only provided the legal and political context for the reorganization of the mine workers' union in 1933, but also helped liberate miners' families from the insecurity they faced, with its welfare state provisions. Miners from this period tended to see their lives as having been improved by the efforts of the two great men, Lewis and Roosevelt, and as having declined since then. In both this paternalistic view of the historical process and a frequently expressed economic determinism which emphasized the influence of the business cycle on their fortunes, they view themselves as spectators, or only in a secondary role as John L's troops.

The consciousness of the hand-loading era miners may be characterized as a particularly contentious craft consciousness which fused class and gender elements. They had a strong sense of rights and prerogatives within the capitalist organization of labour, accepting their status not only as wage labourers but as hard-working, 'brute' labourers who must endure alienating and dangerous working conditions. They took manly pride in being able to do this. On the other hand, their construction of manly identity involved a courage which allowed them to battle the mine guards. They were also convinced of the unavoidable conflict of interests with their employers and the need to fight collectively for even their modest goals of craft autonomy, a family wage and freedom from favouritism, cheating on pay, and oppression in the coal camps. Because of their acceptance of the need for struggle they prized solidarity with other miners, even though the labour process did not particularly promote it. Manliness meant being able to look a manager in the eye, and having 'brotherly' relations with workmates. Although often confident and confrontational in their relations with management in the mines, they had little knowledge of how to fight effectively against increasingly large and remote corporate employers. They appreciated a tough leader who could operate effectively at the national level against these awesome enemies.

This sketch of coal-miners' consciousness in the hand-loading era seems quite similar to what Lockwood terms 'proletarian traditionalism' (1975). However his ideal typical construct does not include the contradictions and complexities which must be considered. For instance, many miners of the hand-loading period in the US who worked for relatively successful and benevolent operators were deferential, even though they lived in occupational communities that Lockwood considered productive of proletarian consciousness. Lockwood also stresses the congruence of work and community for miners, dockers, and shipbuilders in producing a dichotomous power image of class relations (ibid:17–18). It seems to me that one of the generative conditions of conflict consciousness among Appalachian miners of this period was the contradition between workplace autonomy and community paternalistic control (see Simon, 1978).

Class/gender consciousness of miners during rank-and-file mobilization: the 1970s

Miners frequently refer to the views and actions of the older generation as sources of ideas, justifications, and points of comparison:

> 'Our grandaddies fit [fought] for this union'. (M130 1/78)
> 'The coal operators killed my dad'. (M145 7/11/78)
> 'Well the union is, originally more so than now, what's made America really! I mean its done away with slavery, just about'. (M133 15/3/78)
> 'We don't know how to work the way the old-timers did'. (M141 13/3/78)

The emotional proximity of the past is undoubtedly due to the fact that most Applachian miners are the sons and grandsons of miners. Yet conditions in the mines and beyond have changed substantially since then. The frequent reference to the views of miners of a previous era reflects a judgement that they are still relevant. Miners during the 1970s appreciated their fathers' bequest of a union, won with sacrifice and struggle. They accepted the older generation's perception of the operator/miner conflict.

One indication that miners' consciousness in the 1970s involved a melding of class and gender understandings is the expression for a respected miner, 'good strong union man'. It involves a combination of gender and class terms, but each term has both class and gender meanings: a man is only 'strong' if he can take a militant stance, and the union is conceived of as a brotherhood. A good strong union man is contrasted with a 'scab' or 'company suck', who is neither manly nor true to his class.

Listen to three southern West Virginia miners[4] in their forties talk about the difference:

> Dennis: We have a percentage of good strong union men, but even with the scabs you can take good stong leaders and break their backs. See a scab won't rebuke you, if you got a good leader. A scab ain't nothin' but a yellowbelly anyhow. He's the next thing to Judas. . .
> They put it out if you are a good union man, you are out to

destroy production, you're out to destroy the country. That's the biggest lie that a man ever told. Because a real down to earth union man, he wants production.

Don: If you go in or around the mines the good strong union men is the ones that is doing all the work.

Bud: We have to mine the coal that pays our wages.

Don: He [the good strong union man] wants a safe place to work and he wants enough to live on. All poor people are now realizing that that's all there's going to be out of life. If he can stay healthy, if he has got a healthy, safe place to work and he comes home, he's got warm and plenty to eat, that's about all he asks for. That's all I have ever wanted, you know, and plenty of friends. . .

(M127, M145, M146 22/7/78)

These miners see life as a series of harsh tests of manhood which the good strong union man passes and the scab fails. Not only is the work dangerous, strenuous, skilled and dirty, but the daily work experience involves constant managerial attacks. Manhood is won in daily personal combat with the boss and the work.

Since the hand-loading era there seem to have been subtle changes in emphasis in the notion of toughness. Hard work waned slightly in significance, and technical competence became an important require-ment for respect from peers. News of somebody's mistake spread quickly through the mine. Also toughness in 'standing up' to the boss was stressed during the period of mobilization. It seems that miners adopted the norm of autonomy from their fathers, while trying to practice it under a labour process with much closer supervision, requiring constant fighting off of managerial encroachment. Tough-ness involves the courage and skills of this self-defence. The strong labour demand of the 1970s reduced the chances of being fired for this aggressive stance.

For militant miners, manhood also required softness – a supportive, nurturing stance towards one's brothers. The union man is big hearted. Typical male competitive individualism which scorns depen-dency is directed at the relationship with management, while a collective ethic of interdependency is promoted for relations with workmates. Since competitive individualism is a pervasive manly value in the dominant culture (Wilkinson, 1984), miners must struggle to overcome it. They use tough manly sanctions and harsh initiation rites to attack it in members of their work groups (Vaught

45

and Smith, 1980). The discipline of collective production and safety under the current mechanized production process and the ample time for communication reinforce miners' efforts to form a solidary brotherhood. The 'company suck' violates the brotherhood in two ways: he is solidary with the boss and thus not with his union brothers, and he is unmanly because he does not have the courage to stand up to the boss, and thus cannot be depended upon to stick up for a wronged brother. He is also selfish in his relationships with workmates. During the 1970s miners became especially sensitive to the necessity for unity in their rank-and-file strikes. They evaluated each proposed contract in 1978 in terms of its effects on various categories of 'brothers', including the young, older working miners and the pensioners. Since their strength came from unity, any potentially divisive element was seen as weakening.

Although few miners think about it in this way, they have sought to redefine the meaning of masculinity to meet their perceived class needs. Male combativeness is not condoned in relations with mates, but is honoured in relations with class enemies. Commendable behaviour towards mates should include support, caring, mutual respect and love as a form of collective resistance against management.

Union miners see two contending world views extant among miners, which they tend to view as stable character traits. The consciousness of 'good strong union men' involves a calculus of collective betterment, manly 'backbone' to 'stand up' to the boss, and 'big heartedness' to buddies. The 'scab' consciousness of 'company sucks' entails a calculus of individual advantage, unmanly cowardice and selfishness. The good strong union men dream of collective transcendence, of a strong vibrant working-class community which is able to defend its rights in the workplace. The scabs dream of individual transcendence by getting rich.

Miners have a strong sense of class conflict in relations with management in the mines. One miner reported his response to a foreman who had tried to establish a brotherly relationship as: 'Let's get one damn thing straight right now! You ain't our damn buddy. You're our enemy!' Even rather conservative union miners see a conflict of interest with their employers over the goals of production and safety. Although some miners view coal operators as especially 'dirty' in their dealings with their employees, many generalize their view of coal companies as their 'enemies' to big business in general, and would endorse the following statement of a moderate miner:

'Actually the big companies in the United States is what run it. They can choke you, they can drown you, they can do what they want to do, if the people let them. And there'd be more of it if they would be let more' (M135 15/3/78).

As the above quote suggests, many miners see the class relationship as a desperate struggle, with high stakes. They have to fight for their lives, their families, their rights and their dignity.

Involvement in struggles with the coal companies over black lung, safety, and labour legislation as well as strikes has provided miners with an opportunity to evaluate the roles of government, the media, and various types of professionals in class conflict. Asked what lessons he learned from a 111-day strike, one miner responded:

'Number one is you know who all your enemies are and never underestimate your enemies. Another good lesson is that the federal government and big business are one and the same. They are like Siamese twins. If you hit one the other hollers'

(M128 3/7/78).

Few miners see the relationship between big business (usually called 'money') and government in the structural terms of Marxist state theorists. Rather, most see the state as responding to pressure as in the pluralist theory, but with big business having the most effective means of influence. Many miners assess the state's role in class conflict by analysing the influences on the personnel in governmental positions. Either they see personnel as having business interests, such as the speculation during the 1978 strike that President Carter must have made investments in the coalfields, or as being easily influenced by the elite. Gender comes into this analysis in the common belief that it takes 'a real man' to withstand seductive and intimidating elite influences, just as it does to stand up to bosses in the mines.

In their desperate struggle against the powerful money interests, miners see the unions as their only source of support:

'The union is the only thing in this whole country that stands up for the working man. If you don't have a union you don't have no rights at all' (M139 16/3/78).

Since the union is so important in the class struggle, miners must make sacrifices to save it from being destroyed.

'These men might as well face it. They are going to have to fight. They are going to fight or they are going to die!' (M141 13/3/78).

To fight, miners feel they need courage, toughness, and weapons. They see the strike as their primary weapon. When laws and slack demand for coal labour make it ineffective, they are discouraged; 'I don't care how good a man is, if he ain't got no weapon, he can't fight' (M139 16/3/78). Miners see the contract, governmental safety regulations, guns and other forms of physical intimidation as other important weapons in their arsenal. They differ in the degree to which they disapprove of illegal or violent actions, but most approve of them in extreme circumstances, because they perceive the stakes to be so high and legal sanctions open to them have been blunted by the companies.

Although most of my respondents saw the system as enduring and were suspicious of revolutionary ideologies, the experience of rank-and-file mobilization during the 111-day strike and of the symbolic aid from other unions and farmers encouraged some to think that rank-and-file power could force major societal changes. They saw working people as historical actors who through their unions had brought about a wider distribution of the fruits of their labour and of human rights. In that situation they tended to view their role defensively as fighting off a business and governmental attempt to crush the unions:

> 'If you keep all the unions together, then you can beat the companies. But if you don't we're going to end up on the short end' (M147 18/3/78).

But some thought more expansively of beating the enemy once and for all:

> 'I mean if you ain't a big man you're liable to get stomped in the mud in this country. And it is getting worse. But what they don't know is rank and file still runs the governnment same as the union. And I want to see the day when the United States marches on that D.C. up there and cleans it out. And the Bible says it will happen. We're going to throw them all in the Potomac. All them rich dudes is going down in the Potomac with their money in their pockets 'cause they'll be afraid to leave it' (M141 13/3/78).

Miners' consciousness of class beyond the coalfields is typically derived from few sources of information. Their union provides one source, and the conglomerate owning their mine may provide another, but on many issues they rely on local newspapers and television. Since their experience is powerfully affected by macropolitical and economic developments, such as government reactions to national strikes and the secular trend towards the export of manufacturing jobs, they pay close attention to these developments. They tend to evaluate national events according to assumptions about class relations as they experience them and have been taught about them by their fathers. Though their images of a national class structure tend to be vague, their impressions about class relations are sharp.

Miners' consciousness of the national class system once again seems to fit Lockwood's model of 'proletarian traditionalism', since it seems to be generated by class relations experienced at the mines and in miners' communities, and is a dichotomous power model. However, there are indications that macrostructural developments have caused revisions in their image and that it is a profoundly strategic assessment arising from a problematic of collective action.

This brief description of the main contours of the gender-specific class consciousness of Appalachian miners during a period of mobiliza-tion suggests that they had developed an analytic and emotional frame for understanding the world from the earlier generation of miners and from their work and community experiences. Their consciousness involved a fusing of class and gender perspectives into a particularly aggressive and solidary conflict class consciousness and notion of manliness. In the enthusiasm of mobilized rank-and-file power, some even had visions of achieving a society in which workers exercised more power.

Changes in the consciousness of miners with the 1980s coal employment crisis

In attempting to undestand the coal emloyment crisis which has had such a devastating effect on their lives, miners are presented with two competing interpretations: the corporate and the union. The corporate explanation was available from President Reagan, coalfield newspapers, coal associations and many coalfield politicians. It con-tended that American unions, especially the miners' union, had become too strong and had bargained up wages, benefits and working conditions to the point where American coal was no longer competitive on the world market. Unions had protected lazy, unproductive workers and wasteful work practices, which had led to massive inefficiencies. The solution offered included cutting labour costs by lowering wages and benefits, increasing managerial control, and destroying unions. The United Mine Workers of America tried to counter this explanation with one of its own, arguing that miners had not priced themselves out of the market, but that the market had been fundamentally altered by forces beyond their control. They pointed to the fact that while US coal had been losing out to foreign coal, the labour costs of US coal had decreased due to a doubling of productivity. They detected a corporate plot to destroy domestic unions and reduce labour costs by producing in low wage, low tax, lax regulation countries. Their answer was protectionism: saving US jobs by reducing imports.

Although varying in their analyses, miners have tended to combine elements from both these explanations, because they each resonate with their experiences. They look back on the 1970s, from the perspective of the present crisis, as a time in which they did live 'high off the hog' compared with their parents and grandparents, and as a time when they did exert considerable power over the labour process. They remember protecting unproductive workers and defending unproductive practices and now view the tighter discipline under which their parents worked as necessary. On the other hand, they see a corporate plot to destroy their union by opening non-union mines and importing coal. They experience this directly in the closure of large union mines and the subleasing of the coal rights to small non-union operators, or the investment in large new, government-protected 'scab' mines which pay above the union scale. In the strategic debate about contract concessions the strongest voices in favour come from the unemployed and the strongest voices against from union organizers, who are already having difficulty talking union to non-union miners with above union wages. But most miners are reluctant to give up hard-won gains which are a measure of their collective achievements.

Miners' assessment of the present crisis is accompanied by shifts in their gender-specific class consciousness. Perhaps the most dramatic change in consciousness is in emphasis on the two criteria of manliness. While in 1978 the stress was on a miner's ability to face up to the boss, now it is on how hard a worker one is. Thus gender identity has become less class combative. This change has been accompanied by an altered use of history. Whereas in 1978 the elders were cited for their struggle against operator oppression, they are now revered as hard workers. The new generation of miners hired in the 1970s, then lauded for their militance, are now seen by many as a cause of the downfall of the industry and of the union because they were not interested in working for their buddies' welfare. In times of crisis, harmony of interests with precarious operators becomes more plausible and hard work is stressed as a way to keep the company in business and protect jobs.

The brotherhood has begun to unravel as a result of the lay-offs and the inability of the union to protect jobs. Unemployment means that bonds are not reinforced by the daily work experience. It also means that miners do not have the disposable income to participate in many leisure activities with peers. They are thrown back on kin support networks for survival. Miners who are still working appreciate the precariousness of their position. They resist the demand of the brotherhood that they should refuse overtime while others are laid off. Instead they try to get all they can, to provide a nestegg for their families for when they are sacked. They have reluctantly and with a bad conscience adopted the calculus of individual advantage in place of the calculus of collective betterment they believe in. In the crisis, when collective struggle seems implausible, family loyalty takes precedence over loyalty to the brotherhood.[5]

Miners seem also to have re-evaluated the exercise of rank-and-file power. At the peak of rank-and-file mobilization during the 1978 strike, miners considered themselves to be powerful, able to win the strike and possibly to force more far-reaching structural changes. The perceived failure of that strike caused them to re-evaluate their power position with respect to their corporate opponents. Ten years of gathering crisis has convinced most that the companies are practically invincible.

As the past president of a local branch at a Consol mine puts it:

'Well, you take West Virginia. They can shut it down. They don't care about the conditions. In ten years, you're going to see things pick back up. Has it hurt the company? No! It's just made them more powerful. 'Cause they control me. They don't want to let the control out to the people. You keep the people down, it makes them stronger. As long as they can keep the labouring class of people down, they're going to. The more desperate people get, the more they can make. It's more or less like in a communist country. *There*, the government controls you. But *here*, your companies control you to a certain extent.' (M224 15/1/87)

They see the possibility of change due to an upswing in the business cycle or the election of a Democratic president, but view either development as being beyond their power to influence. Without change, many see their union being destroyed in the near future.

As miners perceive the diminishing power of the rank and file, they reassess militance. The wildcat strikes of the 1970s which were seen in 1978 primarily as a noble attempt by miners to fend off operator aggression are now typically seen as foolish and often ignoble, a view the operators had all along. Rank-and-file power is also questioned by way of increasing criticism of union democracy. Although not optimistic, miners hope that their union leaders will be able to find a way out of the present crisis, since they perceive themselves as powerless to accomplish the feat. Thus they want to give their leaders as much power as possible. They want a smart, tough manly leader to win the battle they can no longer win themselves. Many hoped that the miner-lawyer, Rich Trumka, whom they elected union president would fit the bill.

These perceptions of the balance of power affect miners' thoughts about appropriate strategies. There is strong support for the union's protectionist policy. Miners know that the energy corporations are operating globally, but their lack of knowledge of miners and their unions in other countries makes it difficult for most to imagine a transnational brotherhood of miners, even though the logic of class conflict leads a number to recognize the necessity. Instead they feel very keenly the sapping of their strength by competition with 'slave labour' and want protection from it. As one put it:

'My strategy would be to put tariffs on these coal imports, but when it is cheaper to get coal shipped from Africa to Florida than it is to rail it from West Virginia, there is something *wrong*. They need to get that balanced out somehow. That would help your home people'. (M241 8/6/87)

Many accept the media portrayal of US foreign policy as international welfare and insist that charity should begin at home. They are indignant that hungry mining families who are losing their homes are being taxed to give foreign aid to obscure an unappreciative people. A number of union militants supported Reagan's aggressive foreign policy and military build-up for reasons of national pride. Few see US foreign policy as designed to maintain the vast international low wage labour pool which destroys their bargaining power.

A few miners, especially those that have been involved in recent collective struggles, see some possibility of successful collective strategies. A striker from Matewan, West Virginia, foresaw a coalition of unions electing people who would represent workers' interests.

'They holler "solidarity, solidarity, solidarity". We proved what we, the UMWA, could do in Mingo County. You take a big state like Kentucky, I mean Governor Martha Lane is Kentucky's scab protector. You take the Mine Workers, the Steel Workers, telephone workers, railroaders. You have a mass meeting of the officials in one room and they would sit down and evaluate each candidate. What can they do for solidarity, not what can they do for my union or my little group? They pick who they want. Each union give their political arm the authority to endorse these people. That is the only way you are going to have labour represented. Divided we are too little. You have to get solidarity. . .

'Then you can work your way on up to these senators and congressmen. Then you got the power that you need in Congress and the Senate to get some of these bills passed to protect human rights or get some of the ones that hurt us cancelled. Get it back where it represents the working class of people and not who's got the most money in the bank or who is willing to spend the most to buy a job' (M241 8/6/87).

A miner whose community shut down a small non-union operation at the head of their hollow imagined a general strike to force the government to work for the people.

'If our union could ever get in with enough different unions, auto and all them and put pressure on this country at one time, they would get something done. Stop this country still! It would be a heck of a thing to do to stop a whole country but it's going to take something. It's going to take people with enough backbone to stand up. Say 'OK, government, now you want to run it, you run it'. Let them do your jobs. You could put a squeeze on any country. It think that's about what it's going to take. In other words it's going to be a stinking war between the rich and the poor' (M232 23/3/87).

Miners resist working in non-union mines or leaving for the low-wage non-union jobs in the South because, according to their gender-specific class consciousness, these jobs would deprive them of the working conditions they have fought for, the brotherhood they cherish and their sense of self-respect.

Miners' work-related gender-specific consciousness is not very helpful in developing alternative strategies. Miners see their power as deriving from their position as wage labourers. When there is no demand for their labour, most see themselves as powerless. Collective strategies that involve finding new sources of power and new allies, such as women and other male workers, are unimaginable for those without experiences with these kinds of struggle. They also reject visions of the future which detach them permanently from the underground brotherhood, the basis for their proud class/gender identity. In the crisis, the miners' union does not seem to be formulating any collective struggle strategies for an economic transition from coal.

CONCLUSION

In assessing the implications of the above description of the developing class/gender consciousness of male Appalachian miners, I will first consider some ways in which gender interacts with class in that consciousness, and then explore the implications of the changes in consciousness I have traced for theories of the development of class consciousness.

Class and gender elements of miners' consciousness

Miner toughness

Wilkinson lists the traits constituting toughness in American culture as mastery, dynamism, competence, self-defence, competitiveness, endurance in dangerous and stressful situations, will-power and autonomy (1984:7). These traits resonate with the special meaning of the term as used by miners. The core meaning for miners seems to be a mental and physical stance toward the world, it is a cognitive and performance style focused on combat. Whereas survival strategies of subordinate people may involve invisibility and subtle, passive resistance, or ingratiating one's self to the powerful, toughness for miners involves a declaration of independence from, and a challenge to, the authority of the bosses. It includes class and gender elements which both reinforce and contradict each other. While toughness in American culture stresses competition with other men (Howell, 1973; Wilkinson, 1984), miners direct combat toward their class enemies, the representatives of mine management. Socialization to masculine toughness, especially in the coal-mining subculture, teaches men many of the conflict skills of verbal and physical combat, bluffing and strategic thinking useful in taking a militant stance toward management. For a vulnerable working-class man confronted by a powerful enemy, learning to be tough allows him to act in defence of rights, rather than out of fear. The tough miner can thus achieve a relationship with the boss which is consistent with a conflict class consciousness. On the other hand, fighting with the boss has been a test of masculine identity.

Tough-mindedness is the attendant cognitive style disciplined for conflict. It involves distilling the implications of information for the conflict. Tough-mindedness involves impatience with complex analyses which impede action. It involves facing the facts, even if they are intimidating, for unrealistic assessments lead to ineffective action.

It values practical experiential knowledge rather than abstract knowledge. The latter tends to be ridiculed as impractical and mistrusted as manipulation by class enemies. However, the experience of having a union leader, Arnold Miller, who came from the ranks but was perceived as not being sophisticated enough to hold his own in the elite world has led many miners to value 'book learning' as well as practical experience. Tough-mindedness demands that one's analysis be harnessed to an iron will, backbone.

Willis (1979) has observed that the masculine toughness of British factory workers is easily co-optable, and is thus a block to class consciousness. Since tough men are preoccupied with defence of their dignity, they can be mollified with a managerial apology rather than structural change. I have found a similar concern for the style of command among coal-miners. They tend to go along with a boss who asks, and to fight one who orders. On the other hand, miners conceive of their dignity as involving preservation of an expansive set of rights. These include free speech, freedom to do the job the way they want without supervision, freedom to make judgements about their own safety, to work as fast as they want, to strike when they want, together with high wages, family health care and pensions. Aggressive assertion of these rights is, to put it mildly, an impediment to management's control. Miners make little distinction between rights to personal dignity on the job and citizens' rights beyond the job. All of these rights have to be protected by struggle against the powerful. Hebert Gintis (1980) has argued that in the West the class struggle has been waged in terms of human rights versus property rights. Although sometimes co-optable with gestures, coal-miners' tough defence of expansive human rights catapults them into this struggle.

The tough, conflictual class consciousness of male miners was relatively well adapted to the boom conditions they faced in the 1970s. With changing conditions, however, miners have experienced a disjuncture between consciousness and action. The militant collective contestation survival strategy, in a period of lay-offs, mine closure and a demobilized rank and file, becomes increasingly vulnerable to capitalist reprisal. Survival strategies and their attendant consciousness are also labelled by bosses and dealt with accordingly: the 'good strong union man' is a 'troublemaker', the 'company suck' is a 'good man'. Miners know that their consciousness is not a private affair, and that it can have powerful ramifications. In the present crisis miners who wish to avoid being labelled a 'troublemaker' and yet retain the concomitant combative class consciousness feel very uncomfortable with concessions they must make at work. As one miner put it, 'Sometimes you have to eat crow to survive' (M229 22/1/87). To relieve the painful sense of hypocrisy, some miners begin to adjust their consciousness towards a more harmonious view of employer–employee relations.

Possibly because standing up to the boss is no longer a practical test of toughness, being able to do hard work, to endure discomfort and to brave danger is regaining the importance it had during the hand-loading era. This test gives the work significance in the achievement of manliness. In this way, celebration of toughness becomes an impediment to seeing their class interests as opposed to those of capital. Only the most conflict-conscious are fully aware of this and resist it consistently.

Toughness undermines class solidarity in three ways. Firstly, it is a manly virtue; women are not generally viewed as tough, and so cannot be worthy members of the brotherhood and are ignored as class allies. Secondly, to the extent that toughness is a posture of independence from influence, it may make it difficult for miners to compromise and cooperate as a group. Thirdly, miners' desire for tough leaders can be a block to class consciousness. They tolerate the undemocratic practices of a leader as an extension of the toughness they want and as a way to intimidate hopelessly weak miners into taking the proper militant action. In the process they tend to ignore the structures of class unity and accountability of leadership, setting themselves up for betrayal by their leaders. In the national political arena their quest for a tough leader led some of the younger militant miners to vote for anti-union Ronald Reagan in 1980 because of his tough stance toward other countries.

Male toughness as construed by Appalachian coal miners has contradictory effects on their class consciousness. Toughness supports, prepares, and endorses class combative actions which enhance conflict class consciousness with its emotional dimensions of courage and indignation at attempts at subordination. It is packaged with a tough-mindedness disciplined to struggle. On the other hand, it excludes women, tends to be competitive and ignores some important aspects of class analysis.

Male bonding and class solidarity

Male bonding can pose an impediment to class solidarity, by encouraging miners to perceive a bond with male managers. This happens to some degree in the shared hostility of foremen and male miners to the introduction of women into the mines. But miners guard against these claims to solidarity with class antagonists by defining brotherhood as excluding bosses. They include the ability to fight the bosses as a membership criterion.

Class solidarity is also obstructed by the male competitiveness and perceived sense of superiority (Gray, 1984). Miners struggle to overcome this by stressing the importance of the brotherhood of miners. Although they participate in competitive games, they strive to set limits and sanctions against behaviour that threatens unity. They have been so successful over the decades that they have been able to unite beyond the workplace and to conduct wildcat strikes across multistate regions, in spite of opposition by union leadership. During these periods of mobilization their solidarity has inspired visions of social transcendence of the class system, but not of the gender system. With mass unemployment in the 1980s the underground brotherhood became frayed and miners focused more on their role as family breadwinners. Thus crisis may corrode class and gender solidarity.

The biggest block that the miners' brotherhood erects to class solidarity is its exclusion of women. Since women are considered to have essentially different and to some degree opposite traits from men, they are seen as outsiders and are viewed with suspicion. Although there are many examples of male miners who have welcomed women miners into the brotherhood, rather than see the brotherhood weakened, it seems to be a provisional membership. Wives have joined strikes and other union struggles on an episodic basis but are typically not welcomed to union meetings and are not thought of as forming part of the group. Their abilities are not used well and strategic thinking typically does not include them. In fact militants often see wives as blocks to militant actions because their presumed preoccupation with paying the bills leads them to put pressure on their husbands to go back to work. In an important way miners now have less in common with their wives than was the case for their parents in the coal camps. They do not jointly face the operator as landlord, store-keeper, and controller of services in the community, as the coal-camp family did. Some militants imagine overcoming this problem by bringing wives into the union but have been discouraged from pushing this project by membership resistance. In the 1980s, mass unemployment unified the experience of husbands and wives appreciably.

Subordination at work versus superordination in the family

There is a contradiction for the male worker under patriarchal capitalism between his subordinate position at work and his superordinate position in the family. Miners often express indignation at the unmanly subordination they experience at work. On the other hand, the patriarchal family position may compensate for the subordination to the boss. Cockburn (1983) and Willis (1979) argue that because men feel they owe their role as breadwinner to their employer, they are likely to be grateful, especially when jobs are scarce. The breadwinner role discourages militant action which might jeopardize the job or interrupt the cash flow. But miners have often struggled for a family wage, job security, better safety and benefits in order to fulfil the breadwinner role adequately. These demands have tended to counter exploitation, but have been resisted by companies. The companies' resistance has led miners to regard capital as being opposed to their attempts to provide for their families, heightening their sense of class conflict. Their gender consciousnesss reinforces this consciousness.

Images of leadership: paternalism versus collective leadership

The experience of most of my respondents with rank-and-file mobilization and class conflict had led to profound disillusionment with the whole gamut of authority figures. Reform union president Miller, President Carter and governers of coal states were seen to be on the side of the operators. Judges who issued injunctions for the operators, and police who 'baby sat' scabs while harassing strikers were also perceived to be partisan. The supposedly neutral role of the state according to dominant ideology was critically reassessed. This led to a blanket condemnation: in terms of the miners' gender-specific class consciousness, 'None of them stood the test'.

Few thought of the solution in terms of building structures of collective leadership or of accountability to the working class. The neglect of such an option may have been partly due to their recent disillusionment with a rank-and-file group which had been secretly led by a Maoist sect. The most important factor seems to have been their reading of their experience with union presidents. From their class/gender perspective, Lewis was a tough man who could stand for the membership, while Miller was weak and had sold them out. In making this judgement they ignored the accommodationist actions of

Lewis and the benefits they had won under Miller. Although few had experienced Lewis's rule, they viewed him as the leader nobody could control, who had remained true to his followers and who thus commanded their respect and obedience. The way miners read the historical evidence was influenced by their own experience with class conflict. They know it takes 'backbone' to stand up for their buddies at the mine, and increasing sophistication to fight effectively against lawyers, company executives and government bureaucrats. They wanted a leader to 'stand behind' them, backing the rank-and-file demands, and at the same time in front as the 'big man' enforcing discipline, taking charge. During the 1970s a number of younger miners were concerned about the problem of creating a new autocrat, but since standing up to corporate executives and presidents would take combat skills they lacked, they wanted a paternalistic champion to do right by them. Their class/gender consciousness directed them toward the search for a tough, educated man. As the conditions became more intimidating in the 1980s, so the miners' perceived need for a champion increased. They elected as union president tough-talking Rich Trumka, hoping that his mining experience and law degree would mean he was prepared to fight the companies effectively.

The evidence I have collected from Appalachian miners indicates that their gender consciousness is an adaptation of the prevailing American male gender consciousness, resonating with their militant conflict class consciousness. Miners' gender consciousness reinforces their class consciousness, stiffening their class militance with masculine toughness, and cementing their solidarity with male bonding. The impulse of labourers to struggle with bosses is reinforced by viewing subordination to capital as being beneath their manly dignity. Because of its aggressive defence of this dignity, the militant stance is more consistent with cosmopolitan and local definitions of manliness than an accommodationist stance.

This consciousness contains contradictions. Miners' gender consciousness impedes working-class consciousness by the exclusiveness of the 'we' group, conceived as the brotherhood of male miners rather than all working people, the dependence on a paternalistic union leader, manly pride in alienated labour, and in superiority over women.

The contradictions in this consciousness make it more dynamic. They create tensions which disrupt its solidity. Emphasis within the set of themes may change without completely disrupting accepted truths, viz. the recent change of emphasis in the definition of manliness, from standing up to the boss to hard work, which accompanied the demobilization of the rank-and-file movement and the crisis in coal employment.

The development of consciousness

How do changes in context cause changes in consciousness? Perry Anderson writes: 'the context determines the consciousness' (1968:4). My data also suggest a powerful influence of context on miners' consciousness, but since the influence is complex and is affected reflexively by consciousness, I would avoid the verb 'determine.' Viewed from an epistemological problematic, one might expect changes in consciousness to accompany changes in material conditions, in sources of information about these conditions and in available interpretations. I have described the changes in material conditions. In the 1980s demobilization of the rank-and-file movement and mass lay-offs weakened the rank-and-file communication network, thus making miners more dependent on the media and the union leadership for news and interpretations. With the election of Trumka as union president, the perspective of the union leadership placed greater emphasis on the conflict of interests with the coal companies than under the previous regime.

There has been another profound secular change in information about class relations. Although the coal market has always been affected by remote developments in the regional and national economies, the increasing globalization of that market over the past decade makes this source of change in miners' class position even less accessible. Paralleling this change has been an increasing remoteness of the employer, the class opponent. Capital units have expanded from the coal camp with its live-in operator, to the national coal company, to the national conglomerates, to transnational conglomerates. These developments have caused a form of sensory deprivation for miners in developing their class consciousness and have made them more dependent on second-hand information filtered through other parties' ideological lenses. But as sensory deprivation theory suggests, another response is to project preconceived formulations on to the blank screen. Miners seem to use both these strategies in combination. From their image of class conflict and the information they get from the union, some project a global conspiracy of corporations to assault the living standard and power of American workers. Others conclude from their experience with high wages and wasteful practices during the 1970s and from the information they receive from the media that miners have bargained themselves out of competition.

Another point to make about the relationship between changing the scenery and changes in consciousness is that consciousness is not a passive reflection of the scenery. With the radical changes in the class and gender relations of coal mining in this century there has been an amazing continuity in consciousness. Some analyse this as a result of cultural inertia, but other working class subcultures have changed quite radically with changing conditions. The changes often do not come until the next generation, which views its parents' perspectives as quaint and inappropriate to the changed conditions. One reason for the continuity is undoubtedly that with all the change some basic relations remain similar in form. Miners have a continuing sense of class conflict, largely because they have continued evidence that coal operators often do not operate in their best interests. They therefore see a continuing need for the union, in spite of its present weakness and past mistakes. Since gender is such a powerful source of identity and since aggressive masculinity is celebrated in the dominant ideology, the gender element of miners' consciousness is a source of resistance to change. Although the elements of gender consciousness may be adapted slightly to new conditions, major change would cause an identity crisis for many.

The problematic of action points to another important cause of change in consciousness with change in conditions. As noted above, consciousness is developed out of people's efforts to solve the problems in their daily lives. It is the general frame in which strategic assessments are made of present conditions which suggests courses of action. I have argued that the gender-specific class consciousness of male miners was relatively well adapted to the conditions they faced in the 1970s. With changing conditions, however, miners have experienced a disjuncture between consciousness and action. The militant collective struggle survival strategy, in a period of lay-offs, mine closures and a demobilized rank and file, becomes increasingly vulnerable. Survival strategies and their attendant consciousnesses are labelled by bosses and dealt with accordingly: the 'good strong union man' becomes a 'troublemaker' and may be sacked and blacklisted. By contrast, the 'company suck' becomes a 'good man'. In the crisis of the late 1980s, miners who wished to avoid the 'troublemaker' label and yet retain a combative class consciousness saw what they had to do to make a living as being disreputable. They may accept it as what has to be done to survive. For example, I found a greater tolerance for 'scab' behaviour among even the most militant miners in 1987 than was evident in 1978. To relieve the painful sense of hyprocrisy, some miners began to adjust their consciousness towards a more harmonious view of employer–employee relations.

For the unemployed miners there is also a disjuncture between consciousness and action. Their gender-specific class consciousness is honed in the workplace. Its manly pride in work judges their unemployment harshly. They are in the unmanly role of sitting at home and living off others. What is the effect of being a fish out of water on their consciousness? Almost all the unemployed express a grim demoralization. Their present detachment from their source of power in work and the experience of a long series of defeats by the operators since the 1978 strike leads them to see the macrostructure as being unchangeable by a weak rank and file. A few determined militants cast about for signs of weakness in the operators or hope for an upswing in the business cycle, or that when things get bad enough miners will be forced to unite and fight. Most hold on to a somewhat modified class gender consciousness, while accepting the dominant definition of the situation, which deems collective action as being counterproductive. This leads to paralysis. The comparison between the dreams of social transformation of miners during the rank-and-file mobilization and the present sense of stony structures suggest the close relationship between social imagination and the experience of power, while casting doubt on the incrementalist model.

NOTES

1 Perry Anderson's explanation of the revival in support for Gaullism after the 1968 uprising is an illustration of the use of this theory:

> The voter in the polling booth is pre-eminently private, atomized, serialized as Sartre has put it. In the occupied factory, in the Soviet-style [sic] assembly, political life is public, collective; individuals may form fused groups. It is not surprising that the parliamentary elections produced a massive victory of Gaullism. In the polling booth every worker may lose his [sic] class. The choice [by the French Communist Party of the ballot box rather than occupation of the factories] was not simply between two kinds of tactics but between two kinds of consciousness and ultimately, two kinds of society.

(1968:4)

2 After one of the most thorough reviews of the literature, Marshall (1983) concludes:

. . .energies and resources should be channeled in the direction of intensive, longitudinal ethnography, in which different aspects of consciousness are located firmly in the contexts of class practices – everyday work at the factory, leisure time at home and in the club, the rent protest, the strike – and conceptualized at the outset as inherently dynamic phenomena. Such studies must be based on the realization that class consciousness, like class itself, is a relational phenomenon. It does not exist as a separate entity with a reality *sui generis* but only as a consciousness *of* something: of the structures that impinge on workers' lives and opportunites for action within these. The necessity of uncovering the diverse ways in which components of an awareness and evaluation (or consciousness) of the social order are taken up, employed, and perhaps disregarded, requires intensive observation and interviewing of respondents over an extended period of time. Qualitative techniques alone, among sociological research methods, are capable of uncovering the relationship between attitudes and actions that is class consciousness.

(1983: 290)

3 My description of the development of the class/gender consciousness of Appalachian miners is based chiefly on almost 200 lengthy (1½ to 4½ hours) semi-structured interviews with 100 underground miners and 30 miners' wives which my wife, Ruth, and I conducted between 1978 and 1990. Twenty-five of the miners were interviewed at least two times and several eight times. The interviews were conducted principally in central Appalachia – southern West Virginia, eastern Kentucky and western Virginia. Oral history interviews and autobiographies of miners who worked during the first three decades of the twentieth century (Brophy, 1964; Kelly, 1986) are used to sketch the consciousness of miners during the hand-loading era. I conducted observations of a number of the respondents in various settings such as at work, on picket lines, at union meetings, at family meals, at church, at health clinics and at a trial for a wildcat strike.

4 The names have been changed.

5 The pain of this violation of the principle of brotherhood is underscored by the attempts to reaffirm it during the 1989–90 Pittston strike. Over 40,000 miners struck in solidarity with the Pittston strikers, and material aid poured in to the strikers from other miners.

REFERENCES

Adorno, W. *et al.* (1950) *The Authoritarian Personality* (New York: Harper & Row).

Allen, V. L. (n.d) 'Consciousness and Experience: The Case of Miners and Dockers in Britain'.

Anderson, P. (1968) Editorial Introduction, *New Left Review* 52, Nov–Dec.

Baretz, M. (1955) *The Union and the Coal Industry* (New Haven: Yale University Press).

Bituminous Coal Operators' Association (BCOA) (1977) 'Statement

Presented at the First Session of the National Bituminous Coal Wage Agreement Negotiations', Washington, D.C., October 6.

Blackburn, R. and Mann, M. (1975) 'Ideology in the Non-skilled Working Class', *Working Class Images of Society*, by M. Bulmer (ed.) (London: Routledge & Kegan Paul).

Branscome, J. (1978) 'Annihilating the Hillbilly' in *Colonialism in Modern America: The Appalachian Case*, H. Lewis *et al.* (eds) (Boone, N.C.: Appalachian Consortium Press): 211–27.

Brook, E. and Finn, D. (n.d.) 'Working Class Images of Society and Community Studies'

Brophy, J. (1964) *A Miner's Life*, edited and supplemented by J.D.P. Hall (Madison: University of Wisconsin Press).

Chapman, D. (1983) *Energy Resources and Energy Corporations* (Ithaca, N.Y.: Cornell University Press).

Coal Data (1985) (Washington, D.C. National Coal Association).

Coal Facts (1985) (Charleston, W.V.: West Virginia Coal Association).

Cockburn, C. (1983) *Brothers: Male Dominance and Technological Change.* (London: Pluto Press).

Corbin, D. (1981) *Life, Work and Rebellion in the Coal Fields: The Southern West Virginia Miners, 1880-1920* (Urbana, Ill: University of Illinois Press).

Dix, K. (1977) *Work Relations in the Coal Industry: The Hand-Loading Era, 1880-1930* (Morgantown, W.V.: Institute for Labor Studies, West Virginia University).

Dix, K. (1988) *What's a Coal Miner to Do? The Mechanization of Coal Mines* (Pittsburgh, Pa.: University of Pittsburgh Press).

Eyerman, R. (1982) 'Some Recent Studies in Class Consciousness' *Theory and Society*, 11:541-53.

Fantasia, R. (1988) *Cultures of Solidarity: Consciousness, Action, and Contemporary American Workers* (Berkley, CA: University of California Press).

Gintis, H. (1980) 'Communication and Politics: Marxism and the "Problem" of Liberal Democracy', *Socialist Review* 10: 189-232.

Goldberg, R. (1981) 'Dissatisfaction and Consciousness among Office Workers: A Case Study of a Working Women's Organization', Ph.D. dissertation, American University.

Goldthorpe, J. *et al.* (1968) *The Affluent Worker: Industrial Attitudes and Behaviour* (Cambridge: CUP).

Goodrich, C. (1925) *The Miners' Freedom: A Study of the Working Life in a Changing Industry* (Boston: Marshall Jones).

Gordon, C. (1990) 'Pittston and the Political Economy of Coal', *Z Magazine*, February: 95-100.

Gray, S. (1984) 'Sharing the Shop Floor: Women and Men on the Assembly Line', *Radical America* 18:69-88.

Green, J. (1978) 'Holding the Line: Miners' Militancy and the Strike of 1978', *Radical America*, 12:2-27.

Hart, N. (1989) 'Gender and the Rise and Fall of Class Politics', *New Left Review*, 175:19-47.

Hume, B. (1971) *Death and the Mines: Rebellion and Murder in the United Mine Workers* (New York: Grossman).

Howell, J. (1973) *Hard Living on Clay Street* (Garden City, New York: Anchor).

Jacoby, R. (1978) 'Political Economy and Class Unconsciousness', *Theory and Society*, 5:11–18.

Johnson, L. (1976) 'Reflections on Women and Appalachian Culture', *Win Magazine* 12, August 19:9–10.

Kelly, E. (1986) 'The Life of a Coal Miner', unpublished manuscript (Beckley, W.Va).

Knights, D. and Collinson, D. (1985) 'Accounting for Discipline in Disciplinary Accounting: A Case Study of Shopfloor Resistance to Management Accounts and Its Disciplinary Outcomes', presented at the Inter-disciplinary Perspective on Accounting Conference, Manchester.

Lee, H. B. (1969) *Bloodletting in Appalachia* (Morgantown, W.V.: West Virginia University Press).

Lewis, H. (1970). 'Coal-Miner's Peer Groups and Family Roles', paper read at American Anthropological Association Meeting, San Diego, California, November.

Lewis, H. *et al.* (1978) 'Family, Religion and Colonialism in Central Appalachia', in *Colonialism in Modern America: The Appalachian Case*, Lewis, H. *et al.* (eds) (Boone, N.C: Appalachian Consortium Press): 113–39.

Lockwood, D. (1975) 'Sources of Variation in Working-Class Images of Society' in *Working Class Images of Society* by M. Bulmer (ed.) (London: Routledge & Kegan Paul): 16–31.

Long, P. (1985) 'The Women of the Colorado Fuel and Iron Strike, 1913–14' in *Women, Work, and Protest: A Century of U.S. Women's Labor History* by R. Milkman (ed.) (Boston: Routledge & Kegan Paul): 62–85.

Mann, M. (1970) 'The Social Cohesion of Liberal Democracy', *American Sociological Review* 34:423–39.

Mann, M. (1973) *Consciousness and Action Among the Western Working Class* (London: Macmillan).

Marshall, G. (1983) 'Some Remarks on the Study of Working-Class Consciousness', *Politics and Society*, 12(3) 263–301.

Morris, R. T. and R. J. Murphy (1966) 'A paradigm for the study of class consciousness', *Sociology and Social Research* 50, April: 297–313.

Nyden, P. (1974) 'Miners for Democracy: Struggle in the Coal Fields' Ph.D. dissertation, Columbia University.

Ollman, B. (1972) 'Toward Class Consciousness Next Time: Marx and the Working Class', *Politics and Society* 3:1–24.

Ollman, B. (1986) 'How to Study Class Consciousness. . . And Why We Should', paper read at American Sociological Association Meeting, New York. September.

Parkin, F. (1972) *Class Inequality and Political Order* (New York, Praeger Publishers).

President's Commission on Coal (1980) *The American Coal Miner: A Report on Community and Living Conditions in the Coal Fields*, Washington D.C.

Seltzer, C. (1977) 'The United Mine Workers of America and the Coal

Operators: The Political Economy of Coal in Appalachia, 1950–1973'. Ph.D. dissertation, Columbia University.

Simon, R. M. (1978) 'The Development of Underdevelopment: The Coal Industry and Its Effects on the West Virginia Economy, 1880–1930'. Ph.D. dissertation, University of Pittsburgh.

Simon, R. M. (1983) 'Hard Times for Organized Labor in Appalachia', *Review of Radical Political Economics*, 15:3 Fall.

Stewart, K. (1981) 'The Marriage of Capitalist and Patriarchal Ideologies: Meanings of Male Bonding and Male Ranking in U.S. Culture' in *Women and Revolution* by L. Sargent (ed.) (Boston: South End Press): 269–311.

Swinney, D. and Metzger, J. (1986) 'Expanding the Fight Against Shutdowns', *Labor Research Review* 5:99–112.

Suffern, A. E. (1926) *Coal Miners' Struggle for Industrial Status* (New York: Macmillan).

Vanneman, R. and Cannon, L. (1987) *The American Perception of Class* (Philadelphia, Pa: Temple University Press).

Vaught, C. and Smith, D. (1980) 'Incorporation and Mechanical Solidarity in an Underground Coal Mine', *Sociology of Work and Occupation* 7: 159–87.

Westergaard, J. H. (1975) 'Radical Class Consciousness: A Comment', in *Working Class Images of Society*, by M. Bulmer (ed.) (London: Routledge & Kegan Paul): 251–6.

Westwood, S. (1985) *All Day, Every Day: Factory and Family in the Making of Women's Lives* (Chicago: University of Illinois Press).

Wilkinson, R. (1984) *American Tough: The Tough-Guy Tradition and American Character* (New York: Harper & Row).

Willis, P. (1977) *Learning to Labor* (New York: Columbia University Press).

Willis, P. (1979) 'Shop Floor Culture, Masculinity and the Wage Form', in *Working Class Culture* by J. Clarke *et al.* (ed.) (London: Hutchinson): 185–98.

Yarrow, M. (1979) 'The Labor Process in Coal Mining: Struggle for Control', in *Case Studies on the Labor Process*, by A. Zimbalist (ed.) (New York: Monthly Review Press): 170–92.

Yarrow, M. (1982) 'How Good Strong Union Men Line It Out: Explorations of the Structure and Dynamics of Coal Miners' Class Consciousness', Ph.D. dissertation, Rutgers University.

Yarrow, M. and Dorris, J. (1985) 'Work, Leisure, and Social Cohesion: The Changing Basis of Coal Miner Solidarity', in *Transitions to Leisure* by B. G. Gunter *et al.* (eds) (New York: University Press of America): 71–88

Yarrow M. (1986) 'Capitalism, Patriarchy and "Men's Work": The System of Control of Production of Coal Mining' in *The Impact of Institutions in Appalachia*, Proceedings of the Appalachian Studies Conference, by J. Lloyd and A. G. Campbell (eds) (Boone, N. C. Appalachian Consortium Press): 29–47.

2

TECHNOLOGY AND THE CRISIS OF MASCULINITY

The gendering of work and skill in the US printing industry, 1850–1920*

Ava Baron

INTRODUCTION

Research on the labour process has been based on the assumption that work belongs to men. The feminization of work has been treated as problematic, while its masculinization has been taken for granted. This study of the printing industry assumes that the masculinization of work requires explanation. The absence of women workers, rather than their presence, is the starting point for this investigation of occupational change. This is not a study of women workers or of women's work, but of the broader question of the ways work and skill are gendered.

Gender has remained largely invisible in research on the labour process because the categories scholars have used to study workplace conflicts (whether class relations or impersonal market forces), while purportedly gender-neutral, instead have universalized men's experiences. Feminist research has provided valuable correctives to this male-centred approach. Numerous case studies now document the significance of gender for understanding women's work. Despite this attention to women's work, a satisfactory explanation of the persistence of gender segregation of work and women's labour market inequality has not yet been developed. Debate continues as to whether women's subordination is central to capitalist production, a vestige of pre-capitalist patriarchal ideology, a consequence of

* This chapter is based on my manuscript, 'Men's Work and the Woman Question: The Transformation of Gender and Work in the Printing Industry, 1830–1920'. An earlier version of this essay was published as 'Contested Terrain Revisited: Technology and Gender Definitions of Work in the Printing Industry, 1850–1920,' in Barbara Wright *et al.* (eds), *Women, Work, and Technology: Transformations*, (Ann Arbor, MI: University of Michigan Press). The author thanks David Knights and Andrew Sturdy for their comments on this version.

men's efforts to maintain patriarchal privilege or a result of women's reproductive role.[1]

Much feminist research on the labour process, explicitly or implicitly, has employed a series of conceptual dualisms – capitalism/patriarchy; public/private; production/reproduction; men's work/women's work – that assumes that class issues are integral to the first term of each pair and gender is important only to the second.[2] Based on the theory of two separate but interacting systems of capitalism and patriarchy, analysis of gender was thought to require a theory logically independent of class. This provided a rationale for many studying work to bracket as unimportant to their investigations the mass of feminist research on working women and the sexual division of labour.[3] By failing to challenge the framework of class analysis as gender-neutral, research on women has been allowed to remain marginalized and research on male workers has remained unaltered.

Recent feminist debates have failed to transcend the capitalist-patriarchy conundrum, in part because we still lack an adequate theory of gender identity and its role in creating and reproducing relations of power (J. Scott, 1988; Collinson and Knights, 1986). Gender involves more than relations between men and women; it is integral to class relations among men workers and between workers and their employers (Baron, 1991a).

This study explores the relationship between the process of deskilling of male craft work and its demasculinization by focusing on the controversies over the gender and skill definitions of work in newspaper composing rooms in the United States before and after the introduction of typesetting machines in the late nineteenth century. It shows that the transformation of work not only jeopardized male printers' craft respectability, it threatened their masculinity as well. Analysing working men's efforts to construct and defend a collective gender identity helps us to understand more fully the relations between workers and employers, the organization of work, and the process of occupational gender segregation.

Printing is an ideal focus for the study of gender and work because it was much discussed in the nineteenth and early twentieth century public debates over what occupations were appropriate for women. Different answers to this so-called 'woman question' were put forth by employers and workers, middle-class reformers and machine manufacturers. Its resolution was viewed by workers and by employers as critical in the development of the printing industry. Although women represented a small minority in the printing industry until recently, the intense debate over whether printing constituted woman's work throughout the period of this study highlights the significance of gender for the organization of printing.

In the decades between the 1830s and 1880s, with increasing intensity, publishers made various unsuccessful attempts to employ technology and to displace male with female compositors in their composing rooms. In the late nineteenth century, after many years of trying, publishers were finally successful in developing a typesetting machine, the Linotype, which restructured the work and promised to displace the skill of the hand compositor. The implications of the Linotype were considered 'truly revolutionary' (Loft, 1944:43). Despite this, publishers' attempts to introduce women as Linotypists failed. Composition remained in the hands of men and the powerful typographical union. Indeed, as we shall see, male printers sought to control the implications of the new technology in ways that would enhance craft respectability, while reserving the work for men. Such efforts required them to redefine the meaning of masculinity and to alter the relationship of their gender identity to work.

Gender and the workplace

Harry Braverman's (1974) analysis of the capitalist labour process profoundly affected research on work. According to him, capitalists need to control the labour process in order to optimize their profit from purchased labour power. To this end, capital reorganizes production to separate mental from manual labour, or more accurately, conception from execution. Through a process of 'deskilling' managers cheapen the value of labour by introducing technology or otherwise redesigning work to minimize the need for workers' knowledge and skill. Inspired by Braverman, researchers studied the deskilling of work in the nineteenth and twentieth centuries in fields as diverse as coal-mining, tailoring, office work, computer programming, law and medicine.[4]

Braverman's work has been widely criticized for overstating deskilling as an imperative inherent in capitalist production and for underestimating workers' resistance. Research has increasingly showed that workers have *actively* resisted transformations of production that might have reduced their control over work and thereby have actually shaped the organization of work (Montgomery, 1979; Edwards, 1979; Wood, 1982).[5] Such research has provided valuable insights. But scholars have too often applied a gender-blind analysis to the transformation of work, technological change and workplace conflicts. Gender has not been considered integral to the study of the workplace. Most analyses of the work process have used gender as a synonym for women and have either provided a separate section for 'women's work', or have relegated the entire matter to footnotes.

Men's work experience was the starting point of most investigations of the labour process. From such a vantage point women were seen as the tools used by capitalists to deskill work.[6] Skill has been conceptualized as something men have, and which women lack.[7] As a result, this research has reinforced the view that the feminization of jobs is synonymous with deskilling of an occupation, while the displacement of women by men means upgrading.

Feminists took Braverman's idea of the ideological nature of skill categories further by exploring the extent to which divisions of male and female workers into skilled and less skilled jobs are artificial. Anne Phillips and Barbara Taylor (1980), for example, made an important contribution to our understanding of skill by exploring how men satisfied their gender interests by using their organizational strength to control the definition of jobs. But in their analysis the ideological construction of skill remains separate from an understanding of the development of occupational categories. Instead of examining the ways gender and skill labels developed historically, they argued that women received lower pay and less prestige for the work they did simply because it was women performing the work: that is, women bring their unequal status to the jobs they do. Their explanation for women's subordinate economic position hinges on the existence of a societal gender ideology that through some unspecified mechanism works its way into the sphere of production. The significance of gender differences and the identification of those differences still require explanation. Why does gender have the power to affect wages and job status in ways which lead men to organize against women's entry, or capital to use gender as a divisive lever?

Recent research has begun to show how gender affects the way work is organized, the skill categorization of job tasks and the forms of authority and supervision in the workplace as well as the status and wages of jobs.[8] Studies show how management have employed notions of femininity to control female factory and office workers, and, in turn, how women's resistance was often rooted in their gender identities.[9] This was an important step toward developing an understanding of how capitalism is constructed by gender. But an examination of occupational gender segregation should be an integral part of analysis of the labour process, even when the occupation being studied is and has been considered men's work.

Research on the transformation of work has ignored the crises it posed for men, not simply as workers, but specfically as male workers. The process of deskilling, the separation of mental from manual work, has been one of demasculinization as well. Deskilling represented a crisis of masculinity, a crisis for male workers simultaneously as men and as workers.[10]

Despite centuries of history written from a male perspective, we know little about the construction of masculinity. While a few studies of male workers provide some insights, our knowledge of working-class masculinity remains fragmented and incomplete. We have barely begun to uncover the ways working men's gender identities have influenced the development of union policies and working-class politics.[11]

Cynthia Cockburn's (1983) study of British printers underscored the importance of examining gender when studying male workers. She demonstrated the ways men sought to protect their interests 'as men' to the detriment of women. Yet, like most research utilizing a dual systems theory of capitalist–patriarchy, the concept of gender remained oversimplified. Cockburn rightly points out that gender cannot be reduced to ideology. However, efforts to uncover the material base of patriarchy assume a static set of gender interests, even though its articulation may be conceived as variable.[12] By focusing on male workers' material interests, dual systems analysis is limited to weighing the relative impact of one set of interests over another. Studying the historical conditions that heighten the idiom of sexual difference in the discourse of working-class men would help to move forward debates on male unionists' policies to exclude women workers, by seeing them as more than conspiracies of men to dominate women or as serving the functional needs of capital.[13]

The view that men shape work to protect their gender interests assumes that gender is monolithic, rather than multidimensional and internally inconsistent. The view also assumes that men are omnipotent – that they know what their gender interests are and that they have the power to construct the world the way they want. But these very questions require historically documented answers. Research needs to question male power, rather than assume its existence, and to examine its limitations and its variations among different groups and classes.

Most importantly we need to scrutinize how gender is embedded into seemingly gender-neutral 'class' issues such as wages, skill, and the labour process. Efforts to enhance women's position in waged labour have ever been torn between demands for equality (to be like men) and claims of differences. But the meanings of equality and of difference have themselves been the stuff of class struggle, as this study of US newspaper printing exemplifies.[14]

The chapter is organized in the following way. Firstly, the gendered nature of the struggle between male printers and their employers is discussed in the context of hand typesetting, which preceded the introduction of Linotype machines. The subsequent and gradual process of technological change is then briefly reviewed. The following section reviews the controversies over gender and skill definitions associated with the Linotype. This leads to a discussion in the next section of the outcome in terms of the transformation of shopfloor relations, and a redefinition of masculinity.

HAND TYPESETTING AND MASCULINITY, 1850s–1880s

In the old 'hand-set' days, before the introduction of typesetting machines in the 1890s, the printer, often called the compositor or typesetter, read the manuscript, selected and set the type, justified the lines and made up pages, read proofs and corrected the type, and prepared the formes of type for the press. The men of the typographical union considered themselves skilled craftsmen, proud of their work and its traditions.[15]

To these printers, waged work was itself a measure of manliness, essential to a man's role as a family provider. A man's degree of manliness could be gauged by the size of his wage (Willis, 1979; Matthaei, 1982). Further, the men considered the particular nature of the work involved in printing and its occupational culture as masculine. The 'woman question' – the appropriateness of women working in the printing industry – therefore provoked extensive discussion and debate among union printers (Stevens, 1913: 421–40).

Women printers threatened men's high wages and their role as family providers. Women printers, men claimed, increased the available labour supply and reduced men's bargaining positions with capital, making men 'impotent' in their war against capital.[16] In turn, a reduction in men's wages jeopardized their position as family providers and threatened them with a further loss of degrees of manliness (NTU Convention, 1854, in Stevens, 1913:423). But men printers saw capitalists, not women, as attacking their manhood. Women's entry into 'masculine employments' made women 'tools of employers who desire to use them as instruments of robbing their husbands, fathers and brothers. . .' Union men advised women to:

> pause and reflect upon the sad results of this last attempt to make them accessory to their degradation. . .for without their aid, the effort will fail – and then husbands, fathers and brothers will still be enabled to maintain the dignity of labor, and to hold the position of providers and protectors. . .
>
> (*Finchers'*, Oct. 1, 1864)

Employers, however, insisted that typesetting was distinctly 'woman's work'. During the second half of the nineteenth century, publishers increasingly employed women typesetters to do hand composition of the relatively simple columns of text known as 'straight matter' (Herron, 1905:18; Abbott, 1910:255). This kind of typesetting constituted over two-thirds of the work for newspapers. In the 1850s and 1860s publishers recruited women from the textile and clothing industries, gave them a six-week training programme and set them to work as typesetters (Baron, 1982). As one publisher explained:

> We are completing our arrangement to avail ourselves of the labor of female printers and we are quite confident that typesetting is to become one of the regular employments of women, . . .to the very necessary help of the most oppressed and most needful of all working people, the feeble seamstresses.
>
> (c. 1853, in Munsell, 1860: 3)

According to one estimate in 1864, thousands of women were being instructed as printers in New York City, Philadelphia, and New England. One publisher concluded: 'by the first of next year the female compositors will be crowding their male brethren to the wall and will monopolize the entire work' (*Chicago Post*, 10 April 1864).

Employers and middle-class women reformers, such as Susan B. Anthony, during the 1850s and 1860s claimed that the work was gendered, but that it was feminine.[17] They emphasized its intellectual aspects as being particularly feminine. Intellectual work was feminine because it was light, clean and easy, they argued, while manual work was masculine (Penny, 1863; *Harper's*, XXXVII, June–Nov. 1868:530).

A second, contradictory, claim put forth by employers and reformers was that the work required particular aptitudes or characteristics that only women had. The work itself was not gendered; instead it required certain kinds of workers. They considered printing 'peculiarly adapted' to the inherent aptitudes of women. From the publishers' vantage point, women were 'admirably suited for the work, having a nicety of touch which would enable them to manipulate type with greater facility than men' (*IP*, III, 8 May 1886:470).

Men printers, by contrast, thought printing conferred masculinity on those who worked in it. They considered printing a 'manly art' because it combined intellectual and manual labour.[18] While men conceded that women could do typesetting and cited examples of women who could compose with rapidity and precision, still they argued that women *should not* be printers (*PC*, III, Dec. 1868:293). Men argued that women printers would become 'unsexed' by engaging in typesetting (*Finchers'*, 1 Oct. 1864). They pointed to the danger to women's morals of reading the material being typeset, which might contain matter 'eminently unfitted and highly improper for the perusal of modest young women' (NTU Convention, 1854, in Stevens, 1913: 423). Also, men argued that women would lose their femininity by working alongside men, by hearing the language men use on the shop floor, and by contact with the aggressive, masculine nature of shop floor culture.[19] The tramping system, applying for work at the houses of call, the social drinking while waiting for work, and a host of other rituals enhanced the masculine features of the work culture (Baron, 1982; Cockburn, 1983).

Men printers described the 'awful consequences' which would result to women themselves and to society by placing women to work in newspaper composing rooms.[20] As they put it: 'For our part we should be loth to see a daughter or sister of ours confined to the atmosphere of a morning paper office,. . .We should be loth, too,' they stated, for her to be in a workroom, 'Where she is apt to associate, or come in contact with, men and youth of every grade of morals. . .' (*Finchers'*, 1 Oct. 1864). Contact with the world 'in the same method that man finds necessary would have a pernicious effect upon her [woman's] morals' ('Printers' Manifesto', 1854, in Stevens, 1913:427).

Despite the union men's claims about the jeopardy to women's morals by working as printers, in the 1860s the International Typographical Union established a policy of equal pay for equal work regardless of sex and admitted women into the union on the same terms as men.[21] Men saw admitting women into the union as an extension of men's roles as protectors and providers. Union men considered equal pay for equal work 'chivalrous and generous to the women' (*The Printer*, August 1864). The union would protect women from being used as the tools of unscrupulous capitalists. As some union men argued: 'The men of our local unions. . .should throw around their sisters the protecting power of their organizations, and tell unscrupulous capitalists who thus use the female to degrade the male, that it can be no longer.'[22]

Thus gender was an issue for printers even before the Linotype heightened the salience of the 'woman question'.

INTRODUCTION OF THE LINOTYPE, 1885–1905

The speed and output of printing presses increased dramatically during the nineteenth century.[23] As a result, the bottleneck in printing became the composing room, where type was set by hand just as it had been in Gutenberg's day, a slow and tedious process. Throughout the century many typesetting machines were invented, but none were widely adopted, despite their speed. The high capital outlay required for most typesetting machines, generally $3,000 to $5,000 each, was a major deterrent.[24] Employers had to weigh the potential for expanded productivity against enormously increased capital investment.

The tremendous growth of the newspaper industry in the 1880s changed this picture. Newspaper circulation increased from 9 million in 1880 to 18 million in 1890 and 37 million in 1900 (NYS Department of Labor, 1902:162). The number of newspapers in the US increased from 2,302 to 20,285. At this time, chains and mergers were common and the industry became increasingly concentrated. The publishers of the large newspapers sought the capabilities of typesetting machines and had sufficient capital to afford them.[25]

The Linotype patented in 1885, became the standard mechanical typesetting system for newspaper composition in the early twentieth century.[26] Like other typesetting machines the Linotype utilized a keyboard resembling a typewriter. But instead of the key releasing a type character it released a small brass matrix, which was a mould for casting the type character. When enough matrices collected in the assembler to form a line, margins were justified. Then the operator pushed a lever to start the casting mechanism which poured molten metal into the moulds, creating a 'line o' type' called a slug. After casting the used matrices were mechanically distributed back to their appropriate channels to await reuse. After the slug was used it was melted for future recasting.

The success of the Linotype was not assured from the outset. Many options were available to publishers in the 1880s; even in the 1890s publishers debated the merits of the different typesetting machines. When the American Newspaper Publishers' Association studied the various machines available in 1891, it concluded that other models were either cheaper or faster than the Linotype (ANPA, 1892). According to the Test Committee Report, the Linotype '. . .fell far short in the general result of accomplishing what had been claimed for it by its owners and others.' (Report on Machine Compositiors, *Newspaperdom*, I, 1892–93:16–21).

The early Linotypes were extremely crude machines, constantly breaking down. Sometimes newspapers that had adopted the machines found them so unreliable that they discarded them and reverted to hand composition (*IP*, VI, Oct. 1888). Extra machines and expert mechanics had to be kept on hand in case of breakdown,[27] therefore only the large metropolitan dailies could afford to experiment with the Linotype (Barnett, 1926:4). It was not until significant changes were made in the Linotype after 1900 that it became practical and was adopted on a wider scale (Byrn, 1970:167).

The Linotype's success cannot be attributed to its revolutionary technical ideas. It was not the first machine to combine composing and casting, but earlier machines had remained undeveloped for lack of financial backing (Moran: 1965). The Linotype received financial support from the publishers of the *New York Tribune, Chicago Daily News,* and *Louisville Courier-Journal* (A. Lee, 1937:122). The *New York Tribune* installed its first Linotype in 1886. Others began to install Linotypes in 1889, following an extended strike over publishers' unilateral reduction of wages (US Bureau of Labor, 1904:35).

To promote the machine in the 1890s, the Mergenthaler Company, the Linotype manufacturer, set up schools to train operators. These trainees were sent as strikebreakers to help publishers during strikes and lockouts. (Dumas, 1931:247). The company made it clear to the International Typographical Union that it '. . .intended to install the machines at all hazards and to fight if necessary to do so' (US Bureau of Labor, 1904:35). But eventually the ITU and the Mergenthaler Company negotiated an agreement, the company agreeing to remain neutral in disputes between the union and employers, and to refrain from training a force of operators to be used as strikebreakers. The ITU agreed to encourage its members to learn the machine and not to interfere with its introduction. When affiliated locals struck to oppose the introduction of the Linotype, the ITU interceded and at least in one case the ITU sent in union men from other locals to break the strike (US Bureau of Labor, 1904:35–36; Loft, 1944:49).

CONTROVERSIES OVER THE GENDER AND SKILL DEFINITIONS OF LINOTYPE WORK

The ITU's acceptance of the Linotype set into motion conflicts with employers regarding the machine's implications. The initial introduction of the Linotype into newspaper composing rooms created considerable unemployment of hand compositors.[28] The ITU sought to secure Linotype operation for union members; to replace the piece-rate wage system with a time scale; to obtain wages equivalent to what had been earned with hand composition; to reduce the working day to eight hours; and retain control over hiring and firing, their right to set the production norm and their certification of competence (Dumas, 1931:244; Loft, 1944:48). Central to the union's strategies was its effort to define the Linotype as a skilled masculine process. But in this they met with significant resistance from employers.

Both employers and men printers made claims about the specific inherent characteristics of men and women and the work they were capable of, but they articulated different versions of masculinity and femininity. The union claimed that the work was intrinsically masculine, and that women did not have the necessary abilities to do the job. Employers, however, claimed that women were ideal Linotypists because the work required typically feminine characteristics, such as steadiness and dexterity. For over thirty years following the introduction of the Linotype the typographical union and employers battled over the gender and skill definitions of the new occupation.

Linotype as women's work: the employers' view

The Linotype, like most of the mechanical typesetting machines of the period, was created to do straight compostition only (Baker, 1933: 117). As far back as the 1870s, publishers had expressed a strong interest in typesetting machinery especially for use by woman operators. The *Typographic Journal* (II: June) in 1870 stated:

77

The composing machine is now an accomplished fact. Its precise construction is at present not definitely settled, but as certainly as the next dozen years will come and pass away is it that a composing machine will be used in every printing office. We cannot foresee the effect of this invention, but we may say that it cannot fail to exert a very important influence upon the question of the employment of women as compositors. The machine is specially suitable for female use.

Even before mechanical typesetting technology was developed, employers viewed it as a logical extension of women's work as hand compositors. To the publishers, all typesetting machines, regardless of specific design, were suitable for female use.

Use of the keyboard appeared to open up the work of printing to educated women. Unlike publishers' recruitment efforts of the 1860s, which had focused on uneducated foreign-born women from the clothing and textile industries (Baron, 1982), publishers in the 1890s sought to recruit literate native-born American women from stenography and typewriting backgrounds. (Barnett, 1926:26).

Many of the typesetting machines were marketed as being suitable for women with little training. Linotype advertisements showed women operating the machines, to emphasize the ease with which the machines could be operated. Advertisements and articles in the *Linotype Bulletin* portrayed monkeys, blind people, deaf mutes, and one-handed operators as expert and efficient operators of the machine.[29] Employers and the machine manufacturer claimed that women typists and stenographers could efficiently operate the machine with little or no training on the Linotype itself. As one publisher put it: 'There is apparently no reason why women can not operate typesetting machines quite as well as can men. They are especially apt at the work if they have already acquired proficiency at the typewriter. . .' (EP, 5:15, 30 Sept. 1905). As testimony before an arbitration board, a publisher exhibited a Linotype keyboard. He then showed an uncorrected galley proof claiming his stenographer had produced it on the Linotype after less than ten days' experience (ANPA Bulletin 1249, 15 Jan. 1904).

Employers built on their earlier claims that typesetting was work that was respectable for women because it was intellectual. An article on 'Woman's Work and Wages' (*Harper's*, 37, June–Nov. 1868) considered the position of typesetter or compositor to be 'one of the most pleasant, respectable, and profitable occupations' for women.

These claims were bolstered in the 1890s by contemporary changes in clerical work, particularly with the introduction of the typewriter and growing feminization of office work (Davies, 1982).

Because publishers identified keyboard work on the Linotype as essentially the same as work on a typewriter, they claimed that both required the same worker abilities and characteristics. They then tried to establish that Linotype work was unskilled because it did not require extensive special training on the keyboard. Women Linotypists, recruited from the pool of available typists, received no recognition for the keyboard training they had already, and so could be paid less because the work did not require skill: typing skills were assumed to be natural feminine abilities that women brought to the work.[30]

Linotype as men's work: the union's view

Linotype work heightened dilemmas for male printers. The bases of their definition of masculinity in their work were progressively disintegrating. The physical strength requirements of printing eroded during the nineteenth century through the division of labour and technology. The physically demanding presswork was accomplished by specialized pressworkers and steam-powered presses with hoists. The mental aspects of their work were either threatened by increased supervision and management control, or defined as analogous to clerical work and therefore effeminate.

Men may have accepted the Linotype in part because it diminished rather than increased opportunities for women printers (Abbott, 1910:258). The percentage of women on machines was lower than on hand composition. In 1884, just a few years prior to the Linotype, one quarter of Boston's compositors were women (*IP*, II: October 1884:43). Yet nationwide, by 1900 only 15 per cent of printers and compositors were women, and by 1904 only 520 women operated typesetting machines – about 5 per cent of the total in the US and Canada (Barnett, 1926:28). The typesetter who specialized in straight matter, not the all-around craft printer, was displaced by typesetting technology; 95 per cent of the unemployed printers in 1899 had specialized in straight composition (Annual Report, ITU Convention, 1899, in Tracy, 1913:577).

Men printers supported the Linotype over other machines precisely because it posed less of a threat to their class and gender positions. While other machines separated the setting of type from justifying lines and from distributing type, the Linotype made typesetting a single integrated operation. The Linotype appeared to enhance craft respectability because it did not subdivide the work and because it made typesetting a more masculine process by adding typecasting to the typesetter's job. At the same time, unlike machines that used type characters or kept the typecasting as a separate mechanism, and so kept the operator apart from the heat, dust and discomfort created by the typecasting, the Linotype required the operator to contend with the extreme heat and gas fumes produced by the pot of molten metal located near the operator's seat. Men embraced the Linotype because its dirty work made it less respectable for women (NYS BLS, 24th AR, 1906:xciii).

Printers disagreed with employers' and machine manufacturers' claims about the skills and characteristics required for proficiency as a Linotype operator. According to Lee Reilly, a printer-operator, 'to be rapid and competent requires training as a printer'. The assumption that typists made efficient machine operators, he called 'a delusion'. (*Newspaperdom*, II:11, March 1894:425).

In an effort to deal with the crisis of masculinity posed by the new job process, men began to redefine the source of masculinity. In contrast to earlier years when men claimed the work itself was masculine, after the Linotype they claimed there was 'no sex in labour'. Work did not embody gender; only workers did, and some workers could do the work that others could not do. 'In some varieties of work, the strength of a man is required, or endurance which is too exacting for the female frame. In others, the greater delicacy of manipulation which women can give is demanded' (*Unionist*, XXIV:14/2/01:26). Further, men held on to the belief that they had skill and masculinity, even if the job did not. Inherent masculine characteristics, not just acquired skills, were needed for machine proficiency, therefore men made better operators than women.

Sexual difference between men and women as workers was heightened and redefined in biological terms. Women, men printers argued, could not do the work because women were physically inferior, lacking the necessary mental abilities and the natural temperament needed. Men pointed to their ability to lift heavy formes, and to change the machine magazines as evidence that physical strength was needed for the work. Although the operator rarely actually did these tasks, they claimed it was important that they could do them. But most significantly, men printers claimed that the work required endurance that women lacked.

For the men, endurance was important because it symbolized their intellectual and physical superiority over women. Endurance was used to distinguish hand composition, which they had formerly acknowledged women could do, from machine composition which they claimed women were not capable of doing. They argued that the higher speed attained on machines made the work more exhausting than hand composition, and therefore both mental retention and physical endurance were required (US BLS, 1906:742).

Men printers were forced to emphasize the physical attributes necessary for the job because keyboard work – where the definition of the work as intellectual resided – was increasingly associated with natural female attributes. As a NYC printer described the work in composing rooms in 1903:

> Typesetting is exhaustive work. Standing hour by hour brings on backache and in some men varicose veins and swollen feet. Sitting on the high printing office stool doubles the typesetter up, constraining his arm motions and interfering with his digestion
>
> (NYS, BLS, 1906:xciii).

Gender, productivity and worker competence

In the conflicts over the gender and skill definitions of the new job created by the introduction of the Linotype, a new standard of worker competence and measurement of worker performance developed. Prior to the Linotype, a completed apprenticeship certified competence and was a prerequisite for union membership (US Industrial Commission, 1901:583).

The introduction of the Linotype intensified conflicts over wages and the pace of work. Rather than workers' competence being established upon entrance into the union, publishers required workers to prove their competence on a daily basis at work – to work up to the production standard – in order to acquire and retain their jobs. The replacement of piece rates with time wages, initially supported by the union, ironically further exacerbated conflicts over the pace of work and the production norm.[31] Employers increasingly sought to control and measure the output of each individual employee. Employers encouraged speed contests, adopted bonus systems and some even measured the output and speed of each employee with a device attached to the machine. The president of the American Newspaper Publishers' Association encouraged publishers to adopt the techniques of scientific management to improve production and to reduce workers' control.[32]

Working men's efforts to resolve the crisis of masculinity led them to redefine competence in terms which heightened the demands on them both as men and as workers. In earlier decades they stressed the difference between men and women printers in terms of morality and training. By contrast, in the 1890s men viewed competence as deriving from particular biological traits they had as men, which women lacked, enabling men to work faster and for longer periods. These definitions of masculinity in terms of speed and endurance, however, meant that men workers had to prove themselves as men on an on-going basis. As the US Bureau of Labor Statistics (No 67:707) stated in 1906, 'the effects of new processes and machinery in modern industry has been to enhance quantitative skill while decreasing the relative importance of qualitative skill'. In other words quantitative skill – worker speed and productivity – required endurance (which men purportedly had) and became more important than qualitative skill, which included manual dexterity and intellectual ability (which women supposedly had). By cooperating in publishers' construction of the new technology as requiring endurance and speed, men printers locked themselves into new standards of masculinity, as well as into speeding up production.

Thus men's desire to prevent their work from being defined as analogous to that of typists enmeshed them in speed contests for greater productivity. As the US Bureau of Labor Statistics (No. 67, 1906:721) explained:

> The high average speed maintained by Linotype operators is the foremost factor in preventing the displacement of men by women in this line of work. When the machines first came into use there was a great fear among the printers that female stenographers would work the machines, a fear arising from the close resemblance of the keyboard of the Linotype to that of the typewriter. While it is true that women learn to operate the machine readily they have not the endurance to maintain continually the speed which men maintain.

GENDER, THE IDEAL WORKER AND AUTHORITY RELATIONS AT WORK

An exclusive focus on deskilling diverts attention from the construction of the social relations of production, and the role gender plays in identifying what characteristics employers consider important and reward. Publishers attempted to control work by establishing new criteria for the 'ideal worker' in newspaper composing rooms. Redefining masculinity and its relationship to work was central to establishing these criteria.

While men printers articulated the requirements of the machine in terms of endurance, publishers focused on the characteristics of workers that would transform the social relations of the workplace. For publishers, traditional notions of craft manliness interfered with production and with management's control. The masculine work culture of the pre-Linotype years enhanced printers' control over the work process. For union printers their job was their 'property' and they had the right to control it and set the work standards (Porter, 1954). For example, the union was the arbitrator of labour-employer disputes. Even in the initial years of the Linotype, the Union set the 'dead line' or minimum standards of competency (US Bureau of Labor, 1904:54)

In the 1850s and 1860s, men's work culture had been consistent with the characteristics of hand composition. The old method, particularly on newspapers, required a good deal of slack time while waiting for work, followed by incredible rush periods. There was little pressure to be a steady worker and to work consistently, because extra workers were taken on during the busy periods. This work schedule was compatible not only with drinking and gambling, but also with tramping from city to city in search of work, and with a less disciplined attitude towards work time and dependability. The American Newspaper Publishers' Association complained of the problem of disciplining printers who were 'incompetent, insubordinate, and intoxicated' (ANPA *Labor Bulletin* 358, 1 July 1911). Employers found men printers to be 'supremely offensive in their manners; uncleanly in their personal habits; filthy in their language' (*IP*, 11:10, Sept. 1885: 439).

Publishers sought to enhance managerial authority by seeking out and rewarding workers with the 'proper' behaviour traits and personality characteristics along with technical skills (Edwards, 1976). By redesigning work, publishers hoped to redefine the equation of masculinity with printing work and thereby to transform authority relations. Publishers used the Linotype as leverage to make this transformation. They emphasized that the machine required work styles and worker characteristics that were distinctly different to those needed for hand composition. Because the Linotype lessened the rush before press time, employers argued that the work required more consistent rates of speed over longer periods of time. The Linotype reduced the need for temporary substitutes so that the 'tramping system', in which workers travelled from town to town searching for short-term work, ceased to exist. To optimize production on the machines, publishers claimed, required sobriety, which they made a condition of employment (McCann, 1901:81) Typesetting with the machine, according to management at the *New York Herald*, changed the nature and pace of work, and as a result: '. . .the great magician Progress has summoned the new printer to the helm, and the old printer in consequence passes from the scene of his former usefulness, perhaps to death, surely to oblivion' (*FE*, 111:64, 16 May 1895:9).

As publishers established the speed capability of the machine they became more concerned with continued steady operation and therefore sought workers 'of steady, moderate speed who can be relied upon rather than "record breakers", who are too nervous, irritable, and prone to "lay off" ' (US Bureau of Labor, 1904:76). A 'good operator' was not one who could 'set a word, or two or three words, very rapidly' but one who could 'maintain an evenness of speed' (*LB*, June–July, 1905:123). The change in work styles and characteristics was reflected in changes in attire:

> The contrast between the careless attire and prodigal habits of the old-timer and the garb and deportment of the machine operator is marked. The latter are neatly dressed, bright, active, and of steady habits, and their general appearance would suggest a large class of students rather than newspaper compositors.
>
> (*FE*, 111:64, 15 May 1895:9)

Women, publishers claimed, had the right work habits and proper charcteristics for work on the Linotype: women were dextrous, sober and dependable (Mass BSL, 1895:41–5).Employers preferred women clerical workers as Linotypists because they considered these women neater, quicker, more industrious, more loyal and more trustworthy than men printers.[33] Women received lower wages than men because the characteristics that made them ideal workers publishers claimed were part of women's natural temperament and aptitudes, rather than acquired skills.

Publishers' efforts to transform printing into women's work following the Linotype untimately failed. According to NYS Department of Labor survey in 1926, only fifty-three out of seventy-seven newspapers in the state replying to the survey employed women workers. Of the total of 150 women employed, only sixty-nine were Linotype operators, a few worked on other forms of typesetting machines, while the bulk of women in newspaper printing worked as proof-readers (NY Dept. of Labor. Industrial Bulletin, Nov. 1926:37). Publishers had accepted the union's claims about the need for workers capable of physical endurance. As one article in a publishers' journal put it: 'Standing at case handling type is no fit employment for a delicate or impaired physique, but demands strength of body as well as clearness of brain power' (*EP*, 13:5, 19 July 1913:97).

There were many reasons for the publishers' failure, particularly their inability successfully to recruit female typists. The demand for clerical workers, particularly typists, expanded rapidly in this period.[34] The relatively higher wages for women in clerical work, combined with perceptions of office work as being more respectable, made typesetting less attractive to educated women.[35]

Nevertheless, publishers were successful in transforming the social relations of printing into forms they found more acceptable through a complex process which included redefinitions of masculinity and shifts in the relationship between gender and work. Men printers, for their part, could only successfully maintain their craft and manly respectability by redefining the meaning of masculinity and work.

CONCLUSION: MASCULINITY AND THE GENDERING OF WORK AND SKILL

This chapter has emphasized the importance of examining masculinity to understand more fully how work was organized, how skill was defined and how workplace conflicts developed and were resolved. Research on men's work by focusing on class and by excluding gender has resulted in a distorted historical vision of the transformation of capitalist production.

In the case presented here I have shown how both men printers and their employers struggled over the definition of masculinity and its relationship to work. Gender was not only socially constructed, it was politically contested. The 'contested terrain' identified in previous studies of the labour process is a gendered terrain. The outcome of these struggles over gender definitions affected class relations as well as relations between men and women.

This study casts doubt on the view that working-class men organized to exclude women from skilled jobs, based on a pre-capitalist ideology of gender difference. It documents a transition not only in definitions of gender, but in the ways working men sought to establish a gender identity through work. Prior to the development of mechanical typesetting, union men had based their control over the labour process and male privilege in terms of what men did. Engaging in the work of printing itself conferred masculinity on the participants.

Publishers had long contested printers' control over work and had challenged the working men's view of printing as 'men's work', but it was not until the introduction of the Linotype that men printers were forced to redefine both the meaning of masculinity and its relationship to work. The new technology set into motion a struggle over the gender and skill definitions of the occupation of Linotypist. Given the changes in the work process and the strategies used by employers, men printers found the foundations for their class and gender identities increasingly precarious. Men printers began to legitimate their control by making explicit claims to their innate superiority over women. Now men premised workers' control and male privilege on what men were as men, rather than what they did as workers, as before. Union men and publishers reached a 'negotiated settlement'. While publishers accepted definitions of the new work as masculine, the meaning of masculinity and its relation to work were significantly revised in ways that established new terms of authority between them and union men. Working men maintained their positions as privileged craft workers, but the new definitions of masculinity required them continually to prove themselves at work. In class terms this meant they accepted the speeding up of work; in gender terms this meant that their gender identities were formulated in ways that left them insecure. Thus this research adds further credence to the view that examining how workers create a gender identity is important to understanding class relations and strategies.

Feminist theory has tended to assume antagonistic relations between men and women workers and to define the issue of gender inequality as an all-or-nothing battle. My study indicates rather that tensions between men and women within capitalism have been variable. In the case presented here, conditions rooted in the transformation of capitalist production which threatened men workers' gender and class identities resulted in heightened sexual antagonisms and an emphasis on biological sexual differences. Men printers' masculine identity was not mere ideology that trickled down from other classes. Rather, working men participated in the construction of their gender identities. The rhetoric of sexual difference incorporated into union men's thinking influenced their views of gender equality, and the union policies they pursued – to the detriment of both their class and gender interests.

The conflicts between men printers and their employers discussed here are only a part of the process by which work and class relations in the printing industry were gendered. I have not discussed women's participation in this process. What I have said does not imply that women necessarily accepted the gendered terms of work, or the arguments and claims made by men printers and employers. Indeed, the protest of women printers against night work legislation in New York City during the first two decades of the twentieth century, and their success in getting some legislation repealed, indicates otherwise (Baker, 1969; Lehrer, 1987). Further study should explore the limitations on men's and capital's power to construct gender by examining women's resistance, reinterpretation, and negation of their construction as 'other'.[36]

NOTES

1 See, for example: Barrett, 1980; O'Brien, 1981; MacKinnon, 1982; Brenner and Ramas, 1985; Lewis, 1985; Hamilton and Barrett, 1986; Crompton and Mann, 1986; Walby, 1987; and Acker, 1989.

2 Heidi Hartmann (1976) formulated the capitalist–patriarchy paradigm upon which much subsequent work has been based. See, for example: Eisenstein, 1979; A. Scott, 1986; Cockburn, 1983; Cohn, 1985; Milkman, 1987.

3 For a more detailed critique of the dual systems approach, see: Baron, 1991a and Baron, 1989.

4 Carter and Carter, 1981; Kraft, 1977; Baron, 1983; Baron and Klepp, 1984; Davies, 1982; Zimbalist, 1979a; Crompton and Jones, 1984.

5 Researchers have given far less attention to the ways male workers acquiesced to capital or participated in the production of class relations that operated to subordinate them. For exceptions see: Burawoy, 1979; Knights and Collinson, 1985; and chapters in this volume.

6 Braverman did not develop an explanation for the relationship between deskilling and the feminization of the labour market; he simply attributed it to women being an ideal reserve army of labour (Beechey, 1982).

7 A fundamental feminist critique of Braverman and most research on the labour process concerns the use of the concept of 'skill'. Examination and clarification of this concept is central to understanding occupational sex segregation (see Phillips and Taylor, 1980; Beechey, 1982).

8 For an overview of the British literature, see Rose, 1986. For discussion of issues raised by scholarship on gender and skill, see Thompson, 1983.

9 See, for example, essays in Baron, 1991b; Benson, 1986; Cooper, 1987; Blewett, 1988.

10 Historical and sociological research on male skilled workers typically ignores issues of masculinity. See, for example: Zeitlin, 1985; Zimbalist, 1979b; Roberts, 1976. Cockburn, 1983 is an exception. For a more extended discussion of this problem in the American literature on workers, see Baron, 1991a.

11 Research on working-class masculinity is developing rapidly. See essays by Mary Blewett, Ava Baron, Nancy Hewitt, and Ileen DeVault, 1991 in Nichols and Beynon, 1977; Willis, 1977; Cockburn, 1983; Baron, 1989; McClelland, 1989; Johansson, 1989; Baron, 1991b; Yarrow, in this volume. For discussion of the significance of gender for working-class politics, see Benenson, 1984; Alexander, 1984; Rose, 1986.

12 The motive force of a separate sex/gender system has been variously identified as efforts to control women's labour power in the home (Hartmann, 1981), men's desire to control women's reproduction (O'Brien, 1981) and sexuality (MacKinnon, 1982), to name just a few.

13 For discussion of the concept of gender and its usefulness for understanding work, see: Baron, 1991a; J. Scott, 1988.

14 This chapter focuses on newspaper publishers and printers. Other branches of the industry, such as book and job printing employed distinctly different work processes and technologies. Linotype had its greatest impact on the newspaper branch. For discussion of the different work processes and concerns of the various branches before 1880, see Baron, 1982.

15 Presswork and typesetting had become distinct operations by the 1850s. For more information on printers' occupational culture and union membership in these decades, see Baron, 1982.

16 Address to US printers, 1850, in Lynch, 1925:24; *NY Tribune*, 17 July, 1854, in Stevens, 1913:427.

17 Publishers of women's reform papers such as *The Una, The Lily*, the *Literary Journal*, and *The Revolution* advocated making typesetting women's work and often hired women, but at lower than union wages (Baron, 1982).

18 *PC*, I, 1 Feb. 1867:161/II, Nov. 1867:328. 'Clean', 'intellectual', delicate work, not involving physical labour was considered feminine (S. Eisenstein, 1983:79). Willis (1977) found that working-class boys in England in the current period defined manual work as masculine and desirable, and mental work as effeminate. Cockburn (1983:139) found that contemporary British printers believe white-collar work makes a boy's masculinity suspect.

19 *IP*, 11:3, Oct. 1884–Sept. 1885, 109–10. Rubin (1975) explains that women are 'the subject of a traffic among men' that enhances men's solidarity with each other.

20 'Women in Printing Offices', Letter to the Editor, *Sunday Dispatch*, c.1853, Munsell, IX, 1860:96.

21 Report of the Special Committee on Female Compositors, ITU Convention, 1867, in Stevens, 1913:428–9: Baron 1982.

22 Majority Report, Special Committee on Female Compositors, ITU Convention, 1867, in Stevens, 1913:428–9.

23 Newspapers began using steam-powered cylinder presses in the 1830s

and 1840s, web rotary presses in the 1860s, and stereotyping in the 1860s.

24 Dumas, 1931. The first patent for a typesetting machine was granted in England in 1822. J. Thompson (1904) lists over 70 different typesetting machines developed before 1904.

25 *EP* 8:30, 23 Jan., 1907; A. Lee, 1937, 165–209; J. Lee, 1923, Barnett, 1926. In 1910, thirteen chains operated 62 papers; in 1923, 31 chains operated 153 (A. Lee, 1937).

26 Most typesetting machines were used in newspaper offices, and most of these were Linotypes: in 1904 there were 5,491 machines in newspaper offices, and 1,638 in book and job offices (Barnett, 1926; US BLS 1906: 743n).

27 In smaller plants (with fewer than four machines) the Linotypist became responsible for these tasks (Kjaer, 1929: 45). The new function, directly connected to the Linotype, with machinist-operators representing both functions, created a conflict between two interested internatonal unions – the ITU and the International Association of Machinists, both claiming jurisdiction over the Linotype machinist and machinist-operators (Tracy, 1913).

28 Machine composition reduced the number of typesetters required for the same amount of work. According to a US Department of Labor report, three or four out of every five jobs were eliminated with the introduction of the machine. However, by the early twentieth century the industry's expansion, and the increase in the average number of newspaper pages, began to offset the machine's impact on unemployment (Kjaer, 1925:10–11).

29 *The Printer*, VI:6, July 1865:88; *IP*, VI:7, April 1889:580; *Newspaperdom*, III, Sept. 1894: 122; March 1894: 425: *IP*, V:6, March 1888:442; 'Monkey Operates a Linotype', *LB*, VI: 9, Sept. 1910: 66; 'A Blind Linotype Operator', *LB*, IX:11, Nov. 1913:183; 'Operating the Linotype with the Left Hand' *LB*, XIV:6, Sept. 1917; 'Deaf Mutes Made Good Linotype Operators' *LB*, XIII:12, July 1917:179.

30 'Women and the Linotype: The Machine Offers a New Employment for the Fair Sex', *FE* 361, 26 Jan. 1901:7; 'The Woman Compositor', *Newspaperdom*, 2, 1893–4:241.

31 Loft, 1944:45; Barnett, 1926:10. According to Edwards (1979) management cannot maintain control over output with the piece-rate wage system, since workers retain the ability to resist.

32 *EP*, I:2 Nov. 1901:8; 'A Record Broken', *FE*, 4:22 March 1894:9; US Bureau of Labor, 1904:38, 43; Report of the 25th Annual Meeting of the ANPA, NYC, 26th April 1911, 25–6.

33 Mass, BSL, 1895:29, 41, 45; *IP*, II, Oct. 1884:33; US Dept of Labor, II, 1897:255.

34 Clerical positions increased nineteen-fold between 1870 and 1920. The job category of steno/typist alone increased from 154 in 1870 to 615, 154 in 1920 (Davies, 1982:178–179; DeVault, 1985;).

35 Women hand compositors prior to the introduction of the Linotype earned less than copyists; in 1884 women copyists in Boston earned an average weekly wage of $7.00, while women in printing and publishing

earned an average of $6.61 (Wright, 1969:83). Assuming a woman printer worked 50 weeks in 1884 she would have earned $330/year. The average wage of women printers in 1900 was $310/year. Men printers in 1900, however, earned $610.97, considerably more than women.

Ileen Devault (1985) found that at the turn of the century clerical workers in Pittsburgh were frequently the children of skilled workers. On working-class women's views on respectability, see S. Eisenstein, 1983).

36 I discuss these issues in my book manuscript, 'Men's Work and the Woman Question: The Transformation of Gender and Work in the Printing Industry, 1830–1920.'

REFERENCES

Abbott, E. (1910) *Women in Industry: A Study in American Economic History* (New York: D. Appleton & Co.).

Acker, (1989) 'The problem with Patriarchy', *Sociology* 23 (2); 235–40.

Alexander, S. (1984) 'Women, Class and Sexual Differences in the 1830s and 1840s: Some Reflections on the Writing of a Feminist History', *History Workshop Journal*, 17, (Spring) 125–49.

Andrews, J. B. and Bliss, W. D. P. (1910) *History of Women in Trade Unions.* Volume X of *Report on the Condition of Woman and Child Wage-Earners in the United States.* Hearing, 61st Congress, 2d Session. Senate Document 645. (Washington, D.C.: GPO).

American Newspaper Publishers' Association (ANPA) *Bulletins/Labor Bulletins/Proceedings*, 1902–1920

American Newspaper Publishers' Association (ANPA) (1892) Report to ANPA by Committee in Charge of Type Composition Machines Tournament Held in Chicago, Ill., Oct. 12–17, 1891 (New Haven, Ct: Tuttle, Morehouse & Taylor, printers).

Baker, E. F. (1933) *Displacement of Men By Machines; Effects of Technological Change in Commercial Printing* (New York: Columbia University Press).

Baker, E. F. (1969) [1925] *Protective Labor Legislation with Special Reference to Women in the State of New York* (New York: AMS Press).

Barnett, G. E. (1926) *Chapters on Machinery and Labor* (Cambridge, M.A.: Harvard University Press).

Baron, A. (1982) 'Women and the Making of the American Working Class: A Study of the Proletarianization of Printers', *Review of Radical Political Economics*, 14 (3) (Fall): 23–42.

Baron, A. (1983) 'The Feminization of Legal Work: Progress or Proletarianization', *Legal Studies Forum*, VII (2–3):330–57.

Baron, A. (1987) 'Deconstructing Capitalist-Patriarchy: A Case for Studying the Gendering of Work', paper presented at the Social Science History Association, (October)

Baron, A. (1989) 'Questions of Gender: Deskilling and Demasculinization in the US Printing Industry, 1830–1915', *Gender and History*, 1 (2) (Summer):178–99.

Baron, A. (1991a) 'Gender and Labor History: Learning from the Past, Looking to the Future', in Baron, A. (1991b).

Baron, A. (1991b) (ed.) *Work Engendered: Toward a New History of Americal Labor* (London: Cornell University Press).

Baron, A. (1991c) 'An "Other" Side of Gender Antagonism at Work: Men, Boys and the Remasculinization of Printers' Work', in Baron A. (1991b).

Baron, A. and Klepp, S. (1984) ' "If I Didn't Have My Sewing Machine": Women and Sewing Machine Technology' in Jenson J. and Davidson, S. (eds), *A Needle, A Bobbin, A Strike: Women Needleworkers in America* (Phila: Temple University Press).

Barrett, M. (1980) *Rethinking Women's Oppression: Problems in Marxist Feminist Analysis* (London: Verso and New Left Books).

Beechey, V. (1982) 'The Sexual Division of Labour and the Labour Press' in Wood, S. (ed.): 54–73.

Benenson, H. (1984) 'Victorian Sexual Ideology and Marx's Theory of the Working Class', *International Labor and Working Class History,* 25, (Spring): 1-23.

Benson, S. P. (1986) Counter Cultures: Saleswomen, Managers and Customers in American Department Stores 1890-1940 (Urbana, Ill.: University of Illinois Press).

Blewett, M. (1988) *Men, Women, and Work: A Study of Class, Gender and Protest in the Nineteenth Century Shoe Industry.* (Urbana, Ill.: University of Illinois Press).

Braverman, H. (1974) *Labor and Monopoly Capital: The Degradation of Work in the Twentieth Century* (NY: Monthly Review Press).

Brenner, J. and Ramas, M. (1985) 'Rethinking Women's Oppression', *New Left Review,* 149, (Jan-Feb): 33-71.

Burawoy, M. (1979) *Manufacturing Consent: Changes in the Labor Process Under Monopoly Capitalism* (Chicago: University of Chicago Press).

Byrn, W. (1970) *The Progress of Invention in the Nineteenth Century* (New York: Russell and Russell).

Carter, M. and Carter S.B. (1981) 'Women's Recent Progress in the Professions, or Women Get a Ticket to Ride After the Gravy Train Has Left the Station', *Feminist Studies,* 7 (3) (Fall): 477–504.

Cockburn, C. (1983) *Brothers: Male Dominance and Technological Change* (London: Pluto Press).

Cohn, S. (1985) *The Process of Occupational Sex Typing: The Feminization of Clerical Labor in Great Britain.* (Phila: Temple University Press).

Collinson, D. and Knights, D. (1986) ' "Men Only": Theories and Practices of Job Segregation in Insurance', in Knights and Willmott (eds): 140–78..

Cooper, P. (1987) *Once a Cigar Maker: Men, Women and Work Culture in American Cigar Factories, 1900-1919* (Urbana, Ill.: University of Illinois Press).

Crompton, R. and Jones, G. (1984) *White Collar Proletariat: Deskilling and Gender in Clerical Work* (Phila: Temple University Press).

Crompton, R. and Mann M. (eds) (1986) *Gender and Stratification* (Cambridge: Polity Press).

Davies, M. (1982) *Woman's Place Is At the Typewriter* (Phila: Temple University Press).

DeVault, I. (1990) 'Sons and Daughters of Labor: Class and Clerical Work in Turn-of-the-century Pittsburgh, 1870s–1910s' (London: Cornell University Press).

Dumas, C.J. (1931) 'When the Linotype Came: How the Craft Was Stirred by the Appearance of the First Successful Composing Machine Forty Years Ago', *Typographical Journal*, 79 (Sept.): 242–8.

Editor and Publisher, 1901–14 (*EP*).

Edwards, R. (1976) 'Individual Traits and Organizational Incentives: What Makes a "Good Worker?"' *Journal of Human Resources*, XI (Winter): 51-68

Edwards, R. (1979) *Contested Terrain: The Transformation of the Workplace in the Twentieth Century* (New York: Basic Books).

Eisenstein, S. (1983) *Give Us Bread, But Give Us Roses: Working Women's Consciousness in the United States, 1890 to the First World War* (Boston: Routledge & Kegan Paul).

Eisenstein, Z. (ed.) (1979) *Capitalist Patriarchy and the Case for Socialist Feminism* (New York: Monthly Review)

Emery, E. (1950) *History of the American Newspaper Publishers' Association* (Minneapolis: University of Minnesota Press).

The Fourth Estate: A Weekly Newspaper for the Makers of Newspapers, 1894–1920 (*FE*).

Francis, C. (1917) *Printing for Profit* (New York: Bobbs Merrill).

Gamarnikow, E., Morgan, D., Purvis, J., and Taylorson, D. (eds) (1983) *Gender, Class and Work* (London: Heinemann)

Hamilton, R. and Barrett, M. (eds) (1986) *The Politics of Diversity: Feminism, Marxism and Nationalism* (London: Verso).

Hartmann, H. (1976) 'Capitalism, Patriarchy, and Job Segregation by Sex', *Signs*, 1 (3) Part 2 (Spring supplement): 137–70.

Herron, B. M. (1905) *The Progress of Labor Organization Among Women; Together with Some Considerations Concerning Their Place in Industry* (Urbana, 1ll: University of Illinois Press).

Inland Printer, 1884–1920 (*IP*).

International Typographical Union (1871) 'Report of the Corresponding Secretary', Proceeding of the 19th Annual Session of the ITU, Baltimore, Maryland, (June 5-9) Phila: Cooperative Printing.

Johansson, E. (1989) 'Beautiful Men, Fine Women and Good Workpeople: Gender and Skill in Northern Sweden, 1850–1950', *Gender and History* 1 (2) (Summer): 200–12.

Kjaer, S. (1929) *Productivity of Labor in Newspaper Printing*, US Department of Labor, Bureau of Labor Statistics, Bulletin 475. (Washington, D.C.: GPO).

Knights, D. and Collinson, D. (1985) 'Redesigning Work on the Shopfloor: A Question of Control or Consent?', in Knights D., Wilmott, H. and Collinson, D. (eds), *Job Redesign: Critical Perspectives on the Labour Process* (Aldershot: Gower: 197–231).

Knights, D. and Wilmott H. (eds) (1986) *Gender and the Labour Process* (Aldershot: Gower).

Kraft, P. (1977) *Programmers and Managers: The Routinization of Computer Programming in the United States* (New York: Springer-Verlag).

Lee, A. McC. (1937) *The Daily Newspaper in America: A History of*

Newspapers in the United States Through 250 Years, 1690-1940 (New York: Macmillan).

Lee, J. M. (1923) *History of American Journalism* (Garden City, NJ: Garden City Publishing).

Lehrer, S. (1987) *Origins of Protective Labor Legislation for Women 1900-1925* (Albany: SUNY Press).

Lewis, J. (1985) 'The Debate on Sex and Class', *New Left Review* 149 (Jan-Feb): 108–20.

Linotype Bulletin, 1902-20 (*LB*).

Loft, J. (1944) *The Printing Trades* (New York: Farrar and Rinehart).

Lynch, J. M. (1925) *Epochal History of the International Typographical Union* (Indianapolis: ITU).

Massachusetts Bureau of Statistics of Labor (1895) *25th Annual Report*, Part 1, 'Compensation in Certain Occupations of Graduates of Colleges for Women'.

McCann, J. W. (1901) 'Linotypes in Newspaper Offices: Comment on Changed Conditions', Columbia Typographical Union, *Yearbook*

MacKinnon, C. (1982) 'Feminism, Marxism, Method, and the State: An Agenda for Theory', *Signs* 7 (Spring): 515–44.

McClelland, K. (1989) 'Some Thoughts on the "Representative Artisan" in Britain, 1850-1880', *Gender and History* 1 (2) (Summer): 164–77.

Matthaei, J. (1982) *An Economic History of Women in America: Women's Work, the Sexual Division of Labor and the Development of Capitalism* (New York: Schocken).

Milkman, R. (1987) *Gender at Work* (Urbana, Ill.: University of Illinois Press).

Montgomery, D. (1979) *Worker's Control in America: Studies in the History of Work, Technology, and Labor Struggles* (Cambridge: Cambridge University Press).

Moran, J. (1965) 'An Assessment of Mackie's Steam Type-Composing Machine', *Journal of the Printing Historical Society*, I:57–65.

Mott, F. L. (1941) *American Journalism: A History of Newspapers in the United States Through 250 Years, 1690-1940.* (New York: Macmillan).

Munsell, J. C. (1860) 'Biographical Sketches of Printers and Editors, Strikes and Conventions of Journeymen, State of the Trade, etc., Albany', *Printers' Scraps*, Typographic Library, Manuscript Division, Columbia University IX.

New York State, Bureau of Labor Statistics (1886) 4th *Annual Report*.

New York State, Bureau of Labor Statistics (1906) 24th *Annual Report*.

New York State, Department of Labor (1926) *Industrial Bulletin* (November).

Nichols, R. and Beynon, H. (1977) *Living with Capitalism* (London: Routledge and Kegan Paul).

O'Brien, M. (1981) *The Politics of Reproduction* (London: Routledge and Kegan Paul).

Oswald J. C. (1928) *A History of Printing* (New York: D. Appleton & Co).

Penny, V. (1863) *The Employments of Women: A Cyclopedia of Woman's Work* (Boston: Walker, Wise & Co).

Phillips, A. and Taylor B. (1960) 'Sex and Skill in the Capitalist Labour

Process', *Feminist Review*, 6 (Oct.): 79–88.

Porter, A. R., Jr. (1954) *Job Property Rights: A Study of Job Controls of the International Typographical Union* (New York: King's Crown Press).

Printers' Circular and Stationers' and Publishers' Gazette, 1866–90 (PC).

Roberts, W. (1976) 'The Last Artisans: Toronto Printers, 1896–1914, in Kealey, S. and Warrian, P. (eds), *Essays in Canadian History* (Toronto: McClelland and Stewart, Ltd.).

Rose, S. (1986) 'Gender at Work: Sex, Class and Industrial Capitalism', *History Workshop* 21 (Spring):113–31.

Rubin, G. (1975) 'The Traffic in Women', in Reiter, R. (ed.), *Towards an Anthropology of Women* (New York: Monthly Review).

Scott, A. M. (1986) 'Industrialization, Gender Segregation and Stratification Theory', in Crompton and Mann (eds):154–89.

Scott, J. (1988) *Gender and the Politics of History.* (New York: Columbia University Press).

Stevens, G. A. (1913) *New York Typographical Union# 6: Study of a Modern Trade Union and its Predecessors,* New York State, Department of Labor, Bureau of Labor Statistics, *Annual Report,* 1911. (Albany: J.B. Lyon).

Sumner, H. L. (1910) *History of Women in Industry in the United States,.* Volume IX of *Report on the Condition of Woman and Child Wage-Earners in the United States,* hearing, 61st Congress, 2nd Session. Senate Document 645. (Washington, D.C.,: GPO).

Typographical Journal, 1889–1920 (TJ).

Thompson, P. (1983) *The Nature of Work: An Introduction to Debate on the Labor Process* (London: Macmillan).

Thompson, J. S. (1972) *History of Composing Machines* (New York: Arno Press).

Tracy, G. A. (1913) *History of the Typographical Union, Its Beginnings, Progress, and Development* (Indianapolis: ITU).

Turpain, A. (1908) 'The Development of Mechanical Composition in Printing', *Smithsonian Report for 1907* (Washington D.C.: GPO).

US Bureau of Labor (1904) 11th Special Report of the Commissioner of Labor, *Regulation and Restriction of Output,* 58th Congress, 2nd Session, House Document 734.

US Bureau of Labor, Bureau of Labor Statistics (1906) #67, Vol. 13, (November).

US Department of Commerce and Labor, Bureau of Labor (1903) *Bulletin,* VIII.

US Department of Labor (1897) *Bulletin,* II.

US Industrial Commission (1901) Hearing Before the Industrial Commission. *Report of the Industrial Commission on the Relations and Conditions of Capital and Labor,* Vol. VII: Manufactures and General Business and Testimony taken November 1, 1899 (GPO).

Walby, S. (1989) 'Theorising Patriarchy', *Sociology* 23 (2):213–34.

Willis, P. (1977) *Learning to Labour: How Working Class Kids Get Working Class Jobs* (Westmead: Saxon House).

Willis, P. (1979) 'Shop-floor Culture, Masculinity, and the Wage Form', in Clarke, J., Critcher, C. and Johnson, R. (eds), *Working-Class Culture. Studies in History and Theory* (New York: St Martin's).

Wood, S. (ed.) (1982) *The Degradation of Work? Skill, De-skilling and the Labour Process* (London: Hutchinson).

Wright, C. D. (1969) *The Working Girls of Boston* (New York: Arno Press).

Zeitlin, J. (1985) 'Engineers and Compositors: A Comparison', in Harrison R. and Zeitlin, J. (eds) *Divisions of Labour* (Urbana, Ill.: University of Illinois Press).

Zimbalist, A. (ed.) (1979a) *Case Studies on the Labor Process* (New York: Monthly Review Press).

Zimbalist, A. (1979b) 'Technology and the Labor Process in the Printing Industry', in Zimbalist, A. (1979a): 103–26.

3

INDUSTRIAL DISCIPLINE
Factory regime and politics in Lancaster*

Alan Warde

INTRODUCTION

This chapter is a case study of industrial relations in a town in north-west England during the twentieth century. Lancaster is a medium-sized city in Lancashire, north of the textile belt. While having a continuing role as a regional service centre, the town became heavily industrialized in the late nineteenth century. Thereafter a substantial factory proletariat emerged, largely semi-skilled and un-skilled workers, employed primarily in the production of linoleum and, later, artificial fibres. The paradox of politics in Lancaster is that despite its proletarian population, the labour movement remained extremely weak. In neither industrial nor electoral politics did labour have an impact commensurate with the character of the population. Ironically, it was only with the deindustrialization of the city in the later 1960s that labour showed any collective strength.

By means of a critical appropriation of Burawoy's concept of 'factory regime', the specific local situation is examined in order to explain the deep quiescence of workers in Lancaster's manufacturing establishments. The case study shows that other mechanisms besides control over the labour process affect industrial discipline and political responses to work. Those other mechanisms are as yet weakly theorized, but the operation of labour markets, the nature of the reproduction of labour power and the external political environment are all important.

The first section of this chapter reflects on the theoretical contribu-

* This is a slightly revised version of the paper published by *Work Employment & Society*, 3 (1) (1989) 49–64. Thanks to Richard Brown, editor of the journal, and to Paul Bagguley, John Davies, Mike Savage and John Urry for comments on an earlier draft of this paper. Thanks also to ESRC for support for research into Lancaster history as part of the Changing Urban and Regional System initiative.

tion of Michael Burawoy's *The Politics of Production*, which offers probably the most coherent recent analysis of the broader determinants of the politics of production. The following section gives a brief summary of industrial development in Lancaster. Next, some reservations are registered about explanations of the quiescence of factory workers in terms of paternalism. The paternalism/deferential dialectic does not explain consent in the town. Instead, in the fourth section, the absence of industrial conflict is attributed to a number of institutional forces that rendered workers heavily dependent upon local employers. The conclusion suggests some ways of refining theoretical approaches to the politics of production.

BURAWOY IN THE CONTEXT OF THE LABOUR PROCESS DEBATE

Burawoy's main achievement is his dissection of the political aspects and implications of daily life at the workplace. He escapes the wooden political projections of Braverman by focusing his conceptual categories more directly upon real situations of political alignment over the organization of work. Although Burawoy spent a lot of time on empirical studies of work (even to the extent of getting his hands dirty), and in some ways is best known for his earlier vivid descriptions of the experience of engineering work (e.g. Burawoy, 1979 and 1988) he has developed a firm project of connecting power at the workplace with power outside it. He identifies both how the external environment alters relations-in-production and how relations-in-production might, through political action, alter external and internal social relations. Theoretically, Burawoy succeeds in incorporating the political dimension directly into the concepts employed in analysing work practices, his concept of factory regime epitomizing his concern with power relations.

Burawoy's central conceptual innovations derive from drawing a sharp distinction between the labour process (the technical aspects of the division of labour in production) and the 'political apparatuses of production'. The latter refers to the ever-present *political* moment in production, to what Burawoy more usually calls 'factory regime', *the means used to regulate struggles around the relations of domination in any workplace* (1985:87). The forms and dynamics of the 'politics of production' vary in accordance with the type of factory regime. This conceptualization brings contestation around power relations to the very centre of the analysis of work and makes it necessary to identify all 'means used to regulate struggles', whether or not they involve personal interaction between superiors and subordinates in the workplace itself. One of Burawoy's main contributions is to demonstrate a close link between state politics and the politics of production, charting changes over time in factory regimes and differences across modes of production. Another strong point is his identification of an interdependence between state intervention, factory regime and the reproduction of labour power. This observation is best supported by his comparative analysis of the politics of production in capitalist, state socialist and neo-colonial states. But his case can also be sustained by looking at variations within modern capitalist societies, too. For instance he argues that state intervention in welfare provision has been a major cause of the emergence of 'hegemonic' factory regimes in the twentieth century. In annulling market despotism (the 'pure' type of capitalist employment relation, in which the worker is entirely dependent upon wage labour for subsistence) the degree of dependence of labour upon capital is reduced. This alters the character of factory regimes by changing the nature of the political apparatuses of production. It follows that other ways of reproducing labour power may also affect the nature of the factory regime. Among the examples Burawoy cites are the company state, patriarchalism and paternalism. The implication of this is that more attention should be paid to the determinants of the 'political apparatus', or factory regime. There are, in practice, a variety of means by which factory regimes are conditioned and maintained.

There are a number of general difficulties with *The Politics of Production*. Consideration is given only to manufacturing industries, with an almost total focus on male employees and industrial class struggles. His very vocabulary makes it difficult to see its relevance to service industries or to female work-forces. Along with most Marxist analysis, the specificity of gender divisions is ignored. This seems unnecessary given his valuable insight about the relationship between industrial discipline and modes of reproduction of labour power which, in principle at least, gives access to questions about the links between household arrangements and the workplace. In fact it is only men's workplace struggles that are analysed.

Other problems, more specific to my case study, also arise. Firstly, Burawoy seriously underestimates the significance of labour market conditions, which cannot be reduced to the labour process or the political apparatus of production. Theoretically, the power of the wage relation must be recognized as a factor in the maintenance of industrial discipline. A number of people have pointed to the importance of labour markets in terms of understanding relations at the point of production (Littler and Salaman, 1982; Storper and Walker, 1983) and it is essential that sophisticated understanding of the operation of labour markets be incorporated into the analysis of industrial discipline. This is one of the things that the Lancaster case study emphasizes. The employment relation, the particular conventions or procedures under which workers are able to sell their labour power, is a critical constraint upon the politics of production.

Secondly, to ignore labour markets makes it difficult to appreciate any spatial or local aspects of the politics of production. Yet the nature of the local labour market and impact of the local political system often have immediate consequences for factory discipline. The industrial restructuring thesis associated with Doreen Massey (Massey and Meegan, 1982; Massey, 1984; Cooke, 1989) has demonstrated that there is considerable geographical variation in the types and incidence of class struggles. Successive rounds of capital accumulation deposit labour forces with particular, localized histories of organization and resistance. This, in turn, has effects upon current industrial and urban politics, a sophistication beyond the conceptual grasp of Burawoy's formulation (see also Warde, 1988). Careful examination of localities gives a more precise appreciation of the complexities of industrial struggle.

Thirdly, the links between factory regime and ways of reproducing labour power, though clearly demonstrated in some instances by Burawoy, are weakly elaborated theoretically. The demonstration revolves around the effects of central state intervention through welfare reform in obtaining consent within factories. Important though this is, Burawoy remains impervious to local variations in the manner of reproducing labour power and the complexity of interactions between household, community, state and factory.

Finally, the range and complexity of factory regimes are underestimated, though this may be simply a function of the level of abstraction at which Burawoy's analysis is posed. In actual practice there are a great many means of regulating struggles around the relations of domination in workplaces; the case study of Lancaster gives some indication of this.

THE QUIESCENT INDUSTRIAL PROLETARIAT OF LANCASTER

In this section I offer a very brief sketch of some aspects of the development of capital–labour relations in the manufacturing industries of Lancaster during the twentieth century. Subsequently I shall try to explain the particular character of the local relations of production in terms of mechanisms that have regulated the relations of domination in the town's workplaces.

Lancaster is a small city, population about 50,000 in 1951, surrounded by a very extensive rural hinterland. It was an established commercial and service centre in the eighteenth century when it was a port for the Atlantic trade, but this declined thereafter. It was late to industrialize, its principal industry, oilcloth manufacture (primarily linoleum), expanding only after 1880. The production of artificial fibres became important in the inter-war years, and by the mid-twentieth century these two industries provided about 20 per cent of local employment and over half the manufacturing jobs. Lancaster was not, then, an integral part of the Lancashire textile industry, having few people working in cotton and a comparatively low rate of women's paid employment for the region. The town also had certain service functions, a market in a rural hinterland and some public administrative agencies.

Despite its service functions, the local work-force was primarily a proletarian one during the first half of the twentieth century. The 1951 census recorded 36 per cent of the population in social classes IV and V, a considerably greater proportion than average.[1] This fact reflects the nature of the labour processes in both oilcloth and artificial fibres production. In the linoleum firms there were relatively few craftworkers – only some engineers, a few engravers, etc. There was a considerable amount of heavy, unskilled, manual labour. Semi-skilled tasks tended to be learned on the job; More (1980:114) considered linoleum production a good example of the system of 'following up', with industry-specific skills being learned from experience. From the 1930s most linoleum-producing firms engaged Bedaux, the leading scientific management consultants in the United Kingdom (Littler, 1980: Appendix), which is indicative of a routinized labour process. In Lancaster several other firms also used the Bedaux system, including the largest artificial silk producer.

The most remarkable feature of the industrial development of Lancaster was the quiescence of its working class. There was scarcely a single strike of local workers thoughout the period 1900–64. Neither of the two largest factories in the town (Williamsons and Storeys, both manufacturers of linoleum and oilcloth who between them employed about 35 per cent of the town's work-force in 1921) experienced a single strike. Nor did the Cellulose Acetate Silk Company, the largest artificial fibre producer. The widespread implementation of the Bedaux system in Lancaster met with nothing more than a half-day strike at Standfast Dyers. Besides that, of the large manufacturers, only Nelsons, another of the in-migrant firms of the inter-war period, experienced a brief and unsuccessful strike in 1938 (see Warde, 1990). Before the 1960s strikes were confined to a small proportion of the Lancaster work-force. The woodworkers at the furniture manufacturers Waring and Gillow took action occasionally, including during the General Strike. Asylum workers, the railwaymen and certain groups of municipal employees did likewise. And occasionally engineers in Lancaster would withdraw their labour, but only as a result of national instructions and even then those in the linoleum industry were likely to refuse to strike. In the circumstances it is unsurprising that the town council's strategy to attract new industry in the 1930s was to advertise the cooperativeness of local labour.

Industrial quietism was paralleled by low levels of support for left-wing politics. The party politics of the labour movement suffered a grave defeat in 1911 at the hands of Lord Ashton, the owner of Williamsons, from which it never recovered (see Todd, 1976; Warde, 1990). Labour politics lay dormant for nearly twenty-five years – the Labour Party, for instance, scarcely ever contested local elections. After the Second World War Labour was still weak, the Lancaster constituency only once having returned any but a Conservative MP between 1923 and 1987. Piepe *et al.* (1969), using aggregate data analysis to isolate places that deviated from the class-party model of voting, showed that in 1955 the Conservatives took 11 per cent more of the vote than would have been predicted on the basis of the class composition of the city, making it the most deviant, pro-Conservative constituency in Britain.

EXPLAINING QUIESCENCE

Lancaster's low levels of labour resistance have usually been explained in terms of paternalism and deference. Various historical accounts have seen local employers as paternalists (see Gooderson, 1975;

Myall, 1976) and the main modern study of workers in the town, Martin and Fryer's *Redundancy and Paternalist Capitalism* (1973), a study of the first round of mass redundancies at Williamsons in 1967, offered an analysis in terms of deference. There are both conceptual and empirical reasons for being dissatisfied with explanation in terms of the deferential dialectic. The concept of paternalism is incoherent and over-extended; and, empirically, deference is highly qualified, partial and infrequent in its incidence.

The term 'paternalism' is marked by its imprecise usage, a variety of distinctions often being overlooked. It is necessary to distinguish paternalism as an industrial strategy from paternalism as a political strategy. The latter I will refer to as 'civic benevolence', noting that it is only indirectly directed towards control at work. It is important also to recognize different styles of industrial paternalism, at the least to distinguish liberal, benevolent and sometimes populist forms from authoritarian, often moralistic, disciplinarian sorts. Additionally, there is a significant difference in the logic of the operation of power between personal and corporate forms of industrial paternalism. The personal type entails face-to-face relationships, personal obligation, indulgence and situational deference, and might be said to rest on a type of traditional authority. The corporate type entails more negotiated exchange of benefits with welfare provision becoming part of the employment contract; the paternalist relationship becomes an institutionalized and routinized exchange.

Serious analysis of the effects of the implementation of industrial paternalist strategies is lacking. Probably the most important misperception of the effects of industrial paternalism lies in the presumption that it will have the same effects on workers' wider political affiliations as it does on their behaviour in the workplace. This is to draw too simple a parallel between workplace relations and wider political commitment. This point is recognized by Newby (1979), who argued that among his sample of East Anglian agricultural labourers deference was not a unified, deeply held set of attitudes of broad significance in social and political life, but rather a situational reponse, behaviour systematically deployed when required. This way of approaching deference is corroborated by the failure of various surveys to uncover instances of consistent deferential images of society, as was postulated by Lockwood, or of widespread diffusion of deferential attitudes (e.g. Roberts *et al.*, 1977). These considerations lead to the surmise that workers have been attributed deferential political orientations largely because they do not engage in open class conflict. Newby's comments in the conclusion to his *Deferential Worker* (1979) about farm labourers may be even more true of some industrial workers:

> . . .only a small proportion of agricultural workers can be considered as deferential workers in the sense that they adhere to a reasonably consistent deferential image of society. The deference which is often attributed to the agricultural worker can therefore be seen to rest largely upon a fallacious inference made from his largely quiescent social and political behaviour. This quiescence, however, must be seen to result from the agricultural workers' dependence rather than from his defer- ence. The dependence of the agricultural worker upon the farmer for employment, and in many cases for housing in addition, militates against the overt expression of dissatisfac- tion, except in the most individualistic and negative of ways, like the move to another job.
>
> (1979:414)

It is my contention that quiescence of much industrial labour emanated from dependence rather than deference. In the case of Lancaster, Urry (1980) showed that the survey evidence reported by Martin and Fryer (1973) did not establish the prevalence of defer- ence. Nor does evidence of industrialists' practice in the town confirm the widespread use of industrial paternalism. Before the later 1930s there is no real evidence of the existence of industrial paternalist practices at all. From the 1880s until 1911 there was a significant pattern of civic benevolence on the part of the main employers, but almost nothing by way of concessions to their own workers. The single exception to this was Williamsons' practice of not laying workers off completely during periods of bad trade, and of offering sinecures to some older workers in lieu of pensions. In the 1930s industrial paternalism did emerge with one of the new firms, the Cellulose Acetate Silk Co. Ltd., making a variety of welfare-type provisions for its employees. As a self-congratulatory article in the local newspaper, reflecting on twenty-five years of the firm's existence, noted:

> In addition to the ample facilities which the Company provides for recreational and social enjoyment the management has also endeavoured to assist employees to make provision for the

future by the inauguration, at heavy cost to the Company, of a comprehensive pensions and life assurance scheme.

This scheme was launched as part of the progressive policy of the firm as long ago as 1932 when such schemes were far less common than they are today. . . Employees also enjoy a fortnight's holiday with pay plus six statutory bank holidays.

(*Lancaster Guardian and Observer*, 19 May 1950)

It would seem that Storeys also around this time began to offer some company provision, including sports facilities, a social club and a small amount of housing for key workers. There was, however, no sign of Williamsons, or any of the other major manufacturing employers, having made substantial provision for their employees.

Since the deferential dialectic does not account for worker quiescence it seems worth exploring an alternative explanation in terms of the 'conditions of dependence' which workers faced in Lancaster. These conditions of dependence are integral to the regulation of struggle within the workplace

CONDITIONS OF DEPENDENCE

It is possible to isolate several key mechanisms that operated in Lancaster that may account for the extreme quiescence of the factory work-force. Combined together, they provided very effective means of regulating struggles around the relations of domination in the workplaces of the city. However, they are political apparatuses that cannot be reduced to labour processes, nor do they figure prominently in the literature on managerial strategies. Their combined effect was to render industrial workers powerless, or at least to raise to a very high level the potential costs of overt resistance. The general features of the system of economic power in the town persisted from around 1905 right through to the 1960s. Of course changes did occur, but they did not significantly tilt the balance of power towards labour.

Lancaster has always been a relatively isolated and self-contained labour market. With the exception of the nearby urban district of Morecambe and Heysham, Lancaster is situated in the middle of a large rural hinterland, twenty miles from the nearest towns – Preston to the south and Kendal to the north. In the first half of the twentieth century, Lancaster provided the bulk of opportunities for factory employment in the area and the vast majority of the town's workers were local residents. In this way employers had a captive labour force:

migration was the only serious option to the factories for most working-class people.

On its own this would have been unimportant if there had been open competition between many employers for labour in the area. However, Lancaster was also a dominated labour market, i.e. from the first decade of the century to the 1930s a single industry (oilcloth manufacture) comprising two establishments (Williamsons and Storeys) employed a very substantial proportion of the local workforce. Probably about 35 per cent of the employed population in 1921 worked for one of these two firms. The other major industrial employer of the late nineteenth century, the Carriage and Wagon Works, having begun to run down its operations in Lancaster in 1902, closed finally in 1909. Williamsons and Storeys collaborated in exploiting their dominance in the labour market to the full. They recognized the same unions – craft unions only. They agreed wage levels – a practice which continued through into the 1970s. They also operated exclusive internal labour markets, which was probably the most effective mechanism of all deployed to control workers. Each of these mechanisms is now discussed in more detail.

General unions

There were elements of a 'divide-and-rule' strategy in the major employers' attitudes to trade unions. The unions of skilled workers were acceptable – both Williamsons and Storeys recognized engineering, engraving and weaving unions, paying the regional wage rates for such trades. But apart from a brief period at the end of the First World War, unskilled workers remained non-unionized until the 1960s (Todd, 1976). This was not for want of attempts to recruit on behalf of the general unions. Clynes, the official of the National Union of Gas Workers and General Labourers responsible for Lancaster, frequently came to the town before the First World War, registering his dismay at the lack of support in the linoleum firms. During the inter-war years labour movement speakers continued to comment on the disturbingly low levels of unionization locally. When attempts were made, they foundered.

Williamsons and Storeys simply refused to countenance general unions. Williamson seemed to need to do little more than announce that he would not employ union members. In the context of his despotic relationship to his workers, this was probably sufficient. He was reputed to use a telescope at his home to watch workers arriving at work in the mornings and he kept a 'black book' recording miscreant behaviour among his workers. In 1911 he dismissed workers for being political supporters of the Independent Labour Party (ILP).

The situation in the linoleum factories seems to have been replicated in the new firms which located in Lancaster between the wars. The brief and unsuccessful strike to obtain recognition for the National Union of Dyers, Bleachers and Textile Workers at Nelsons Silk Ltd. in 1939 was, for instance, handled in a most authoritarian manner (see Warde, 1990).

Wages

The solidarity of the employers in Lancaster was one of the principal features of the town. Throughout the century there is evidence of collaboration over wage levels. Williamsons and Storeys had semi-official agreements about pay. There is, for instance, a revealing letter, marked 'private and confidential', from Storeys to Williamsons about the implications of the introduction of the Bedaux system:

> This, we believe, will mean that some operatives will be paid on a higher scale than those doing a (more or less) corresponding job at your mills, while in other cases the opposite will hold good.
>
> We are anxious to begin working on the new base rates as soon as possible, but before doing so, desire to give you all the information you may wish to have in regard to them.
>
> I understand that we were in agreement on this matter when we discussed it, and I would be glad to have a line from you, confirming this arrangement.
>
> (Lancs. County Record Office, Jas. Williamson & Son Ltd., Sundry letters *re* terms, wages, etc., 1929-1935. DDSy 1295)

As regards craftsmen, the regional offices of the unions would inform Williamsons of changes in agreed rates. Williamsons would usually, though not always, advance or cut the rates for their employees accordingly. They would then send Storeys notification of their decision and the latter would do likewise (see Lancs. County Record Office, ibid). Surviving correspondence between the firms suggest that this was the case until after the Second World War. A local labour shortage in the later 1940s gave some problems, Storeys' directors' minutes recording agreement that *all* information regarding wages be exchanged with Williamsons in recognition of 'changed circumstances in Lancaster when once Williamsons, Storeys and Waring & Gillow were the only three manufacturing firms in the town' (Lancs. C.R.O., Storeys Directors' Minute Book, 25 July 1950, p.266). Thereafter, management met on a regular basis to coordinate wage rates for non-skilled labour. There was, then, no wage competition between employers for the bulk of their manual labour, but rather a united front. This was probably facilitated by the fact that the labour market was both self-contained and dominated by large firms.

Internal labour markets

Probably the most effective mechanism of all maintaining the dependence of workers was the operation of internal labour markets at Williamsons and Storeys. Internal markets are not very well understood. So far as their effects on industrial politics are concerned, the worker reponses produced can easily be confused with the deference frequently attributed to workers in paternalist enterprises. In Lancaster, especially, where there were relatively few alternative opportunities for unskilled workers, the internal labour markets of the two main employers rendered the work-force heavily dependent. Investigation into the organization of Storeys shows that it was very rare for a worker aged eighteen or over to be taken on by the firm – only 13 per cent of the workers taken on between 1925 and 1937 were over eighteen and the majority of those had actually been employed previously by the firm. Thus, there was effectively a single port of entry for labourers. The resulting job-for-life meant that industrial indiscipline was a potentially very costly individual risk, because obtaining a job elsewhere in the area would be extremely difficult. Various devices were used to maintain the exclusivity of the internal labour market, including collaboration between the two employers. One entry in a register of leavers from Storeys gave the reason for the dismissal of a certain Vincent Landor as 'Discharged. We found he had worked for J[ames] W[illiamson] and S[on] and had not left properly (they complained)' (Storeys Leavers' Book, 1897–1907). Such devices were further bolstered by the mode of training in the industry – the system of 'following up' (see More, 1980). In many respects the mechanism of the internal labour market is a more powerful reason for industrial quiescence than the transparent and shocking aspects of Ashton's practices of surveillance and coercion. The cost of industrial or political resistance was frequently too great.

The strength of the main employers, was, then, considerable. Williamsons and Storeys in particular ensured that there would be no unskilled unions, low wages and no mobility between firms. More surprising was the situation after the arrival of new firms in the late 1920s, when Lancaster experienced a period of industrial restructuring. Firms associated with textile manufacture and processing, and especially manufacture of artificial fibres, came to Lancaster, the most important of them being the Cellulose Acetate Silk Co. Ltd., Standfast Dyers and Nelsons Silk Ltd. In consequence, the labour market was tight even at the height of the Slump: only 6.5 per cent men were recorded as unemployed in the 1931 census.

In terms of industrial relations the restructuring of the 1930s had no perceptible effect. Despite the introduction of the Bedaux system of work control, Lancaster remained calm as ever. The principal reason was that employer collaboration and internal labour markets continued to operate. That, mixed with industrial powerlessness of workers, was sufficient to maintain employer domination in the factories. Restructuring had some effect on political mobilization, but almost exclusively as a result of changing behaviour in the politics of reproduction of labour power.

The Labour Party became more active in the late 1930s and began to mobilize some support. As in many place where unions were not very strong, it was issues of consumption (the provision of public welface services, especially housing) which became central in Labour Party politics (see Savage, 1987; Mark-Lawson, 1988), but that was in a context of a general shift in service provision. The older civic benevolence ceased, but during the inter-war years the local authority did not significantly compensate: Lancaster was mean in its provision of services throughout the inter-war years (see Mark-Lawson *et al.*, 1985). Voluntary provision thus continued to play a major role. It was under these circumstances that a couple of companies began to make provision for their own employees, but the shortfall gave Labour the opportunity to mobilize support by pressing for better state provision of welfare services (see Mark-Lawson and Warde, 1987). Still the forces of labour had little political impact. The employers retained high levels of influence over the reproduction of labour power: there was little reduction in the dependence of the Lancaster working class, in a town where job oportunities and labour resistance were so effectively controlled by the major employing organizations. It was only with economic restructuring in the 1960s that the distinctive conditions of dependence of Lancaster workers were removed.

SOME ANALYTICAL CONCLUSIONS

The case study of Lancaster suggests a need for further analytical clarification of Burawoy's general focus on the politics of production. His concept of factory regime is particularly useful: first, in its specific focus on political apparatuses regulating conflict in the workplace; and second, in directing attention towards a complex array of extra-industrial forces, including employer and state intervention in the provision of services for the reproduction of labour power, that served to maintain industrial discipline. However, he underestimates the range of factors that regulate struggles around the relations of domination at work. In Lancaster, local political hegemony, the nature of the local labour market for certain grades of job and the intertwining of internal and external labour markets were all significant. Four general points arise.

First, the Lancaster case leads to a more sophiscated appreciation of one of the ways in which internal labour markets can ensure control in the workplace. Previous literature has been largely concerned with 'job ladders'; internal labour markets are seen primarily as systems of promotion, with greater or lesser parallels to bureaucratic hierarchy (Doeringer and Piore, 1971). The distinctiveness of the Lancaster internal labour markets was more their function as exclusionary devices. To all outward appearances the factory workers of Lancaster's two largest factories must have appeared very loyal, since they tended to remain with same employer for life. However, they had little choice. Employer collaboration, rather than provision of benefits for their employees, produced patterns of life-long employment. In a dominated labour market, employers could use their system of mutual exclusion to ensure factory discipline. It also kept down wages.

Theoretically, it is significant how internal labour markets bridge the gap between labour process and local labour market. Indeed, in this instance, it is difficult to separate out the employment relation from the authority relation. This also constitutes a distinctive way of segmenting labour markets, by reducing the number of jobs available to certain categories of worker.

Second, these reflections on conditions of dependence indicate the extent to which *locality* is implicated in the reproduction of those conditions of dependence. In Lancaster, it was important that the major manufacturing firms at the beginning of the century were local. It was also important that Lancaster was an isolated and self-contained labour market: except where workers were willing to migrate (which they appear to have been loathe to do, in general) their employment prospects depended on the firms established in the town. The spatial element of isolation made it more obvious and easier for employers to cooperate in regulating the labour market. Declining to take workers previously employed by another firm and making agreements on wage levels for process workers were two further mechanisms for control, both strongly facilitated by, and probably impossible in the absence of, clear geographical boundaries.

Third, other aspects of the local social formation also had an impact on behaviour within factories. The patterns of local politics were critical in the establishment of industrial discipline within the factories of Lancaster. The political hegemony established by Ashton in 1911 continued to reverberate even though it was not positively reinforced politically by major employers. That defeat was a confirmation of the powerlessness of the local organized working class and apparently discouraged mobilization thereafter. To the extent that Labour politics made progress it was more in the fields of urban politics, with the housing issue in particular providing a base for mobilization. But as a result of the way in which services for the reproduction of labour power were organized in the town, dependent for a long period from the 1870s until the First World War on the civic benevolence of the employers, Labour's impact even in this sphere was considerably retarded. Gradually the implementation of central government legislation increased the role of state provision and the coverage of the voluntary mode was reduced, though even in the 1970s there remained a powerful voluntary tradition. Under different structural conditions, modes of service provision could have been quite different (see Mark-Lawson et al., 1985), but in the event many of the resources required for the reproduction of labour power, including training, health care, recreation facilities, support for the poor, etc., were provided by voluntary institutions subsidized by the large employers and run by middle-class personnel. Lancaster developed few mutualist institutions of the working class, only the Co-op really achieving much support. Indirectly, class power was exercised and displayed through the public institutions for provision of services.

Finally, the case study indicates how processes of the reproduction of labour power affect discipline in the factory. It was a fundamental proposition of Burawoy that institutional modes of reproducing labour power affected the character of factory regimes. The less workers were dependent on employers for basic conditions of survival, the less authoritarian were employer/employee relations. Thus, in charting the shift from despotic to consensual regimes around the turn of the twentieth century, Burawoy emphasized the role that state intervention in welfare provision had in removing the worst excesses of a system of market despotism. The issue is more subtle.

The concept of the reproduction of labour power is a loose and difficult one, to be employed with care. I use it here merely as a generic, descriptive term referring to the systemic need for workers to be 'adequately' fed, trained, sheltered and transported – mostly processes occurring outside the workplace but ones which remain a matter of central concern to employers as well as employees. In the present context, what is interesting is the relative levels of intervention of the state and especially employers in the process. Historical analysis has shown intervention to be highly variable, with different modes of institutionalization having differing effects upon industrial discipline. Workers are not now, and scarcely ever have been, dependent solely upon wages: if a proletarian is someone who is entirely dependent upon wage labour for subsistence then history has seen few proletarians, and even fewer *male* proletarians. Market despotism is a pure, limiting type of relationship in capitalist society, not a normal condition. In fact, the propertyless draw on a range of resources that contribute to the reproduction of their labour power – *inter alia*, domestic labour, kin networks, mutual aid, state provision and non-wage provision by employers. Employer interventions take many forms: there are work-camps (Burawoy, 1985), factory villages (Pollard, 1964), company towns (Gaventa, 1980; Hareven, 1982), traditional paternalist workplaces (Joyce, 1980), corporate welfare provision (Littler, 1983), company housing (Melling, 1981), tied cottages, (Newby, 1979), civic benevolence and charitable provision. Forms of provision, and the available alternatives, have direct implications for worker resistance: the more there is a system of unitary power, where employers control job opportunities and resources for reproducing labour power, the less powerful are the workers (Gaventa, 1980). The way in which the reproduction of labour power is organized locally is an important determinant of workplace discipline, a key element in the means used to regulate struggles around the relations of domination in any workplace.

The concepts employed by Burawoy need to be further developed through examination of the interaction between labour process, labour market and the reproduction of labour power. The examination of these three mechanisms gives a powerful insight into alternative ways of maintaining industrial discipline.

NOTES

1 In their analysis of the 157 British towns with populations of over 50,000 in 1951, Moser and Scott (1961) showed that only seventeen towns had higher proportions than Lancaster of classes IV and V. Among the towns with *lower* proportions were found the likes of Gateshead, Sunderland and Rotherham.

REFERENCES

Burawoy, M. (1979) *Manufacturing Consent: changes in the labour process under monopoly capitalism* (Chicago: Chicago UP).

Burawoy, M. (1985) *The Politics of Production: factory regimes under capitalism and socialism* (London: Verso).

Burawoy, M. (1988) 'Piece rates, Hungarian style' in Pahl, R. (ed.), *On Work: historical comparative and theoretical approaches* (Oxford: Blackwell): 210–28.

Cooke, P. (ed.) (1989) *Localities* (London: Hutchinson).

Doeringer, P. B. and Piore, M. F. (1971) *Internal Labour Markets and Manpower Analysis* (Lexington Mass.: Heath).

Gaventa, J. (1980) *Power and Powerlessness: quiescence and rebellion in an Appalachian Valley* (Oxford: Clarendon Press).

Gooderson, P. (1975) 'The Social History of Lancaster 1780–1914', unpublished Ph.D. thesis, University of Lancaster.

Hareven, T. (1982) *Family Time and Industrial Time*, (Cambridge: CUP).

Joyce, P. (1980) *Work, Society and Politics: the culture of the factory in later Victorian England* (Brighton: Harvester).

Littler, C. R. (1980) 'The Bureaucratisation of the Shop-Floor: the development of modern work systems', 2 vols., unpublished Ph.D. thesis, London School of Economics.

Littler, C. (1983) 'A comparative analysis of managerial structures and strategies', in Gospel, H. and Littler, C. (eds). *Managerial Strategies and Industrial Relations: a historical and comparative study* (London: HEB): 171–96.

Littler, C. and Salaman, G. (1982) 'Bravermania and beyond: recent theories of the labour process', *Sociology*, 16:251–69.

Mark-Lawson, J. (1988) 'Women, Welfare and Urban Politics 1917–1936', unpublished Ph.D. Thesis, University of Lancaster.

Mark-Lawson, J. and Warde, A. (1987) 'Industrial restructuring and the transformation of a local political environment: a case study of Lancaster'. *Lancaster Regionalism Group Working Paper No. 33* (University of Lancaster).

Mark-Lawson, J. Savage, M. and Warde, A. (1985) 'Women and local politics: struggles over welfare, 1918-1939', in Murgatroyd, L., Savage, M., Shapiro,

D., Urry, J., Walby S., Warde, A. and Mark-Lawson, J. (1985), *Locality, Class and Gender* (London: Pion): 195–215.

Martin, R. and Fryer, R. H. (1973) *Redundancy and Paternalist Capitalism: a study in the sociology of work* (London: G.A. Unwin).

Massey, D. (1984) *Spatial Divisions of Labour: social structures and the geography of production* (London: Macmillan).

Massey, D. and Meegan, R. (1982) *The Anatomy of Job Loss: the how, why and where of employment decline* (London: Methuen).

Melling, J. (1981) 'Employers, industrial housing and the evolution of company welfare policies in Britain's heavy industry: West Scotland 1870-1920', *International Review of Social History*, 26 (3):255–301.

More, C. (1980) *Skill and the English Working Class* (London: Croom Helm).

Moser, C. A. and Scott, W. (1961) *British Towns: a statistical survey of social and economic differences* (Edinburgh: Oliver and Boyd).

Myall, A. E. (1976) 'Changes in Social Control in Lancaster 1913–38', unpublished M.A. Thesis, University of Lancaster.

Newby, H. (1979) *The Deferential Worker* (Harmondsworth: Penguin).

Piepe, A., Prior, R. and Box, A. (1969) 'The location of the proletarian and deferential worker', *Sociology*, 3 (2):239–44.

Pollard, S. (1964) 'The factory village of the industrial revolution', *English History Review*, 79:513–31.

Roberts, K. *et al.* (1977) *The Fragmentary Class Structure* (London: Heinemann).

Savage, M. (1987) *The Dynamics of Working Class Politics*, (Cambridge: CUP).

Storper, M. and Walker, R. (1983) 'Theory of labour and the theory of location', *International Journal of Urban and Regional Research*, 7:1–44

Todd, N. (1976) 'A History of Labour in Lancaster and Barrow-in-Furness 1890–1920', unpublished M. Phil. Thesis, University of Lancaster.

Urry, J. (1980) 'Paternalism, management and localities', *Lancaster Regionalism Group Working Paper No. 2* (University of Lancaster).

Warde, A. (1988) 'Industrial restructuring, local politics and the reproduction of labour power: some theoretical issues', *Environmental and Planning D: Society and Space* 6 (1):75–95.

Warde, A. (1990) 'Conditions of Dependence: working class quiescence in Lancaster in the twentieth century', *International Review of Social History* 25(1):72–105.

4

CLERICAL CONSENT
'Shifting' work in the insurance office
Andrew Sturdy

INTRODUCTION

Through an empirical examination of clerical consent, this chapter addresses two interrelated concerns: the broadly inadequate treatment of subjectivity within labour process literature (cf. Knights and Willmott, 1990) and more specifically, the continuing stereotypical portrayal of clerical workers. With regard to the latter, continued deskilling, hierarchical/gendered segregation and intensification of labour have apparently rendered untenable 'traditional' forms of clerical commitment and cooperation (Braverman, 1974; Tepperman, 1976; Downing, 1980; Crompton, 1983). By contrast, the increasingly conflictual 'worker' orientation implied in such accounts has been challenged. Here, remnants of 'benign' managerial regimes and the persistence and even growth of limited opportunities for promotion have been cited as continuing to provide the basis for an albeit 'compensatory' form of cooperation based on material and/or status privilege (Thompson, 1983; Storey, 1983; Crompton and Sanderson, 1989). In short, clerical workers have been stereotyped as either different to manual workers by having self-control or commitment, or equivalent to them but only in terms of militancy and/or compliance. Both these positions tend to neglect the subjective experience of work and subordination. In particular, a preoccupation with control structures and the (working/middle) class situation of clerical workers prevents a consideration of the possibility that, whether partially 'privileged' or wholly 'proletarianized', clerks may also engage in the types of consenting practice identified among manual workers.

Drawing on case study research in two UK insurance companies, this chapter examines the practice of 'shifting' work, which has parallels with that of 'making out' on the shopfloor as described by

Burawoy (1979). However, his account is subjected to critical examination in an attempt to explore how coincident conflict and cooperation among workers can be understood at the level of individual subjectivity.

The chapter is organized as follows. Firstly this introduction is developed through review of subjectivity and clerical consent in the labour process. In the second section, the case study companies and practice of 'shifting' are introduced. Having identified the practice as a form of compliance that is distinct from 'traditional' forms of clerical commitment, the localized management control structures associated with it are examined. Here, the simultaneously constraining and enabling character of control is shown to account for the compliant yet self-disciplinary nature of work involvement in 'shifting'. In the final part of the section, this apparent tension is explored further, through the observation that the practice is discontinuous or fragile in form, coinciding with resistance and workers' partial penetration of (seeing through) conditions of subordination. It is a form of escape *into* work.

This, principally structuralist, interpretation is then developed in the third section by examining the experience and reproduction of subordination and by introducing a theory of subjectivity that accounts for workers', sometimes compulsive, interest in control through 'shifting' work. Rather than drawing upon a fixed or latent concept of human nature, the practice is shown to reflect and reproduce individuals' self-defeating preoccupation with securing a sense of personal identity and control that denies (and obscures) the impermanence and inter-dependence of the existential and social world (Knights and Willmott, 1983). Worker resistance is then re-examined in an attempt to account for coexistent conflict and cooperation among individualized and interdependent subjects.

Worker consent and subjectivity

The stereotypical picture of a manual worker as adopting a purely instrumental effort/wages orientation and thereby stopping working when coercion is removed (Mann, 1973:23) can be dismissed as oversimplistic (cf. Goldthorpe *et al.*, 1968). 'Work ethic' and related socialization theories present the opposite extreme (Baldamus, 1961; Thompson, 1967; Weber, 1974; Fromm, 1980). Nevertheless, the notion of working hard for self and others' respect and the literature highlighting the significance of gendered and 'cultural' apprenticeships for work amply illustrate the element of self-

116

discipline or willing involvement in the work behaviour of subordinate labour (Sennett and Cobb, 1973:100; Strauss, 1974:85; Willis, 1977; Pollert, 1981). While recognizing the importance of these so-called 'external factors' or 'imported consciousness within the labour process (see the Introduction to this volume and also Sturdy, 1990), the concern of this chapter, like that of Burawoy (1979), is with self-disciplinary cooperation 'produced' through work tasks – workplace consent. By focusing upon labour consent, Burawoy not only helped counter the early neglect of subjective action in labour process literature, but also the subsequent ideologically informed preoccupation with worker conflict and resistance (Thompson, 1983:154). However, the principal contribution of *Manufacturing Consent* was showing how a form of self-disciplinary and cooperative involvement in work is produced, not from ideological inculcation or socialization (value consensus), but through participation in workplace practices or 'games' such as 'making out' (Burawoy, 1979:27). These practices reflect an adaptation to, or 'escape' from, workers' experience of subordination, yet involve a willing engagement in work effort and thereby, paradoxically, actively *reproduce* the conditions of that subordination. They are to be distinguished from 'passive' adaptations where workers attempt to escape from their work activity either mentally, through day-dreaming, indifference or instrumentalism, for example, or physically, by active resistance or work avoidance. In this way, they can be considered as escapes *into* work. It is from the, albeit limited, element of worker 'choice' in this form of adaptation that Burawoy derived the term 'consent' as opposed to 'compliance' (ibid.) Moreover, participation in 'choosing' was also shown to *obscure* from workers the exploitative nature of capitalist production relations (ibid:93).

While Burawoy has been criticized for underplaying the challenge posed to management control by labour resistance (Thompson, 1983: 165–70), the essentially conflictual and unstable nature of the labour process is maintained, in that control structures are seen to produce both conflict ('crises') and cooperation (1979:12 and 89). The latter is derived from the scope for 'choice' or autonomy inherent even in the most subordinating control forms. In this way Burawoy, at least implicitly, regards management control as both enabling and subordinating or restricting for workers (see also Giddens, 1984).

The theme of coincident conflict and cooperation is explored elsewhere in labour process literature by reference to the *structural interdependence* of capital and labour, or the 'control – engage' dilemma (Friedman, 1977; Cressey and MacInnes, 1980; Manwaring and Wood, 1985; Edwards, 1986). For example, Thompson and Bannon note how capital's dependence on labour's exercise of control for profitable production ensures that management seeks to actively involve workers in the labour process. This is, of course, counterposed by the requirement to minimize labour costs through intensification of management control. Accordingly, a whole range of 'overlapping worker responses' or involvements from resistance to consent are apparently accounted for (1985:98–9). However, such determinism is inadequate. Indeed, as noted in the Introduction to this volume, beyond an explanation in terms of their consequences for the structure of capitalism, the actions of labour and subjectivity itself remain largely unexamined in the literature (Knights, 1990). Where they are considered, it is by a, usually implicit, reference to an essentialist view of the human subject as creative and autonomous that is suppressed by the determining structure of capitalism (Marx, 1970; Braverman, 1974; Cressey and MacInnes 1980; Glenn and Feldberg, 1979).

Burawoy recognized the necessity for Marxist literature to clarify its assumptions about human nature (1979:237). Ironically, his own position is somewhat ambiguous. He is critical of Marxist psychology (e.g. Marcuse, 1964) that presents labour as having had its emancipatory potential stripped away by ideological inculcation in monopoly capitalism (1979:200–1,236). Rather, in addition to his emphasis on consent through active participation in the labour process, he suggests that subjugation is incomplete. Following the view of Reich (1972) on the 'impermeability . . . of [the] individual . . . instinctual impetus to liberation' (1979:237) and of the 'spontaneous subjectivity' (ibid:229) of Habermas (1975), Burawoy points to:

> . . . the empirical existence of a human potential for emancipation, to an instinctive compulsion of workers to collectively control the labour process – a compulsion that under capitalism expresses itself in the distorted form of a game.
>
> (1979:237)

This suggests, once more, an essentialist view of the human subject whose expression is distorted. However, elsewhere, he stresses that workers' interests are not 'primordial' (nor the product of socialization), but emerge from the organization of work relations. They are shaped or regulated by management control, but not solely, for this also provides the scope for choice, or for workers' own 'initiatives' (ibid:85–6). It is the exercise of this 'choice' in the construction of games and pursuit of *control* that Burawoy and others leave inadequately examined at the level of the subject.

The aim of this chapter is not to develop a 'full theory of the missing subject' as Thompson urges (1986:17) (see Knights, 1990; Wilmott, 1990) but to expand on Burawoy's work by providing a psychologically informed account of worker consent in practice. While maintaining the critical and structurally grounded perspective of labour process theory, the Marxist traditions of a crudely determined or essentialist view of the subject are discarded without recourse to voluntarism. Rather, workers' practices of consent and their interest in control are accounted for as indentity/security-seeking 'strategies' pursued by individualized and existentially vulnerable subjects (Fromm, 1980; Knights and Collinson, 1985; Knights and Willmott, 1985). This position is derived from literature of an interactionist tradition. Here, subjectivity is not fixed or latent in character, but is continuously produced and reproduced throughout life through the development of self-consciousness and interaction with and, therefore, dependence upon, others (Mead, 1934; Goffman, 1959; Laing, 1961; Blumer, 1969). For example, Berger and Luckman describe the distinctively human relationship to the world as 'open' through which the formation of self occurs as a subjectively and intersubjectively recognized *identity* (1967). Dependence on others combined with the necessary experience of the world as *separate* from self and uncertain, presents a challenge to the sense of self, giving rise to existential anxiety or vulnerability.

> Faced with the precariousness of identity implicit in the unpredictability of social relations, individuals are constrained to construct a 'nomos' that offers a degree of protection from such uncertainty.
>
> (Knights and Willmott, 1985:26)

In other words, in response to this anxiety, individuals attempt to 'close' or contain the experience of 'openness' by constructing an identity or sense of self that denies and obscures the interdependence and impermanence of its constitution.

Clearly, the concept of a 'vulnerable' subject may also be regarded as essentialist. However, in contrast to the fixed character of creativity typically ascribed in Marxist literature, subjectivity may be constituted in many forms or identities. Indeed security-seeking strategies are multifarious but characteristically involve an attempt to *control* or

119

solidify self and/or the social world (including others). For example, in a critical and philosophical account of individual freedom, Trungpa talks of 'trying to grasp' through indifference, aggression and 'passion' (1976:12). Similarly, Sartre describes how individuals construct a 'distance' or sense of order through indifference, domination and/or becoming subordinate to others (1978). More concretely, it may be seen how indifference provides an, albeit precarious, means of denying powerlessness or uncertainty and securing a sense of being in control that is independent of others. Equally, a preoccupation with hierarchical status may provide a fixed location or identity in relation to others.

The constitution of subjectivity through the pursuit of existential security is by no means independent of structures of control. Rather, it is both a condition and consequence of them (Willmot, 1990). This relationship is explored towards the end of the chapter in accounting for the consenting practice of 'shifting' and, more generally, coexistent conflict and cooperation. Before introducing the case study material, the portrayal of clerical workers in labour process and other literature is now reviewed.

The neglect of clerical consent

Not surprisingly, labour process studies of 'white collar' or clerical work parallel the broad development of the debates on manual labour. A structural focus on management control and the degradation of work was followed by an incorporation of subjective action in terms of resistance. However, the parallel is incomplete, for there has been no adequate account of clerical consent. Rather, the reaction to a preoccupation with worker resistance has pointed to the persistence of former paternalist or 'benign' office regimes as a counter to the often exaggerated accounts of the 'factory office'. Partly as a consequence, where consent is referred to, it is by drawing upon traditionalist Weberian views of clerical workers' 'self-control' that arises from a concern with (middle-class, managerial or, at least, privileged) status and compensates for their experience of routine work and blocked mobility – 'the cultural compensations of status' (Thompson, 1983:173). This broadly corresponds to a counterpose stereotype to the one of manual workers, mentioned earlier, where workers 'internalize' employers' work norms and thereby do not stop working if close control is removed or relaxed (Mann, 1973:23)

It is possible to suggest that the contrasting accounts of white collar workers as either self-disciplined or complaint/resistant reflect the long-established trend of polarization within this sector of employment (Klingender, 1935; Lockwood, 1958; Crozier, 1967; Braverman, 1974; Atkinson, 1978; Crompton 1979; Rolfe, 1985). Indeed, it is often useful to divide these workers loosely into one group of primarily male and/or qualified employees with some prospect of promotion and relatively skilled or highly valued jobs and another, the vast majority, with converse characteristics[1]. However both of the aforementioned stereotypes can be found in studies of apparently similar types of workers (Storey, 1983; cf. Crompton, 1983). Moreover the polarity should not concern us here for, whether or not a privileged (or any) 'cooperative' form of status is available/aspired to, the conditions of subordination appropriate to other forms of consent are prevalent in white-collar work generally and clerical work in particular. For example, routine jobs have been common in clerical work for some time (Klingender, 1935; as have workers' adaptations to/escapes from them Lockwood, 1958; Crozier, 1967; Callow, 1968; Benet, 1972; Tepperman, 1976; Kanter, 1977; McNally, 1979; Prandy et al., 1982). Nevertheless, as the following argues, labour process studies, whatever their view of clerical workers, have ignored practices of consent that represent 'escapes' into work.

Studies abound of white-collar workers and of their relative position to manual labour.[2] Here, the intention is not to enter the longstanding debate concerning class location, but simply to account for the emergence of differing views of non-manual labour. The familiar picture of white-collar workers as both materially and symbolically privileged in relation to others draws upon the experience of the earliest nineteenth century clerks, who represented only a very small fraction of total employment. While significant variations existed (Dale, 1962; Anderson, 1976), these clerks tended to work closely, and to identify, with the owners of production, often carrying out what would now be considered as management functions (Lockwood, 1958:22; Price and Bain, 1972; Braverman, 1974:294). Despite the subsequent massive numerical growth (absolutely and relatively), mechanization, rationalization and feminization of white-collar work (ibid.; Crompton, 1979), equivalent views were evident in the 1960s. An extreme example can be found in an article by Sykes (1965) where the working conditions and attitudes of clerical and manual labour are presented in polarity. The loyalty and status and career commitment (self-discipline) of clerks is contrasted with the instrumentalism and antagonism of manual workers who 'do not identify with management and do not adopt, but in fact oppose, its interests' (1965:307). Following Lockwood (1958) and Wright-Mills (1951), Sykes attributes this differential to the workers' relative opportunities for progression[3]. However, he concludes by noting the emergence of the threat of credentialism to the privileged position of the (male) clerks and, therefore, to the polarity in 'clerk–worker' orientations (see also Dale, 1962:99).

These issues are examined more comprehensively in Lockwood's definitive study of white-collar work in Britain (1958). While recognizing the progressive degradation, polarization and rationalization of office work (ibid.:chapter 3), his adoption of a Weberian perspective on class highlighted the continued and significant differences between manual and 'blackcoated' workers. The clerk remained distinctive, enjoying superior working conditions, market position and status (ibid.:55) – a 'privileged type of proletarian' (ibid.:4). Similarly, Crozier's later study on *The World of the Office Worker* showed how, with bureaucratization, 'the paternalism of former times . . . [had] vanished' (1967:17). Increasingly routine jobs and blocked mobility led to adaptations and indifference on the part of some workers. Nevertheless, in addition to a status distinction with manual workers, the division of labour within organizations provided ample opportunity for a 'compensatory' concern with status and prestige that helped to ensure a measure of commitment (1967:103–5).

In contrast to emphasizing the differences between clerical and manual workers, labour process studies have been primarily concerned with locating clerical workers firmly among the ranks of the proletariat as wage labour and with documenting the continued rationalization, degradation and homogenization of office work (e.g. Braverman, 1974:chapter 15). Here, the subjective focus of Weberian industrial sociology is rejected in favour of developing the Marxist proletarianization debate characterized by the work of Klingender (1935) and Wright-Mills (1951). The concern is primarily with structure – 'objective conditions . . . rather than [to] the workers' subjective feelings and identities' (Glenn and Feldberg, 1979:52). Proletarianization is seen to occur through a combined process of deskilling and a reduction in the extent to which the 'functions of capital' are performed (Crompton, 1979:407) – a change in economic class situation (Crompton, 1980; Roslender, 1981:429).

The neglect of subjectivity in favour of structure has been criticized in long-standing debates concerning proletarianization, the unionization of white-collar workers and the nature of their associated class consciousness (Lockwood, 1958:137; cf. Crompton, 1979, 1980; Heritage, 1980; Kelly, 1983; McColloch, 1983; see also Hyman and Price, 1983; Price and Bain, 1983; Crompton and Jones, 1984). However, the concern here is not with unionization nor an explicit class consciousness but with the more wide-ranging neglect of the subject in relation to localized structures of management control. Of course, the analysis of structure alone is a perfectly legitimate academic activity. Nevertheless, as before, a more or less implicit conception of the labour subject as dominated and/or alienated because denied its expressive potential is evident in much of the literature. For example:

> As managerial decisions are substituted for workers' decisions the [clerical] workforce becomes an 'inert' collection of bodies mechanically related to a set of materials and sustained in motion by an external force.
>
> (DeKadt, 1979:71-2)

While the subject remains inadequately theorized, subjective action has been examined in the literature. However, it tends to be conceived only in terms of the two models of office workers discussed above.

Within the first of these two groups there is recognition and observation of the self-disciplinary preoccupation with status among white-collar workers. However, these existing practices, such as identifying with superiors and management and other 'games' associated with styles of dress and material privileges (Tepperman, 1976:12; Barker and Downing, 1980) are perceived as being under threat (Glenn and Feldberg, 1979:68-9). The intensification of management control means that it 'can no longer be masked by the social relations of the social office' (Downing, 1980:287). Deskilling and depersonalization[4] of control is exposing the 'true' status of clerical workers as wage labour. Accordingly, with varying degrees of qualification, these authors highlight practices of resistance (DeKadt, 1979:252-3), observe and predict 'increasing levels of organization and militancy' (Crompton 1983:26; see also Braverman, 1974:34-5; Tepperman, 1976:6-7, 4) and, in the extreme, talk of 'growing resistance sporadically breaking out into militancy' (Barker and Downing, 1980:87).

Such an emphasis on resistance represents a 'leap of faith', founded on the Marxist premise 'whereby the proletariat would be compelled to challenge and transform class society by virtue of its *objective* location in the system of production' (Thompson, 1986:17; emphasis added). Any other response would represent either economic compliance (DeKadt, 1979) or false consciousness. For example, Glenn and Feldberg suggest that 'some workers act as though the older conditions of work still existed' (1979:65). Other accounts appear more sophisticated. For example, Crompton and Jones study of deskilling and gender highlights the continued heterogeneous (cf. 'mass') nature of white-collar workers (1984:210). Moreover, while predominantly concerned with a 'structure of empty class places' (ibid.:40), they attempt to incorporate a subjective dimension to their analysis by drawing upon Gidden's (1982:30) view of the 'human agent' as both 'knowledgeable' and 'capable' (1984:215,237). However, once again emphasis is placed on expressive or resistant responses either in opposition to capital or in the maintenance of advantage (ibid.:237).

While not discounting the importance of worker resistance, such a focus obscures the coexistent self-disciplinary or willing nature of work involvement. Others compensate for this distortion and neglect, but only by reference to the persistence of apparently distinctive or traditional forms of white-collar commitment and cooperation. For example, Thompson begins his review of consent thus: 'Workers do not always need to be overtly controlled. They may effectively "control" themselves *particularly* if they are in white collar or professional jobs' (1983:153; emphasis added). He continues by accounting for the 'greater consent by clerical and professional workers' in terms of their 'orientation to . . . [presumably middle-] class as a totality'. The adaptive, consenting practices performed by clerical workers 'only develop because they are connected to wider conceptions of class, conceptions in which white-collar workers are encouraged to accept the cultural compensation of status for the limits of their position in the hierarchy of rewards' (1983:173).

While Thompson neglects the significance of equivalent self-disciplinary practices among *manual* workers that draw on 'working-class' conceptions of status such as 'dignity' and 'skill' (Sennett and Cobb, 1973), his account provides a valuable corrective to those of the 'factory office' and to 'militant' clerical labour. Similarly, Storey (1983), in highlighting the variability of clerical work conditions in insurance, notes the persistence of the 'social office' (ibid,:7) and 'benign organizational climates' (ibid.:46). Combined with status ('social location') and socialization (ibid.:8), these 'regimes' are seen to account for the observed 'commitment' and 'cooperation' of the clerical workers to their jobs and company (ibid.:43,44 and 47).

Moreover, these orientations apparently persisted despite an overall increase in bureaucratic and technological control in the case study companies (ibid.:44).

Once again then, clerical workers' self-discipline is understood by reference to their privileged position as 'middle-class' employees. Indeed, Storey even overlooks the adaptive nature of work practices wherein status compensates for material reward. Finally, and in common with each of the aforementioned accounts of clerical work, Storey provides no place for other forms of consent. This persistence in the literature of a polarity in the social relations of the 'office' and 'factory' conceals the shared experience of subordination and methods of coping with it other than through overt resistance. Storey, for example, specifically dismisses Burawoy's account of workers being 'diverted by individualistic strategies' as inapplicable to his insurance clerks (1983:45). This chapter, concerning equivalent workers in the same industry, suggests the contrary.

'SHIFTING' WORK IN THE INSURANCE OFFICE

The practice of 'shifting' was identified during exploratory research in two regional branches of insurance companies in the north-west of England. It subsequently became a focus of research attention – examined through observation, semi-structured interviews and a questionnaire. Before outlining the characteristics of 'shifting', the organizational context of the research is briefly described. However, this chapter is concerned more with the micro-dynamics of the practice at the point of capitalist subordination than with explicating its precise location within wider capitalist structures. The latter and related technological and gender relations are partially explored elsewhere (Knights and Sturdy, 1987, 1990; Sturdy, 1990).

The two case study companies have been labelled Powerco and Freelife, in order to preserve their anonymity. They differ in many respects. Powerco is a large 'composite' insurer dealing with all classes of insurance business and employing around 6,000 staff. Freelife is a mutual life assurance office (owned by policy-holders) with about 1,000 staff. However, they do share a similar and typical organization-al structure up to regional branch level with an administrative head office in the provinces, a smaller City base and a network of over twenty branches. The latter act as processing centres, handling enquiries processing proposals, endorsing policies, limited accounts administration, initiating new business and handling claims. It is at this level where the majority are employed and the research is focused.

Here, once more, the companies differ. At the Powerco branch under study, about 200 people were employed in a number of departments e.g. (motor, fire and accident and accounts). Most staff were located within a clerical hierarchy of fifteen grades which was incremental in terms of income, status and 'skill' and, formally at least, represented a 'career ladder'. Each department had a manager/ superintendent (grade 14/15), one or two assistants (10/11) and around four to six section leaders (8/9) who supervised the staff of their section. Below the supervisory grades were seven grades of clerk, mostly women[5].

In contrast, the Freelife branch had only twenty-seven staff who were employed in one of two formally distinct areas: administration and sales (see also Knights and Collinson, 1985). The latter were primarily sales representatives who worked largely out of the office, visiting agents or clients. The former, office staff, were the focus of this research and consisted of ten 'field staff secretaries' who each provided administrative support for one or two particular representatives although they were formally reponsible to the branch secretary/office manager. A branch manager presided over both office and sales staff.

Despite the absence of hierarchical differentiation among the Freelife secretaries, they carried out broadly similar tasks to the Powerco underwriting clerks (up to grade 7) in the motor and fire and accident (F & A) insurance departments. These tasks are common to insurance work generally and are examined in more detail in studies by Rolfe (1985) and Storey (1986). Each group was involved to varying degrees, with written and telephone enquiries, for premium quotations for example. Similarly, both processed insurance pro- posals, policies and renewals and carried out premium calculations, amendments and endorsements. An important difference, however, was that of typing. This made up around 50 per cent of the secretaries' work, whereas at Powerco it was performed in a central typing pool. The restriction of research access in the latter prevented a compar- ative analysis of this type of work. However, the Freelife secretaries certainly engaged in 'shifting' both types of work.

For many Freelife and Powerco staff, 'shifting work', as they called it, was a more or less conscious attempt of coping with the pressure of work. As the name suggests 'shifting' essentially involves getting work (tasks) out of the way – 'behind you', 'cleared', or 'shifted'. Work effort is directed towards the *completion* of a number of given tasks, rather than the tasks themselves. Whilst a range of consenting practices, adaptations and often contradictory orientations was evident from the research, staff from across the spectrum of age, hierarchical grade, work experience and jobs were found to be concerned, and sometimes preoccupied, with shifting work. Its key characteristics are outlined below.

Shifting is largely recognizable from evidence of a desire to complete or, at least, clear outstanding tasks and/or from the associated feelings of frustration at failing to do so, and relief or satisfaction with success.

'I like to try and shift during the day what comes in. When something comes in and stays on my desk for more than two days, I start worrying.'
'I hate work being left and coming in to work in the morning. I want to get through it all in a day.'
'Once you've got it out of the way, you think, "Thank God for that, I've done it." '
'I feel really good when I've done all my work and got my desk cleared.'

Such comments were particularly evident when individuals were asked the explicitly general question of 'what makes a good or bad day at work?'

[. . . good day?] 'When you can get all your work done and your desk cleared. [A bad day?] When you get hassles from above [supervisors], memos, phone calls . . . "bitty days" . . . not being able to get on with things.'

The sense of frustration was directed towards the apparent sources of interruption or other events or people that hinder the completion or progress of work. These include client, clerical or computer errors; the unavailability or loss of required data, e.g. files and computer terminals[6] and, telephone enquiries. Despite being an integral and persistent feature of the job, the latter cannot become the objects of shifting unless they are translated into a written or visible format, such as a note detailing required action. In either case, they frustrate or defer the relief of completion.

The completion of work tasks is also prevented by the fact that some tasks require an input from other workers or clients. For example, processing insurance proposals is often delayed by customers providing insufficient or ambiguous data. However, shifting is most significantly impeded during periods of work backlogs, which were particulary common in Powerco.

> 'Enquiries are very time-consuming. It can be a real hassle when there's been some sort of error' – 'the main thing is we just don't have the time . . . everyone has too much to do – there's pressure all the time. We seem to be forever chasing our tails.'

These various frustrations do not necessarily undermine the interest in shifting, for individuals may differentiate their work tasks and set themselves targets for completion. Indeed, the practice is by no means uniform - different methods and timescales are adopted.

By far the most common method of shifting was aiming to complete the easy, routine, stock, or quick tasks, while putting off the time-consuming and /or difficult tasks.

> 'If a big account comes in and its horrible and its going to take hours to do, I stick it to the bottom of the pile . . . but tomorrow never comes!'

The typicality of this practice provoked a concern among supervisors, for it frequently led to important tasks being delayed, sometimes indefinitely – the 'get back to it tomorrow syndrome'. However, for the staff, it afforded a sense of achievement that was otherwise difficult to secure with high workloads:

> 'I tend to shove those things that need thought to the bottom [of the pile] 'cos I think I've done a lot then at the end of the day.'

Paradoxically, this method reinforced work pressure, by amassing those tasks that were particularly difficult to shift. An awareness of this consequence is implied in the second and least common form of the practice, where 'big bad jobs' are similarly distinguished but tackled first with the remainder put aside. By contrast, in the third main type of shifting, straightforward tasks are isolated and prioritized, but shifted only when a sufficient number has been collected. This defers or, where routine tasks are less common/distinguishable, creates the sense of achievement found in the first method.

The above approaches to shifting may be adopted singly, alternately, or in combination. In addition, they may be directed towards one or a number of time periods. For most clerks, the principal focus was the working day for which targets were set and/or an assessment made at its conclusion. However, in addition to the aforementioned impediments to completion, some tasks particularly those of supervisory grades at Powerco, required hours of work and took days to complete. As a result, individuals' self assessment of shifting progress extended over longer periods. For example, 'getting through the week' is a common concern in employment, where working hours are divided accordingly. The following quotation shows how shifting work is managed to coincide and thereby reinforce this concern,

> '[A good day?] Usually a Friday because on Monday I have work [left] over, by Wednesday, I could be two days, behind – on Fridays, I have less [work] on my desk.'

Here, the intensity of both work and shifting effort varies through the week, reflecting the persistence of a cyclical time orientation that is considered to be characteristic of pre-capitalist production (see Thompson, 1967 and Hassard, 1988). The widespread nature of this practice in Powerco and Freelife was suggested by the peaks in demand for for central computer processing capacity on Friday afternoons (as workers attempt to clear their desks) and Monday mornings (after having failed to do so and before additional work is allocated).

The attention of shifting extends beyond the two predominant timescales of the working day and week. For example, at Powerco there was a monthly panic of activity, in an attempt to clear backlogs. As we shall see shortly, this was more likely a response to management's monthly state of work assessment, than to the division of working time or self-set targets. Finally, a concern with shifting was evident for other readily distinguishable phases of work, such as before going on holiday and at the end of the year. While such concerns were probably widespread, they were raised only by those in the more senior hierarchical positions. In addition to the frequently longer task times in such jobs, the relatively high proportion of unallocated or unexpected tasks, such as verbal queries from staff and clients, and the greater diversity of work, rendered short-term shifting more difficult:

> 'In my situation, I could go for four days without even looking at the work on my desk because of interruptions.'

While supervisors and managers showed signs of engaging in similar practices to their subordinates, the focus on the latter group here is intended to amplify the dissociation of shifting with the traditional forms of clerical commitment outlined earlier.

Commitment or compliance

The completion of work tasks clearly conforms to managerial requir-
ments for productivity and service provision in terms of speed.
Accordingly, the staffs' active interest in shifting work, combined
with the peristent view of insurance workers' commitment to their
work and jobs (Storey, 1983; Batstone *et al.*, 1984), suggests that the
practice could be explained by a willing involvement founded on
informal controls, intrinsic job rewards and/or an association with
privileged status and promotion hierarchies for example. Indeed,
Glenn and Feldberg, in their account of the proletarianization of
clerical work, specifically attribute comments such as 'when I clear up
everything on my desk then it's been a good day' to residual 'internal
motivation', which will be undermined by a 'work-to-rule orientation'
as formal controls progressively displace the personal controls characteristic of paternalism and the 'social office' (1979:65–6). Once
more, we are, albeit implicitly, presented here with stereotypical and
polar assumptions of non-manual and manual workers where the
former are more likely to control themselves. Without necessarily
challenging the changing patterns of control evident in the clerical
sector and Glenn and Feldberg's study, nor their subordinating
consequences, the apparent satisfaction of clearing work does not
reflect the form of commitment they suggest. Indeed, as we shall see,
on the basis of Baldamus' earlier study on manual work, similar
comments could be expected amongst the most deskilled and homoge-
nized shopfloor workers (1961). In this research, any association of
shifting with clerical commitment is undermined by evidence of the
practice among those in the most degraded jobs, and of its coexistence
with practices of work avoidance or resistance. The following
instances are illustrative.

In the Powerco branch, some of the most routine work was
performed by the key-punch operators, where data from the departments was input through keyboards into the main computer. Despite
the demands of great keyboard skill and concentration, the staff were
afforded the lowest status by both management (through grading)
and fellow workers. Finally, the operators' central position in the
batch processing computer system rendered their jobs the least secure
as a new on-line system was developed[7]. Not surprisingly, they
expressed indifference, resentment and/or defiance in response to
this situation. For example, one claimed to be interested only in
'having a laugh' and, with regard to work, to 'just taking it as it comes',

while another resented her low grading, felt overworked and claimed that 'we [the section] won't let them [management and other departments] rush us'. However, both indicated an interest in shifting. The first boasted: 'I always get done what I have to do to in a day', and complained that the 'machines go too slow, its a real pain waiting to get work done'. Similarly, the second claimed: 'I feel pleased when I've keyed in a lot of work.' However, and more generally, individuals' interest in shifting work was not continuous or straightforward as the case, cited earlier of a daily variation of work intensity intimated.

At one point in the research at Freelife, managerial and supervisory pressure on staff to produce was effectively relaxed or suspended for a particular task of transferring client data in paper files to a new computer database. In response to complaints of excessive workloads from the secretaries, head office management waived their completion deadlines. Given that sales representatives in the branch had little interest in the work in comparison to their premium income (commission)-related tasks, direct superordinate control had become negligible. Subsequently, the secretaries' progress in completing the transfer subsided – a backlog of files was left largely unattended. This apparent failure to engage in shifting was not so much a consequence of other work pressures, for the secretaries' complaints were, at least partially, a form of resistance in attempting to avoid a task they considered most tedious. For example , one secretary claimed to finish her work by 2.00 p.m., yet 'would do anything rather that the files [transfer]'.

In fact, both staffs engaged in covert forms of resistance or work avoidance that are characteristic of office-life (see Callow, 1968; Tepperman, 1976; McNally, 1979; Downing, 1980). For example, some Powerco clerks would 'escape' to the maze of filing cabinets, or use the telephone to chat with near neighbours in order to avoid sanctions from supervisory surveillance and /or telephone work. Even under the less strict supervisory regime at Freelife, secretaries would sometimes seek sanctuary in a room used for conducting computerized premium quotations. In addition, at Powerco, some individuals were found to be 'fiddling' their 'flexi-time' clocks. More generally, they would sometimes deliberately fail to correct data errors or deficiences, in insurance proposals, for example (see Taylor and Walton, 1971), in an effort to both avoid and shift work. Indeed, the practice of shifting itself incorporates an explicit form of resistance. For instance the deferring of 'difficult' tasks not only directly conflicts with supervisory instructions to prioritize the oldest work items but, at Powerco at least, was used to deliberately distort figures recording the state of work (the level of outstanding items). In some cases then, shifting work does not involve the completion of tasks in the sense that explicit management service and productivity requirements are satisfied. This will be further considered later in the chapter.

The above account of shifting coexisting with conflictual hierarchical relations undermines a straightforward association of the practice with clerical commitment. Rather, the evidence of work avoidance when direct management controls are resisted and/or relaxed is more indicative of a 'work-to-rule' orientation. This suggests that shifting could be better understood as a form of work effort based on compliance. Accordingly, the remainder of this section examines the particular local structures of control associated with the practice.

The multifarious structures or mechanisms of management control are well documented in the labour process literature. Here, the focus is on those conditions that engender the individual experience of work pressure, against which shifting is directed. This experience incorporates some general form of obligation or motivation to work, plus a knowledge, or visibility, of outstanding work tasks. Clearly, typical individualizing methods of hierarchical (and lateral) assessment and surveillance directed at securing productivity implicitly require task *completion*. Indeed, at Powerco managerial emphasis was placed on this (or, at least, on removing backlogs), to the extent that the state of work was incorporated into all structural levels of personal and bureaucratic assessment. However, such emphasis and direct forms of control were not as evident in Freelife, where patriarchal and personal controls gave rise to the sort of apparently 'benign' regimes described by Storey (1983; 1986). Nevertheless, both staffs shared an experience of work pressure.

In addition to the roles of management and staff in helping to shape market demand and, therefore, the levels of incoming business to be processed, the physical basis of work pressure is maintained by the formulation of, and adherence to, staffing levels or quotas (calculated through the use of work measurement techniques for example) that fail to match processing requirements. Such precision implies an implausible degree of managerial omniscience, particularly in the face of variations in the volume of new business. In practice, work pressure is maintained or increased by a reluctance to recruit that is founded on budgetary controls and by crude or optimistic productivity measurements during periods of rationalization (Knights and Sturdy, 1990). As one Powerco manager commented:

'We don't want people left with no work at the end of the week because that means we're overstaffed!'

With a volume of outstanding work virtually assured, it is rendered visible to the staff by the system (structure) of work allocation. This could be organized using a pool system, where staff drew out work when ready (see Gourlay, 1987:23). However, it is its *individual specificity* that is fundamental to shifting, for this ensures that staff are *individually accountable* for completing tasks. For example, at Powerco, incoming work is allocated by superordinates to specific individuals according to a strict division of labour so that, for instance, one grade 3 motor clerk would handle work arising from, or related to, brokers in the alphabetical group A–D. At Freelife, secretarial work tasks were also clearly divided by the pairing of office staff with particular representatives. Moreover, in both cases, only a limited amount of work was shared out or passed on in times of extreme work pressure. Indeed, at Freelife, considerable quantitative variations in secretarial workloads were sometimes evident. The strict accountability imposed by such a system is illustrated in the, albeit extreme, case from Powerco described below where a clerk had been off work through illness:

'One time, my tray was 10 inches deep in work. . . it's like being punished. It's as if "if you're not in work, then you should be".'

While the structure can be seen to reinforce other individualizing controls such as personal surveillance and assessment, it may also partially substitute for them:

'Here, they [representatives] know that you're going to get your work done so you can have breaks, although not officially.'

The imposition of individual accountability virtually leaves staff with *little choice but* to engage in shifting , for if they fail to do so and/or resist through work avoidance then their workloads would, eventually at least, mount up and result ultimately in client complaints and/or supervisory sanctions. Thus, the clerks' concern with the completion of work tasks could simply be accounted for as a compliant response to structures of individual accountability and visibility. However, on its own, such an explanation is inadequate. Not only does it portray subjects as passive objects, simply responding to economic dependence and other structures of management control, but, relatedly, it fails to account for the self-disciplinary nature of shifting — the interest in, or commitment to, the completion of tasks. Indeed, the following examples suggest that, rather than straightforward compliance, the practice can assume an almost compulsive character, whereby the structure of accountability is, in some way, internalized.[8]

We have already seen how key-punchers at Powerco continued to shift, despite job insecurity, indifference and low status opportunities. In addition, the same staff rejected a 'legitimate' opportunity for work avoidance by the joint union – management recommendation/offer of twenty minute breaks from VDU usage. Despite admitting (in research interviews) to experiencing regular head and backaches, the breaks were opposed:

> '. . .because we're too busy. . . it just wastes time – the machines would be idle for 80 minutes (a day).'

A similar situation arose in other Powerco departments where, following the introduction of on-line processing, an inadequate provision of computer terminals led to a sometimes obsessive desire to 'get on'.

> 'It's really annoying waiting to use them – about 20 per cent of your time is wasted.'

Both cases illustrate the experience of time in a disciplinary linear and commodified form — not to be 'wasted' (see Hassard, 1988:6–11; Thompson, 1967:61 and 80). Indeed, in some cases, Powerco staff were willing to give their time *freely*, in an effort to clear work backlogs. During the period of research, staff in some departments and branches were working seven days a week, mostly earning overtime (despite an overtime ban) but sometimes 'writing off' up to twenty hours per month each as unpaid. Clearly, in this extreme example, career-based commitment for a minority and, with overtime, immediate financial interest, played a part, along with the influence of strict supervisory regimes in some departments. However, the individual preoccupation with relieving work pressure must also be considered. For example, despite critically recognizing the adverse employment implications of overtime and resenting 'working for nothing', one clerk conceded:

> 'Really, it's my own foolish fault for getting over [the maximum number of working hours], but if I didn't do it [write off time] my job would be in a worse state than it is.'

The accountability/helplessness imposed through individualized work allocation is internalized as a sense of responsibility or self-discipline whereby management control structures are obscured or denied:

'There's no pressure on you, you just know that you have to do it [shift] so you do it. . . . It's there in your own mind — you pressure yourself to get things done.'

Such internalization initially at least, can be accounted for by viewing structures of control as subjectively enabling and productive as well as constraining and subordinating. Indeed, the temporal autonomy (Hassard, 1988:11) within the structure of work allocation/account-ability facilitates the realization of a sense of competence and contol (identity) through shifting.

At the same time as leaving staff with little choice but to shift, individual work allocation gives them the 'freedom' to do so. For example, while processing methods in both companies are strictly defined in office manuals and rating guides and through personal or computerized 'quality control' (checking), there is greater autonomy over *when* tasks are performed. This is evident from the variety of methods used in shifting and by the perception of phone calls, for example, as being 'interruptions' or 'intrusions'. Equally, while work allocation renders workloads visible to staff, it also allows staff to see what they have done. The sense of achievement, competence and control derived from such an arrangement has already been noted. It is illustrated in descriptions of 'good days' as being 'left alone' and in the sense of satisfaction in overcoming the obstacles of interruptions and completing work, and in using an individual method to do so.

'[A good day is] when everything has gone smoothly, when you've been able to get through plenty of work, when you feel you've achieved something, can see what you've done.'
    'When you can get it all done and your desk cleared — its great!'

The combination of autonomy or 'choice' and productive compliance as a form of self-discipline is well illustrated in the following comment from a Powerco superintendent:

'The majority of people try to clear up their work because there's a satisfaction of getting it done. . . a sense of achievement purely in terms of shifting the work. Also, they are given work which is given to clear and if they don't then someone will want to know why!'

Moreover, it is fundamental to Burawoy's concept of consent. However, there remains a contradiction to be resolved from the foregoing account of shifting. In addition, the individual interest in competence and control remains unexamined. Both are addressed in the following sections.

An 'Escape' *Into* Work

The practice of shifting has been shown to assume an almost compulsive character whereby, for example, despite the opportunity for a removal or relaxation of direct supervisory control, the 'internalization' of accountability maintained individual commitment to task completion. Conversely, the clerks have been shown to engage in work avoidance or resistance to control, both within the practice itself and when direct controls were relaxed or suspended. The apparent contradiction here may be resolved through the recognition that shifting is a *discontinuous* form of involvement in work that reflects a defensive/escapist adaptation to the experience of subordination and, in particular, of compliance to work pressure. It is a way of securing a competent sense of self in an attempt to relieve the experience of an otherwise subordinate situation.

The 'escapist' nature of the practice is sometimes explicit, as in cases where a paradoxical preference for work pressure is expressed:

> 'I prefer to come in to a bit of a backlog because it makes the day go quicker if you've got pressure – it beats clock watching!'

Indeed, on occasions where work or immediate supervisory pressure is 'laxed', individuals may consciously construct their own pressure.

> 'You create your own pressure because you know you have to do the work.'
> 'I like to have a bit of pressure so I like trying to shift in a day what comes in.'

In this way, shifting differs from many of the familiar adaptations to work, such as the work avoidance practices noted earlier (see also Katz, 1968; Ditton, 1972 and 1979). It is an escape *into*, rather than from, work effort/activity (completion), equivalent to the shopfloor practice of 'making out' (Burawoy, 1979) and almost identical empirically to the relative satisfaction of 'batch traction' identified by Baldamus as a response to work 'tedium' (1961:53).[9] In addition, it shares the self-defeating and paradoxical character of all such practices in that it serves to reproduce the conditions of its emergence — the pressure of work. However, unlike the adaptations decribed by Roy (1960), Katz (1968) and Burawoy (1979), the individualistic nature of shifting meant that it did not form the primary basis of a workplace culture. Possibly as a consequence, it was more clearly a discontinuous form of work involvement.

> In obscuring and securing unpaid labour, games are more effective the more broadly they encompass everyday life on the shopfloor.
>
> (Burawoy, 1979:92)

A discontinuity or fragility in the staffs' commitment to work clearance has already been intimated in the description of the weekly orientation to the practice. Equally, it is evident when staff leave the office.

> 'If I've got a lot to do, I just try and get ahead, but I shut myself off at the end of the day – I don't go home and worry about how much work I've got to do.'

In addition, as we have seen, practices of work avoidance or resistance reflect a partial rejection of the shifting imperative. Nevertheless, in both physically escaping from surveillance and deferring 'difficult' tasks (outside and within the practice, respectively), the implicit intention is defensively to relieve the experience of work pressure. Even voiced expressions of conflict may be shaped by the form of consenting practice. For example, Burawoy described how the workers' experience of 'being screwed' by management was expressed in terms of their bosses' failure to facilitate fully opportunites for 'making out' (1979:66). Similarly, in this research, staff resented management for creating frustrations to shifting, such as providing 'additional' tasks, inadequate numbers of staff and computer terminals and even, for trying to introduce work breaks. However, worker subordination and its dependence upon management's organization of resources is not always so obscured. For example, while neither staffs could have been described as militant, it should not surprise most readers that the clerks recognized management's provision of cheap house loans as a 'ball and chain mortgage'. In addition, some staff readily penetrated the objectives of supervisory surveillance, credentialism and the reductions or containment of staff numbers:

> 'there's a lot more discipline now. . .they are constantly making sure that people are working.'
> 'the company are only interested in making money they're cutting staff and cutting careers and saving money'.
> 'They're just trying to get more out of us.'

Equally, we have already seen how they were sometimes aware of their own contribution to such processes in their recognition of the employment consequences of doing overtime and 'writing-off' hours as unpaid.

Individuals' departure from a consciousness of shifting, either in work avoidance or penetrative reflections, was especially evident where extreme or renewed work pressure was experienced, and during changes towards increased supervisory control. At such times, the (anticipated) sense of competence and control derived from the practice is challenged or undermined. For example, work backlogs beyond a certain size or duration led to some indifference or apathy towards task completion:

> 'If you come in [to work] to a big backlog, you think "God! I've got to do all that today". It puts you off doesn't it?'
>
> 'No one likes being in a backlog – you're motivated when you can see a "light at the end of the tunnel" and you can get it out of the way. Otherwise, you just say "Sod it!" . . .you don't want to work because it won't make any difference, so you don't bother.'

In addition, the apparent relentlessness of work pressure rendered the satisfaction or relief of task completion belittled or short-lived:

> 'You're thrilled to bits because you think you've cleared it and then "Bang!" a load more mail comes in."

It is reasonable to assume, given the regularity of such occurrences, that apathy would result before, once more, resuming the practice of shifting in an attempt to 'escape' back into work completion. As this requires some allocation of tasks, we can now comprehend clerks' qualified preference for work pressure:

> 'A "good" day is being left alone to get on with it, not too much to do but not being bored.'

Either extreme of an 'excessive' or 'insufficient' work-load under-mines the sense of control derived from shifting[10]. The chapter now proceeds by developing an account of the individual interest in control within the context of work pressure.

SHIFTING AND IDENTITY – THE ANXIETY OF WORK PRESSURE

In this section, we return to the clerks' self-disciplinary involvement in shifting by further examining the nature of their experience of work pressure and, therefore, subordination. The individual accountability for productivity achieved through work allocation has been shown to elicit a sense of *helplessness* among clerks against the level of incoming and outstanding work and external sources of interruptions to task completion:

'If you don't talk, you could probably do your work in a day but you get phone calls and interuptions — it just mounts up!'

We have also seen how this is reflected in feelings of *frustration*. Indeed, in a questionnaire, Powerco staff cited work backlogs as being their greatest frustration. This is not surprising, since supervisory pressure also intensified in these periods:

'It's so frustrating that you can't work quicker than you are.'

Accordingly, staff would *worry* over their failure to shift:

'If you leave cases. . . they're always in the back of your mind – you've got to get it done.'

'I hate work being left and coming in to work the next morning.'

Relatedly, it has also been noted how task completion was experienced with *relief.* The combination of these feelings of helplessness, frustration, worry and relief can be described as a form of anxiety that is associated with the compulsive character of shifting, outlined earlier. Thus the practice can now be understood as an attempt to relieve or escape from the anxiety of work pressure and, at the same time to secure a sense of identity and/or control.

Such an account appears consistent with Fromm's social-psychological explanation of the emergence of the work ethic in industrial capitalism. Here, self-disciplinary work effort was seen as a search for a sense of belonging that was rooted in the individual existential traits of aloneness and anxiety – a 'fear of freedom'.

Activity in this sense assumes a compulsive quality: the individual has to be active in order to overcome his feeling of doubt and powerlessness. This kind of effort and activity is not the result of inner strength and self-confidence, it is a desperate escape from anxiety.

(1980:78)

However, Fromm was primarily concerned with the individual vulnerability to 'dominant' doctrines (e.g. Calvinism) and structures, rather than the reproduction of localized practices. Moreover, he portrayed self-discipline largely as complete conformity and thereby neglected the possibility of coexistent conflict (1980:243). In addition, the vulnerability of the subject was seen to result in the distortion of a 'spontaneous' or 'fully developed' human nature (1971:68;1980). Once again then, an essentialist, Marxist conception of the subject is employed. The following develops the concept of existential vulnerability outlined earlier in an attempt to show that both the practice of shifting and coexistent conflict reflect not so much a distortion of human subjectivity as its constitution. It has already been argued that individuals engage in multifarious practices directed towards controlling or solidifying a sense of self (identity) and/or the social world. These security-seeking practices counter an existential anxiety or vulnerability that is founded upon the dual and necessary condition of a dependence on others in the formation of self/identity and the experience of self as separate from others (self-consciousness). The unpredictabilty and variability of social relations renders identity precarious or uncertain. Accordingly, individuals' pursuit of a 'solid' sense of self, of control or 'closure' (Knights and Willmott, 1985), denies and obscures the interdependence and impermanence of its constitution. But how does this view of the continuous (re)production of subjectivity help to account for labour conflict and cooperation as the conditions and consequences of enabling and constraining structures of management control?

Existential anxiety is constantly reinforced through individualizing structures of control (Fromm, 1955; Luckman and Berger, 1964; Knights and Wilmott, 1983; Leonard, 1984). For example, in the context of this research, the structures of hierarchical assessment, accountability and visibility can be seen to intensify a sense of separateness of self from others (Roberts, 1988) and give rise to the particular anxiety of work pressure, for instance. At the same time, control structures facilitate the pursuit of 'closure' and identity by offering the apparent security of 'success, worthiness status and power' (over others) (Collinson and Knights, 1984: 40–41) or, for the most subordinate, some control over the material world at least. For example, with the practice of shifting, the structure of work allocation is 'engaged' in the reproduction of self. Not only does its specificity (and that of the division of labour generally) provide for a sense of job attachment, hierarchical identity (see also Tepperman, 1976:12) or 'belonging' but, as we have seen, its autonomy facilitates the exercise of control over the environment – a sense of self as competent. In short, shifting is directed toward achieving a sense of combined control and identity, 'independence and closeness' (Fromm, 1971:86) or 'autonomy and security' (Knights and Vurdubakis, 1988:31).

While control structures may be experienced as separate from, and independent of, self, they are the ongoing products of action – 'subjects are as much constituted as constituting' (Giddens, 1979; Knights, 1987:26). We have seen how 'shifting', like other adaptive practices (Prandy *et al.*, 1982), reproduces or sustains the very conditions from which it emerges and which it seeks to deny. The practice is also self-defeating in that the inherent uncertainty of the social world ensures that the pursuit of individual control or 'closure' ('certainty') will reproduce anxiety – 'the denial of impermanence imprisons us' (Trungpa, 1976:13). For example, given that there can be no guarantee that one's view of self will be confirmed by others, identity is rendered constantly vulnerable so that subjects will continue to seek security. With 'shifting', we have seen how individuals' control over work tasks is constantly undermined (and also supported) by various circumstances – the actions of others. These are experienced as 'unexpected' and frustrating (anxiety) precisely because the sense of control sought in the practice is one that is independent of, or separate from, others' actions. It is denying of both the impermanence and interdependence of social relations and subjectivity, and thereby perpetuates anxiety. This denial also explains how capitalist social relations are obscured in practices of indifference and consent, for example. By defensively attempting to escape from conditions of subordination, the dependence of self and of a sense of control on the dominant, as on others, is denied. How then, do we account for worker resistance?

The consenting practice of shifting then is self-defeating, in continually reproducing both the existential anxiety and structural conditions of its formation. However, at the same time, the consciousness or commitment of shifting has been shown to be discontinuous, allowing for resistance and reflective and critical penetrations of subordination. Such expressions of conflict were particularly evident where the individual sense of competence or control (security) was undermined by extreme or renewed supervisory and work pressure. In other words, when the self-defeating or self-denying nature of the practice is experienced most acutely, conflict occurs. Indeed, it is commonplace for self-discipline to erode under extreme or 'direct' oppression (Lockwood, 1958; Thompson, 1967; Weber, 1974:152). However, we have also seen how individual resistance through work avoidance, for example and the practice of shifting are equivalent in that both reflect a strategy to relieve work pressure and sustain a sense of control/identity – to secure 'closure'. This equivalence is also recognized by Burawoy in likening the 'game' of 'making out' with that of 'making a revolution' (1979:93). In fact, shifting, like other forms of consent, incorporates resistance or work avoidance. Similarly, and again following Burawoy (1979:66), we have seen how partial penetration of subordination is expressed within the consciousness or 'rules' of consent. However, other moments of critical reflection have been referred to where individuals were apparently not engaged in 'shifting'. Such penetration of the 'presented reality to its underlying conditions' formed a focus in Roberts' study of the 'possibilities of accountability' (1988:2, 9, 5). As an *individual* (cf. 'social') activity it was seen to reflect a way of 'retaining some sense of being in control' (ibid.). Thus, once again, it can be regarded as a self-defeating concern with securing 'closure'.

If, as the above argument suggests, individual practices and expressions of conflict and cooperation can *both* be comprehended as reflecting a defensive preoccupation with securing identity and control, then why is it that cooperation, through shifting, for example, is pursued in favour of overt resistance? Here, we return to the importance of structure, material conditions and mutual dependence outlined in the introduction. For the most part, shifting offers an albeit precarious sense of both economic and symbolic security by productively 'engaging' in structures of salary assessment, the division of labour and work allocation, for example. Given the extent of blocked mobility (see Knights and Sturdy, 1987), any sense of self as hierarchically 'successful' that is pursued through the alternative or additional practice of careerism would soon be undermined, for many. Equally, to confront individually or resist management control structures would, initially at least, expose the sense of powerlessness by contradicting the security derived from them hitherto – income and identity would be threatened. The possibility of securing an alternative identity in resistance is crucially limited by processes of individualization that hinder the formation of a sustained and shared 'culture of resistance' In short:

> Whether or not technologies of power. . .are resisted depends upon the extent to which they confirm or threaten prevailing subjectivities. That the result, especially within the labour process, is so often conformity, compliance or a resigned indifference is partly because of the difficulty in mobilizing collective resistance among individualized subjects.
>
> (Knights, 1987:32)

Indeed, the 'pacifying' effects of individualization are well documented in labour process (Friedman, 1977; Burawoy, 1979; Edwards, 1979; Willmott, 1990) and other literature (Foucault, 1977; Fromm, 1980). Here, we have seen how individualizing structures, such as that of work allocation, reinforce the sense of self as separate, so that the interdependence and impermanence of social relations are denied and obscured in the defensive pursuit of control over self and 'other'. Accordingly, social, interactive and collectivist subjectivities, where there is a 'relatedness to the world' (Fromm, 1971) or a recognition of interdependence (Knights and Willmott, 1985; Roberts, 1988) and of impermanence or fluidity can be presented as providing the existential and prescriptive basis for 'transformative' change. A consideration of the conditions of possibility for such a transformation is beyond the scope of this enquiry, but would at least require an exploration of how the specific and localized structures discussed in the foregoing interrelate with other and 'wider' dynamics of power in contemporary capitalist society (see Sturdy, 1990).

NOTES

1 This research is principally concerned with the latter group, but the limitations of a strictly polar model are suggested by the inclusion of those workers lying towards the former group. Prandy *et al.*, (1982), for example, make significant distinctions between groups of male 'white-collar' workers (see also Crompton and Jones, 1984).

2 For example, see Klingender, 1935; Wright-Mills, 1951; Lockwood, 1958; Dale, 1962; Sykes, 1965; Crozier, 1967; Price and Bain, 1972; Braverman, 1974:chapter 15; Westergaard and Resler, 1975; Anderson, 1976; Tepperman, 1976; Prandy *et al.*, 1982; Kelly, 1983; Hyman and Price, 1983; McColloch, 1983; Crompton and Jones, 1984; Armstrong *et al.*, 1986. More recently, a debate has emerged surrounding the standardiza-tion of employment conditions towards the apparent 'decline and fall of the status divide' between manual and non-manual workers (see Price, 1989)

3 See also Prandy *et al.*, 1982; Crompton and Jones, 1984; Crompton and Sanderson, 1986, 1989. The comparative importance attached by clerks to promotion was undoubtedly exaggerated by Sykes' exclusion of women (segregated) clerks from the study.

4 Glenn and Feldberg (1979), in particular, focus on the transition to an impersonal form of paternalism where, for example, cheap loans and other 'benefits' are provided (see also Tepperman, 1976; DeKadt, 1979:251; Burawoy 1985).

5 In fact the hierarchy conceals a gendered division of labour. In the company as a whole 91 per cent of women are in grades 1–7, whilst 71 per cent of men are in supervisory grades (see Knights and Sturdy, 1987).

6 The practice of shifting in relation to technological change is examined in Knights and Sturdy (1990).

7 During the period of research, their numbers were halved through relocation.

8 The examples are drawn from Powerco, where work pressure was usually more intense than in the Freelife office. However, the self-disciplinary nature of the practice was equally evident in both sites.

9 The parallel between the practices is explored in more detail in Sturdy (1990) and Knights and Sturdy (1990).

10 It is interesting to note Burawoy's parallel observation that when the *uncertainty* of 'making out' was 'too little' or 'too much', workers would withdraw from the practice (1979:89).

REFERENCES

Anderson, G. L. (1976) *Victorian Clerks* (Manchester: Manchester University Press).

Armstrong, P. *et al.* (1986) *White Collar Workers, Trade Unions and Class* (Beckenham: Croom Helm).

Atkinson, W. R. (1978) 'The Employment Consequences of Computers: a User View' in Forester, T. (ed.) (1980) *The Microelectronics Revolution* (Oxford: Basil Blackwell).

Baldamus, W. (1961) *Efficiency and Effort: An analysis of Industrial Administration* (London: Tavistock).

Barker, J. and Downing, H. (1980) 'Word Processing and the Transformation of Patriarchal Relations of Control in the Office', *Capital and Class* 10:64–99.

Batstone, E. *et al.* (1984) 'Technical and Organisation Change at a UK Insurance Company', draft paper, Oxford University.

Benet, M. K. (1972) *Secretary: Enquiry into the Female Ghetto* (London: Sidgwick and Jackson).

Berger, P. L. and Luckmann, T. (1971) *The Social Construction of Reality* (Harmondsworth: Penguin).

Blumer, H. (1969) *Symbolic Interactionism - Perspective and Method* (New York: Prentice Hall).

Braverman, H. (1974) *Labour and Monopoly Capital: the Degradation of Work in the Twentieth Century* (New York: Monthly Preview Press).

Burawoy, M. (1978) 'Towards a Marxist Theory of the Labour Process: Braverman and Beyond', *Politics and Society* 8 (4): 247—312.

Burawoy, M. (1979) *Manufacturing Consent* (Chicago: University of Chicago Press).

Burawoy, M. (1981) 'Terrains of Contest - Factory and State Under Capitalism and Socialism', *Socialist Review*, 11 (4): 83–124.

Burawoy, M. (1985) *The Politics of Production* (London: Verso).

Callow, P. (1968) 'The Clerk', in Fraser, R. (ed,) *Work: Twenty Personal Accounts* (London: Pelican).

Collinson, D. and Knights, D. (1984) ' "Men Only": Theories and Practices of Job Segregation', Society for the Study of Social Problems Conference Paper, San Antonio, USA.

Cressey, P. and MacInnes, J. (1980) 'Voting for Ford: Industrial Democracy and the Control of Labour', *Capital and Class*, 11.

Crompton, R. (1979) 'Trade Unionism and the Insurance Clerk', *Sociology*, 13 (3): 403—26.

Crompton, R. (1980) '. . . a reply to John Heritage', *Sociology*, 14:449—55.

Crompton, R. (1983) 'Women and White-Collar Unionism', Aston/UMIST Labour Process Conference paper, Manchester.

Crompton, R. and Jones, G. (1984) *White Collar Proletariat: Deskilling and Gender in Clerical Work* (London: Macmillan).

Crompton, R. and Sanderson, K. (1986) 'Credentials and Careers: Some implications of the increase in Professional Qualifications amongst Women', *Sociology* 20 (1): 25-42.

Crompton, R. and Sanderson, K. (1989) 'The Gendered Restructuring of Clerical Employment in the Finance Sector', UMIST/Aston Labour Process Conference paper, Manchester.

Crozier, M. (1967) *The World of the Office Worker* (Chicago: University of Chicago Press).

Dale, J. R. (1962) *The Clerk in Industry* (Liverpool: Liverpool University Press).

DeKadt, M. (1979) 'Insurance: a Clerical Work Factory', in Zimbalist, A. (ed.) *Case Studies on the Labour Process* (New York: Monthly Review Press).

Ditton, J. (1972) 'Absent at Work – or How to Manage Monotony', *New Society*, 22:679-81.

Ditton, J. (1979) 'Baking Time', *Sociological Review* 27:157-67.

Downing, H. (1980) 'Word Processors and the Oppression of Women' in Forester, T. (ed.) *The Microelectronics Revolution* (Oxford: Blackwell).

Edwards. P. K. (1986) *Conflict at Work: A Materialist Analysis of Workplace Relations* (Oxford: Blackwell).

Edwards, R. (1979) *Contested Terrain* (London: Heinemann).

Foucault, M. (1977) *Discipline and Punish* (Harmondsworth: Penguin).

Friedman, A. L. (1977) *Industry and Labour* (London: Macmillan).

Fromm, E. (1955) *The Sane Society* (Greenwich, Conn: Fawcett).

Fromm, E. (1971) *The Crisis of Psychoanalysis* (London: Jonathan Cape).

Fromm, E. (1980) *Fear of Freedom* (London: RKP).

Giddens, A. (1979) *Central Problems in Social Theory - Action Structure and Contradiction in Social Analysis* (London: Macmillan).

Giddens, A. (1982) 'Power, the Dialectic of Control and Class Structuration' in Giddens and MacKenzie (eds) *Social Class and the Division of Labour* (Cambridge: Cambridge University Press).

Giddens, A. (1984) *The Constitution of Society* (London: Polity).

Glenn, E. N. and Feldberg, R. L. (1979) 'Proletarianising Clerical Work: Technology and Organisation Control in the Office', in Zimbalist, A. (ed.) *Case Studies on the Labour Process* (New York: Monthly Review Press).

Goffman, E. (1959) *The Presentation of Self in Everyday Life* (Harmondsworth: Penguin).

Goldthorpe, J. *et al.* (1968) *The Affluent Worker: Industrial Attitudes and Behaviour* (Cambridge: Cambridge University Press).

Gourlay, S. (1987) 'The Contradictory Process of Work Reorganisation:

145

Trends in the Organisation of Work in an Insurance Company, 1965–1984', UMIST/Aston Labour Process Conference paper, Manchester.

Habermas, J. (1975) *Legitimation Crisis* (Boston: Beacon Press).

Hassard, J. (1988) 'Toward a Qualitative Paradigm for Working Time', UMIST/Aston Labour Process Conference Paper, Aston.

Heritage, J. (1980) 'Class Situation, White Collar Unionisation and the "Double Proletarianisation" Thesis: A Comment', *Sociology*, 14:283—94.

Hyman, R. and Price, R. (eds) (1983) *The New Working Class? White Collar Workers and their Organisations* (London: Macmillan).

Kanter, R. M. (1977) *Men and Women of the Corporation* (New York: Basic Books).

Katz, F. E. (1968) 'Integrative and Adaptive uses of Autonomy: Worker Autonomy in Factories' in Salaman, F. and Thompson, E. (eds) (1983) *People and Organisations* (Milton Keynes: Open University Press).

Kelly, M. P. (1983) *White collar Proletariat - The Industrial Behaviour of British Civil Servants* (London: Macmillan).

Klingender, F. D. (1935) *The Condition of Clerical Labour in Britian* (London: Martin Lawrence).

Knights, D. (1987) 'Subjectivity, Dualism and the Labour Process', Labour Process Conference Paper, Manchester (revised in Knights, 1990).

Knights, D. (1990) 'Subjectivity, Power and the Labour Process' in Knights D. and Willmott, H. (eds) *Labour Process Theory* (London: Macmillan).

Knights, D. and Collinson D. (1985) 'Redesigning Work on the Shopfloor - A Question of Control or Consent?', in Knights, D. *et al.* (eds) *Job Redesign* (Aldershot: Gower).

Knights, D. and Sturdy, A. J. (1987) 'Women's Work in Insurance: I.T. and the Reproduction of Gendered Segregation in Insurance', in Davidson, M. J. and Cooper, C. L. (eds) *Women and I.T.* (Chichester: Wiley).

Knights, D. and Sturdy, A. J. (1990) 'New Technology and the Self-Disciplined Worker in Insurance', in Varcoe, I. *et al.* (eds) *Deciphering Science and Technology* (London: Macmillan).

Knights, D. and Vurdubakis, T. (1988) 'Insurantial Technologies and the Social Construction of Risk and Subjectivity', Interdisciplinary Perspectives on Accounting Conference Paper, Manchester.

Knights, D. and Willmott, H. (1983) 'Dualism and Domination: An Analysis of Marxian, Weberian and Existentialist Perspectives' *Australian and New Zealand Journal of Sociology*, 19 (1):33—49.

Knights, D. and Willmott, H. (1985) 'Power and Identity in Theory and Practice', *Sociological Review* 33(1):22—46.

Knights, D. and Willmott, H. (eds) (1990) *Labour Process Theory* (London: Macmillan).

Laing R. D. (1961) *The Self and Others* (London: Tavistock).

Leonard, P. (1984) Personality and Ideology: Towards a Materialist Understanding of the Individual (London: Macmillan).

Lockwood, D. (1958) *The Blackcoated Worker* (London: Allen and Unwin).

Luckmann, T. and Berger, P. L. (1964) 'Social Mobility and Personal Identity', *European Journal of Sociology*, V:331-43.

McColloch, M. (1983) *White Collar Workers in Transition - The Boom Years 1940-1970* (Westport, USA: Greenwood Press).

McNally, F. (1979) *Women for Hire* (London: Macmillan).

Mann, M. (1973) *Consciousness and Action Among the Western Working Class* (London: Macmillan).

Manwaring T. and Wood, S. (1985) 'The Ghost in the Labour Process', in Knights *et al.*, *Job Redesign* (Aldershot: Gower).

Marcuse, H. (1964) *One Dimensional Man* (London: Abacus).

Marx, K. (1970) *Capital* Vol 1 (London: Lawrence and Wishart).

Mead, G. H. (1934) *Mind, Self and Society* (Chicago: University of Chicago).

Pollert, A. (1981) *Girls, Wives, Factory Lives* (London: Macmillan).

Prandy, K. *et al.* (1982) *White Collar Work* (London: Macmillan).

Price, R. (1989) 'The Decline and Fall of the Status Divide?', in Sisson, K. (ed.) *Personnel Management in Britain* (Oxford: Blackwell).

Price, R. and Bain, G. S. (1972) 'Who is a White Collar Employee' *British Journal of Industrial Relations*, 10 (3):325–38.

Price, R. and Bain, G. S. (1983) 'Union Growth in Britain: Retrospect and Prospect', *British Journal of Industrial Relations*, 21:46–68.

Reich, W. (1972) *Sex-Pol* (New York: Vintage Books).

Roberts, J. (1988) 'The Possibilities of Accountability', Interdisciplinary Perspectives on Accounting (IPA) Conference Paper, Manchester.

Rolfe, H. (1985) 'Skill, Deskilling and New Technology in the Non-Manual Labour Process', UMIST/Aston Labour Process Conference Paper, Manchester.

Roslender, R. (1981) 'Misunderstanding Proletarianisation: a Comment on Recent Research', *Sociology*, 15:428–30.

Roy, D. F. (1960) ' "Banana Time": Job Satisfaction and Informal Interaction', *Human Organisation*, 18 (4):158–61.

Sartre, J.-P. (1978) *Being and Nothingness* (New York: Pocket Books).

Sennett, R. and Cobb, J. (1973) *The Hidden Injuries of Class* (New York: Vintage).

Storey, J. (1986) 'The Phoney War? New Office Technology: Organisation and Control', in Knights, D. and Willmott, T. (eds) *Managing the Labour Process* (Aldershot: Gower). (Revised version of 1983 paper)

Strauss, G. (1974) 'Workers: Attitudes and Adjustments', in Rosow, J. M. (ed.) *The Worker and the Job: Coping with Change* (New Jersey: Prentice Hall).

Strinati, D. (1990) 'A Ghost in the Machine?: The State and the Labour Process in Theory and Practice' in Knights, D. and Willmott, H. (eds) *Labour Process Theory* (London: Macmillan).

Sturdy, A. J. (1990) ' Clerical Consent: An Analysis of Social Relations in Insurance Work', Ph.D. thesis, UMIST, Manchester.

Sykes, A. J. M. (1965) 'Some Differences in the Attitudes of Clerical and Manual Workers', *Sociological Review* 13 (1):297–310.

Taylor, I. and Walton, P. (1971) 'Industrial Sabotage – Motives and Meanings', in Cohen, S. (ed.) *Images of Deviance* (Harmondsworth: Penguin).

Tepperman, J. (1976) 'Organizing Office Workers', *Radical America* 10:2–20.

Thompson, E. P. (1967) 'Time, Work Discipline and Industrial Capitalism', *Past and Present* 38:56–97.

Thompson, P. (1983) *The Nature of Work* (London: Macmillan).

Thompson, P. (1990) 'Crawling from the Wreckage: The Labour Process and the Politics of Production' in Knights, D. and Willmott, H. (eds) *Labour Process Theory* (London: Macmillan)

Thompson. P. and Bannon, E. (1985) *Working the System: The Shopfloor and New Technology* (London: Pluto).

Trungpa, C. (1976) *The Myth of Freedom and the Way of Meditation* (Shambhala).

Weber, M. (1974) *The Protestant Ethic and the Spirit of Capitalism* (London: Allen and Unwin).

Westergaard, J. and Resler, H. (1975) *Class in a Capitalist Society* (Harmondsworth: Penguin) quoted in Storey, J. (1983):4.

Willis, P. (1977) *Learning to Labour* (Farnborough: Saxon House).

Willmott, H. (1990) 'Subjectivity and the Dialectics of Praxis: Opening up the Core of Labour Process Analysis' in Knights, D. and Willmott, H. (eds) *Labour Process Theory* (London: Macmillan).

Wright-Mills, C. (1951) *White Collar* (New York: Oxford University Press).

5

MANAGING LABOUR
RELATIONS IN A
COMPETITIVE
ENVIRONMENT*

Mick Marchington

INTRODUCTION

The ground on which the labour process debate now takes place has shifted considerably over the last decade, in the period following the publication of Braverman's *Labour and Monopoly Capital*. To a large extent this has been stimulated – in Britain at least – by the annual UMIST-Aston conferences, and by the publication of a series of books emanating from papers presented at these conferences. Although most of these have focused on particular features in the debate (e.g. gender, new technology, management), a more recent addition has been the 'theory' book edited by Knights and Willmott (1990). This publication was extremely timely and focused on a number of themes which are central to the following examination of how consent is developed in workplace labour relations.

First, it reiterated the view that management strategy can vary between different organizations and over time (Friedman, 1990: 177–208). It will be recalled that a key element in Braverman's work was his assumption that Taylorism, and the separation of execution from control, represented *the* fundamental strategy of management (1974: 89), which led consequently to the progressive deskilling of work (1974: 118). A major objection to this argument is that Taylorism represents just one from a number of possible strategies which employers adopt in order to exert control over the labour process (Wood, 1982; Knights *et al.* 1985). In other words, whilst Taylorism

* Some of the data which is referred to in the chapter was collected with the aid of a grant from the ESRC (FOO 23 2226), on which Philip Parker was employed as a research assistant. I am grateful to the ESRC and to Philip Parker for their assistance.

149

may have been – and in some instances patently still is – an approach adopted by employers, it is wrong to assume that this is the only strategy which can be utilized. Second, it reminded us that employers – whilst adopting different strategies for the management of labour – are not always or necessarily obsessed with questions of labour control. Furthermore, it criticized some of the 'management strategy' literature for its (implicit) assumption that employers are both omniscient and omnipotent in their actions (Littler, 1990: 46–94; Edwards, 1990: 125–52). Third, it encouraged students to treat the subjectivity of labour in a more theoretically sensitive and comprehensive manner, focusing specifically on why employees actively contribute, that is offer their consent, to the production and reproduction of the capitalist labour process (see Knights, 1990: 297–335, and Willmott, 1990: 336–78). It is argued that more attention needs to be given to the 'missing subject', that is the employee/worker and his/ her contribution to the creation of specific labour processes (Manwaring and Wood, 1985). Of particular interest here is the notion of 'tacit skills', those attributes which all workers, irrespective of job status, learn by virtue of their experience and then utilize in order to assist or thwart the achievement of managerial objectives. Finally, it stressed that the labour process does not take place in a vacuum, with the workplace somehow separate from the economic, legal, social and political context in which organizations operate (see Thompson, 1990: 95–124, and Strinati, 1990: 209–43, in particular). Of key relevance to this chapter is the link between product markets and labour relations, and the extent to which this is mediated by managerial choice and the actions of shopfloor employees.

These arguments provide the background for this chapter, and for its focus on the production and reproduction of consent in the workplace. We need to recognize (following Burawoy (1979) and others) that workers are not continually engaged in an overt struggle with management, and that many of their actions actively contribute (perhaps unintentionally) to the securing of employer objectives. Equally, most managers spend rather more of their time cooperating with employees than they do fighting with them, a trend which has become even more apparent given sectoral shifts in the economy towards industries where unions have not traditionally been powerful. At the same time, there has been a growth in management-initiated schemes for employee involvement, which are aimed – amongst other things – at eliciting commitment and identification from workers. This investigation of consent should not be misread as reconstituted unitarism, but a belief that labour relations comprise in part a harmony between the different interest groups in any hierarchical organization. Relatedly, it is not the intention of this chapter to 'portray the labour process as a haven of consent' (Manwaring and Wood, 1985: 191), but merely to focus analysis on features which seem to attract rather less attention in most labour process analyses. In short, by concentrating the discussion on the characteristics of consent, the key role of subjectivity (management and employee) in this context and the highly differing circumstances within which organizations compete, it is hoped that the debate can be extended yet further.

The remainder of the chapter proceeds as follows. First, there will be a short discussion about control and management strategy, which is designed to ensure that the subsequent detailed analysis of consent is placed in its proper perspective. Then the argument proceeds to an examination of the characteristics of consent under three separate though interrelated headings: tacit skills/product quality, representative participation, and direct employee involvement/communication. The chapter concludes with a consideration of product market circumstances and the nature of consent.

LABOUR CONTROL AND MANAGEMENT STRATEGY

It was suggested earlier that much labour process analysis views management as preoccupied with issues of control, and that this forms a (or more likely is the) key feature of management objectives. As Wood and Kelly stress, 'the tendency to inflate control to the point at which it becomes the central problem of capitalist management is at variance with most analyses of capitalism . . . which emphasise the pursuit of profit as the directing aim of capitalist management' (1982: 77). Despite the insistence of some writers, employers are not interested in control *per se* (Littler and Salaman, 1984: 64). Part of the problem emerges because there is a confusion between objectives and consequences, a transposing of cause and effect; just because certain decisions have important implications for the management of labour, this does not mean that they have been 'formulated with a conception of the desired labour process prominently or even clearly in mind' (Child, 1985: 108). If this is the case, what place does the labour process occupy within the framework of senior management decisions?

There are broadly three different perspectives on this:

151

(a) That labour is one factor among many which are necessarily considered by senior managers, all of which assume roughly equal prominence (Fidler, 1981; Storey, 1985).

(b) That labour is a factor of secondary importance within the strategic decision-making process, in effect downstream from or consequential upon other decisions about profitability or efficiency (Rothwell, 1984; Rose and Jones, 1985). Within the specialized academic field of labour relations this perspective has informed a number of studies which have examined plant location (Kochan *et al.*, 1984; Whitaker, 1986) or decisions on product development (Marsden *et al.*, 1985).

(c) That labour control varies in importance depending on the issue, and it becomes more important at times of crisis, especially when capital perceives itself to be under threat from labour, for example if labour is able and willing to contemplate industrial action (Littler and Salaman, 1984; Purcell, 1983). More recently, Littler has drawn up a list of factors which might be thought to increase the centrality of labour relations issues in managerial initiatives, although this has not as yet been tested rigorously in practice (1990: 54).

In addition to being criticized for implicitly assuming that control over the labour process is a central preoccupation of employers, people such as R. Edwards (1979) have also been attacked for regarding management as omniscient within contemporary organizations. Of course, there may be circumstances when this is the case, and employers do have well-conceived strategies for the management of labour which are successfully and fully implemented in accordance with original intentions; this is most likely in a rigidly hierarchical organization which refuses to recognize trade unions. Generally, however, this is unlikely to apply to many organizations, because their senior managers either lack the requisite skills or the power to enforce decisions on an unwilling workforce – including supervisors and junior managers (Storey, 1986). Moreover, most of the research on management activity presents a picture in which brevity, variety, and fragmentation are typical features of the working day (Stewart, 1976; Mintzberg, 1973). One of the major problems with analysing complex and sensitive concepts such as management strategy is gaining access at the time when strategic decisions are actually made. In many cases, judgements have to be made on the basis of hindsight, and this increases the likelihood of ascribing rationality to a series of actions merely because the consequences seem to imply such an approach. In addition, the actors themselves may look back and report the process in a more logical manner than was the case at the time.

Even if senior managers do have clearly formulated strategies for the management of labour, it is not certain that they will be able to implement these without modification or resistance; indeed, it is highly unlikely that strategy will be converted unproblematically into concrete practices on the shopfloor or in the office (Purcell, 1979; Brewster *et al.*, 1983). There are many different ways in which strategies may be amended as they are implemented down the hierarchy, as supervisors flout or manipulate rules to suit their own preferences and local needs (so-called acts of commission). In addition, informal practices may develop which are not challenged by managers, creating precedents which can be used later to dispute management rules and policies (Brown, 1973; Armstrong *et al.*, 1981). In short, although it is clearly important to analyse the notion of management strategy, and especially to make allowance for variations in style and philosophy between different organizations, it cannot be assumed that management practices can be 'read-off' from the statements of senior personnel or from broad categorizations of style or strategy. Rather, much greater recognition needs to be given to the inter-subjective character of workplace labour relations, and the key role of workers within this; a theme which will be taken up in a subsequent section of this chapter.

CHARACTERISTICS OF CONSENT

Consent plays a key part in the labour process, for a variety of reasons. First, in order to make commercial use of labour power, employers require more of workers than is typically spelled out in their contracts of employment, whether this relates to technical abilities or the attitude/willingness of employees whilst at work. At all times, even in situations where jobs appear to require little in the way of skill, management remains dependent upon the actions of employees to ensure that production or service is maintained at a satsifactory level. Clearly, this is at its most apparent when skilled work is being undertaken, when quality is the principal selling point of goods, or when employees are in direct contact with customers. Second, notwithstanding significant changes in the British economic and legal environment over the course of the last decade, most employers have continued to recognize trade unions for collective bargaining purposes, and have not chosen to remove their institutional base from the organization. In part, this is probably due to a desire to achieve an 'internal state' (Burawoy, 1979) in which trade union representatives are incorporated by management to the extent that their motivation for taking industrial action is reduced. Equally, however, if employees do choose to withdraw their labour, or engage in a 'work to rule' or 'working without cooperation', management soon finds its ability to maintain production or customer service can be adversely affected. And third, in addition to working with trade union or other employee representatives, many employers have sought to develop involvement schemes which are aimed at communicating directly with individual employees. As we shall see below, these are introduced for a variety of reasons, but most regularly as an attempt to encourage workers to become aware of the commercial and financial environment in which their organization operates, and consequently (so the argument goes) to accept the reasoning behind management decisions.

The following discussion will be organized in a way which differentiates these three sorts of scheme according to its principal source (Knights, 1990: 327). Consequently, the section on tacit skills and product quality can be seen as evolving out of the subjective actions of workers, i.e. to be worker constituted, although many of these have subsequently been formalized by management into schemes such as quality circles or customer care packages. The section on representative participation can be seen to evolve out of jointly-constituted procedures, this is by management and employee/trade union representatives. These tend to be formalized into arrangements for collective bargaining or joint consultation. The third section can be seen as a creation of management, an attempt to 'educate' or inform employees about those aspects of the organization which management regards as relevant and appropriate for communicating down the hierarchy. Such management-constituted schemes would include the cascading of information to employees (such as team briefing or employee reports/videos), or informal techniques by which supervisors seek to persuade employees to accept their plans and proposals. This should allow us to theorize about the nature of consent by acknowledging that it '. . . cannot be reduced to a single measure. The analytical task is to explore its nature and its constitutent parts' (Edwards, 1990: 141). Each of these will now be dealt with in turn, starting with those systems which evolve initially from the actions of employees themselves.

Tacit skills and product quality

The notion of 'tacit' skills has been most clearly articulated by Manwaring and Wood, with their comment that 'even unskilled workers require some knowledge to do their jobs' (1985: 171), and that the description of work as unskilled is a relative and not an absolute term. According to these authors, there are three main dimensions to tacit skills: the process of learning by which skills are acquired through experience (and training); the different degrees of awareness which are required to perform certain activities; the collective nature of the labour process and the necessity for cooperative skills (ibid.: 172–3). Since all jobs, no matter how unskilled in terms of their classification, contain some element of tacit skills, management are relatively dependent on labour for the production of goods and services. Furthermore, the absolute removal of subordinates' initiative 'would render them frequently immovable and inactive, and even more frequently operating inefficiently' (Storey, 1983: 12–13). The notion of tacit skill therefore contains both technical and attitudinal elements; on the one hand, the practical skills employees acquire through experience which enables them to undertake jobs in an efficient manner, and the ability to 'correct' errors in management instructions, and to guarantee continuity of production. Additionally, these skills may be employed in a manner which is supportive of management, either consciously or sub-consciously, or one which is aimed at thwarting the achievement of managerial goals.

There appear to be at least three different ways in which we can tackle the notion of tacit skills. First, as a potential weapon to be used against employers (Cressey and MacInnes, 1980: 14), either as part of a set of collective sanctions or as an individual act against managerial domination. In the case of the former, there have been well-publicized examples from the car industry (Beynon, 1973; Thompson, 1983) whereby employees have chosen to follow a new rule so strictly that it resulted in a major production problem for the company. Similarly, Nichols and Armstrong report cases drawn from the chemcial industry where workers forbore from using thier initiative, as a way of getting back at management for implementing new working practices without their agreement (1976: 69). From the leisure industry, Analoui (1987) describes how night-club employees regularly reacted in a collective but covert manner in order to 'repay' the manager for his insensitivity to a colleague in distress. What unites these rather disparate examples is that they each represent the use of tacit skills *against* the employer, as a form of sanction or struggle in the workplace. They serve to remind management that it continually needs to secure the consent of employees before introducing change, and that managers would be better advised to listen to employees' ideas, which they ignore at their peril.

The second way in which to conceptualize the idea of tacit skills is concerned less with challenges to management, but rather more with employees discovering ways to make life at work tolerable; 'getting by', as opposed to 'getting back'. Of course, this conception is central to Burawoy's (1979) work at Allied, in which the game of 'making out' was responsible for and generated harmony at work, rather than the converse, in which playing the game is dependent upon harmony and a broad consensus about working relationships (ibid.: 81-2). By constituting life as a series of games, capitalist relations are secured, taken as given and immutable (Burawoy, ibid.: 93). Knights and Collinson (1985: 202-21) also found evidence of a practice known as 'making out' in their research at a components factory in Britain, although they were less inclined to see this as forming a basis for consent, preferring the term 'socially organized compliance', which they felt to be a more accurate description of the limited impact which employees have on the system of production, because their actions are principally defensive and reactive. Consequently, rather than challenge the basis of managerial authority, the actions of the workers concerned merely serve to reproduce the very conditions which bolster management control.[1] Thus, on one level, workers apparently consent to the rules of management, whilst the limited nature of their commitment is apparent at another; accordingly, the usage of 'getting by' as a term which accurately reflects their consent (see also Parkin, 1972).

However, employees do not necessarily view their relations with employers from such an adversarial or conflict-based perspective, or as a response to the overwhelming power of capitalism; such conceptions only serve to preserve ideas of a duality between structure and voluntarism, in which workers only release in reaction to managerial domination is via creative and liberating acts. The position of labour is thus romanticized, subjectivity is identified with creativity, autonomy and control, and the worker is then posited as struggling against the powers of a determinative structure (Knights, 1990: 307). As we noted earlier, it is insufficient to examine the labour process merely in terms of conflict, struggle and adaptation (that is getting back and getting by). Analysis also needs to incorporate considerations of consent and commitment, whereby workers may actively contribute to the achievement of management objectives, without questioning whether or not this is appropriate. In short, workers may actually enjoy, for whatever reason, doing their jobs effectively and in a way which improves the process of production; that is, workers my prefer 'getting on' with their jobs, or 'getting on' in their careers to the extent that consent is rather more typical than conflict (see also Sturdy in this volume). As we shall see below, there may be certain conditions which facilitate this conception of consent, but first some examples may help to illustrate the nature of 'getting on'.

'Getting on' is most explicitly illustrated from the research by Buchanan on chemical process operators; he notes that computerized production control technology can 'potentially enhance operator control over the production process and increase managerial dependence on operator skills, knowledge and experience' (1986: 71). He then provides evidence of how the operators had overridden the computer on many occasions, for example when alarms sounded, because they 'knew' there was nothing wrong with the plant. They used their own initiative and experience in concluding that it was the alarm, rather than the plant, which was faulty. As he notes, the operators had 'responsibility and discretion, and their actions had a significant effect on plant output. They retained a key controlling role and exercised a high degree of skill and knowledge to perform their role more effectively' (ibid.: 72). Moreover, 'the effective operation of many computerized devices depends upon skilled operator "feel" or intuition based on experience with the equipment and its functions' (ibid.: 75), an understanding which those not operating the equipment cannot have. Buchanan is not the only researcher to highlight the key role played by chemical process operators in maintaining production, by virtue of their skills and intuition, and many more examples could be provided (see, for example, Batstone et al., 1987; Marchington and Parker, 1988). Management soon becomes heavily dependent on this group of workers because of the high costs of disruption to the process, and in many organizations has been keen to encourage teamwork, creativity and responsibility amongst these workers, usually supported by high levels of pay and operator training.

The evidence to support workers' use of their initiative and discretion to keep work flowing is not confined to the chemical industry, although this does represent an ideal environment in which this type of activity is practised. Other examples come from Knights and Collinson whereby workers ignored management instructions if they felt them to be inadequate or incorrect (op. cit.: 213), and from Jones (1989: 55) and Walker (1989: 80-2). In a quite different context, namely the retail sector, Smith provides examples of how salespeople 'particularly valued their own ability to make judgements about individual customers and to adjust their approach accordingly. They enjoyed making a sale and took pride in the tacit knowledge of the craft' (1989: 158). Although his examples relate to what is termed the craft retail sector (that is, upmarket shops), similar words were used by the checkout operators interviewed as part of my own research in retail superstores (Marchington and Parker, 1990); they often referred to their rapport with individual customers, and to their desire to provide high-quality service even though their wages were not related to sales output, and in many cases their length of service was short.

Why should employees want to use their tacit skills as a way of 'getting on', when there might be more short-term benefits (in terms of rest periods whilst a machine is mended, for example) from failing to use their initiative? At one level, the willingness of employees to cooperate to a greater extent than required by the terms of a contract might reflect little more than simple instrumentalism. On the one hand, employees may be fearful that they will be dismissed for failing to contribute at a higher standard, either immediately or at some later date should the company choose to make reductions in the numbers employed. Alternatively, employees (and especially those who are partially insulated from the external labour market by the operation of an internal labour market) may identify more closely with the fortunes of their current employer, for a variety of reasons. As a number of writers have suggested, employees have at least some interest in the viability of the unit of capital which employs them, and consequently have some commitment to ensuring continuity of production within that organization (Cressey and MacInnes, 1980: 15; Littler and Salaman, 1984: 65). Events during the last decade may well have emphasized the dependence of employees on their current employer, perhaps leading to a greater likelihood of temporary alignments of interests between the parties (Terry, 1986: 175). Whether or not the coalescence is merely temporary, the instrumental attachment of workers must go some way to explaining why they are prepared to cooperate with employers in achieving managerial objectives.

Irrespective of this, individuals may also offer consent at another level, which results from conceptions of their own identity relations, from their own attempts to construct patterns of life which increase or reinforce feelings of self-worth (Knights, 1990; and Sturdy in this volume). To conceive of individuals only in relation to their position at work and within organizational hierarchies is to fail to appreciate people's own motivations and objectives, produced and reproduced through events prior to starting work, as well as in parallel to their experience at work. The prospect of doing a 'good job' – by turning out good quality work, resolving work-related problems, providing effective customer service – is central to much of our socialization and also to many of the activities which we undertake outside of the workplace. This is a theme which has been taken up by some of the North American management consultants (for example, Tom Peters), who argue that workers generally have considerable motivation and commitment, only to be 'turned off' by managers once they arrive at the workplace.[2] In a number of studies, employees (when interviewed) have castigated their managers for a host of mistakes whilst at work, for their lack of understanding of production, for their lack of commitment to the plant or for their failure to listen to the suggestions made by workers (see, for example, Nichols and Beynon, 1977: 139–40; Marchington, 1982: 60; Knights and Collinson, 1985: 212–13).

Of course, employers have not been slow in attempting to appropriate this knowledge and to integrate it into formally constituted schemes for tapping worker opinion, such as quality circles and customer care committees. Although much has been written about the potential of quality circles or quality improvement groups, the extent of coverage in Britain is low; it is estimated that no more than about 500–1,000 organizations have actually instituted this type of scheme; this is in contrast to the situation in Japan, where one million circles are operating. However, there are indications that quality circles have become more extensive since the beginning of the 1980s (Batstone, 1984: 266). Even in those organizations where circles have been instituted, it is suggested that only a small proportion of workers actually take part in them. Overall, more recent evidence suggests that the impact of quality circles has been slight, not only on management decision-making but also on the role and organization of trade unions in the workplace (Bradley and Hill, 1983; Black and Ackers, 1988). Given this, it is hardly surprising that many employees tend to lose interest in the concept of quality circles when it is realized that their impact is minimal.

Customer care programmes are equivalent to quality circles in a number of respects, most obviously in that they aim to tap employee opinion so as to enhance organizational effectiveness. These are most extensive in the private and public services sector (IDS/IPM, 1989). Whilst they may suffer from similar problems to quality circles, customer care programmes may prove more successful for employers because they are specifically related to issues which are highly relevant to the everyday needs and grievances of individual employees. The impact is potentially greater, as well, because employees in these industries are so regularly and continuously exposed to customers, and are more able to identify their own contribution to the work of the organization. In addition, these schemes have generally been introduced into industries which have been less prone to conflict, such as retail.

Overall, therefore, we can see the ways in which employees might utilize their tacit skills, not just to 'get by' whilst at work or to find ways of 'getting back' at their employers, but also to contribute to more effective working practices. This might be viewed as a way of achieving instrumental gains or as a way in which to reinforce their own identity and self-worth.

Representative participation

Despite the sweeping changes in the British economic, legal and political environment during the 1980s, all the surveys indicate a considerable degree of continuity and stability in the arrangements for workplace union organization. Whilst union membership fell considerably over the 1980s (from over 13 million to less than 10 million members), this loss can be largely explained by shifts in the distribution of employment (by sector and workplace size). According to Millward and Stevens (1986: 303), managements in those work-places where union members were present were no less likely to recognize the appropriate unions, and there was little evidence of employers withdrawing rights from those unions which had recognition at the beginning of the decade. Although there was a small number of derecognitions during the 1980s these did not constitute evidence of a full-blooded assault by employers on the structures of trade union organization (see Claydon, 1989). This broad picture of stability is confirmed by other survey evidence (Batstone, 1984; Edwards, 1987) and most of the case study material (Batstone et al., 1987; Marchington, 1988).

As well as continuing to recognize trade unions, the majority of large employers maintained their arrangements for negotiating pay via collective bargaining during the 1980s, albeit with some shifts in the most important level at which this took place (Millward and Stevens, 1986: 229). In addition, a recurrent feature of many private sector deals was the size of pay increase awarded to employees, especially those who were to some extent insulated from the external labour market. As Gregory *et al.* note, 'employers who are reasonably secure in the product market are rewarding those employees who are relatively secure in the labour market' (1986: 230). Consequently, it appears that employers were quite willing to negotiate settlements at above the rate of inflation, provided that their own labour costs did not increase; with increasing usage of more capital-intensive technologies, reductions in numbers employed and a shift towards more flexible labour relations practices, employers were able to offset increased wages by gains in productivity. In other words, trade union representatives were not only able to maintain their institutional presence within organizations, they were also able (principally in the private sector) to negotiate sizeable pay increases for their members. Whether they will be able to maintain a position of centrality within workplace affairs is a rather more problematic question (Marchington and Parker, 1990: 203–28).

Representative participation can be achieved not only through collective bargaining, but also via a union presence on joint con-sultative committees. Most commentators[3] are agreed that these have become more widespread since the early 1970s (Brown, 1981; Daniel and Millward, 1983), and that their extensiveness remained at roughly the 1980 level during the first half of the 1980s (Millward and Stevens, 1986). This does mask some decline in the manufacturing sector of the economy, but once again this is probably due to structural changes in the economy (by sector and workplace size) rather than a tendency for establishments with committees to abandon them (ibid.: 138). A vigorous debate has also taken place about the nature of these consultative committees – whether they have been upgraded so as to undermine trade unions (Terry, 1983), whether they are marginal to events in the workplace (MacInnes, 1985), or whether they can operate in parallel with the machinery for collective bargaining (Marchington, 1987). Whatever the form taken, and much of this depends upon the history of relationships within individual organiza-tions and the environmental context within which employers operate, in each case employee representatives retain some links with management. It is through institutions such as these that managers seek to influence the representatives of the workforce, presumably in the hope that these individuals will subsequently be able to persuade their constitutents of the 'logic' of managerial actions.

In sum, therefore, there is broad agreement that – contrary to some analyses at the beginning of the 1980s – the institutions of workplace union organization held up remarkably well during the Thatcher years (see also MacInnes, 1987). However, we also need to offer an explanation for this level of continuity at a time of considerable economic change and upheaval, as well as make an assessment about whether the nature of shop steward organization changed in those companies which continued to deal with trade unions, even if its extensiveness did not (see Ackers and Black in this volume).

Two sets of arguments seem to be relevant here, one relating to the desire of employers to initiate adjustments in labour relations, the other to their ability to do so. There are at least three sets of reasons why employers may not wish to change their arrangements with the trade unions in the workplace. First, employers may feel that the trade union(s) with which they deal represent a useful channel through which to deal with collective affairs such as pay bargaining, the introduction of new technology, or dispute resolution, and that they consequently help to maintain order and stability in the workplace (Marchington, 1988). This in fact was one of the principal features of Purcell's articulation of a 'strategy for management control in industrial relations', a model based to large extent on the practices of many large employers in Britain towards the end of the 1970s (1979: 27–59). It also has parallels with the idea of management sponsorship put forward at a similar time by Terry (1983), in which employers offered their support for the trade unions as a way of regaining management control over the shopfloor. 'Sponsored' union organization, so the argument goes, would be less inclined to challenge management because they had been effectively 'incorporated' into maintaining systems for the reproduction of managerial control, a sort of 'hegemonic regime' (Burawoy, 1985). Support for this notion might be found in the histories of certain industries (for example, chemicals) or specific companies (for example, Nissan (Wickens, 1987)), although there are also examples of 'sponsored' unions later engaging in industrial action and challenging employers (Willman, 1980). Notwithstanding this, my own research still continues to find examples of employers keen to work with and recognize trade unions in the anticipation that such a policy will lead to better relations in the future (Marchington and Parker, 1990). In other words, despite operating in an environment which might allow them to adopt a more adversarial stance towards the unions, many employers continue to feel that consent amongst shopfloor or office workers is more likely to be achieved by cooperating with and supporting their union representatives, rather than confronting and directly undermining them.

Second, it can be argued that employers are more concerned with issues other than those relating to trade unions and, provided the latter do not present too great an obstacle to the achievement of more strategic goals (such as customer service, for example), their presence can be tolerated. This is even more relevant if trade unions are not engaged in a continual struggle with employers, but rather see cooperation as a more appropriate stance in difficult economic circumstances (Batstone, 1984). As Terry (1986: 177) suggests, the interests of workers and managers may be temporarily aligned, and both worker and management power may be directed along the same lines, for example to ensure company survival or avoid compulsory redundancies. Cooperation may therefore represent an optimum strategy for maintaining strong formal workplace organization now and into the future (Batstone and Gourlay, 1986). Whether or not this is an indication of shop steward weakness or resilience is of course an empirical question to be addressed in different workplaces, but on the basis of a variety of case studies, Terry (1986: 176) suggests extremely tentatively ('hedged about with qualifications') that they are now weaker.

Finally, employers may desist from using their potential power at a time of comparative advantage, for fear of a future backlash from the trade unions should conditions change and stewards seek to settle old scores (Marchington, 1988). Some of the literature on the British car industry seems to suggest that there are instances when this did happen, and that this situation was then exacerbated by harsh management actions towards the end of the 1970s (Edwardes, 1984; Marsden et al., 1985). Some leading industrialists have openly criticized this abrasive management style (Roots, 1982), warning that it may prove counterproductive to alter the long-term character of workplace labour relations. Alternatively, it is argued that 'responsible' workplace union organization and 'responsive' management are mutually reinforcing.

Even if they have the desire to remove the institutional base of trade unionism from the workplace, employers may lack the ability to do so, in the short run. Whilst the overall level of unemployment may signal to employers that a more forceful approach is possible, it is not usually a simple matter to withdraw union recognition, still less to sack all workers and replace them with equally qualified individuals at short notice. Labour market surpluses at a macro level frequently coexist with shortages at a local level (Batstone, 1984; Kelly, 1987). This became even more apparent towards the end of the 1980s, when many were wary of losing high-quality staff as levels of unemployment fell and shortages in the labour market became more marked. Indeed, despite the greater legislative freedoms now at the disposal of employers (especially with regard to the dismissal of strikers, temporary staff and part-time employees) and the more recent recession, many companies continue to expend effort in improving their attractiveness to employees by offering inducements (in terms of pay or crèche facilities, for example).

Second, employers are likely to be cautious in their dealings with trade unions, unless they are convinced they will win or they perceive no alternative to a fight, for fear that they might encounter more severe forms of resistance or give workers a fresh and more effective focus for struggle in the workplace (Marchington, 1982; Batstone, 1984). Irrespective of the state of the legal, political and economic environment at national level, certain groups of workers continue to retain considerable potential power to disrupt the activities of employers, by virtue of the group's centrality and pervasivenes; or by the absence of substitutes for its labour (Marchington, 1982: 94–108). This can occur by virtue of their position in the workflow and the number of links groups have with other parts of an interdependent production/information process, the speed with which actions (or more precisely a lack of action) can disrupt the work of other parts of the organization, or the lack of substitutes for a specific form of labour in an organization. No matter how far some companies may have moved to employ more flexible forms of worker, all employees still retain – as we saw from the previous section on tacit skills – a body of knowledge which can be used against employers if they so desire. Moreover, the latter part of the 1980s also saw an increased willingness by workers to engage in industrial action in support of their claims. Consequently, it is easy to understand why employers have typically (though obviously not always) exercised caution in their dealings with union representatives.

Finally, competitive product markets may actually reduce rather than enhance employer strength, because companies become even more dependent upon continuity of production or service to ensure orders are delivered on time (Kelly, 1987: 279). As we shall see in a later section, although managers may utilize images of the product market in order to persuade employees to accept company proposals, there are distinct limits to this approach in a highly competitive situation when any disruption to service could mean the loss of an order; again, caution may represent a more attractive option for employers than a full-blooded assault on employees and their organizations. Overall, therefore a more competitive product market is a source of both strength and weakness for employers in their dealings with employees.

So far, we have concentrated on the advantages which employers may gain from a policy of supporting the trade unions, that is developing consent, even when the short-term situation appears to militate against this. However, we also need to assess whether trade unions gain anything from cooperative relationships with employers, or whether sponsorship and support merely serve to neutralize their presence in the workplace, rendering them unwilling to challenge employers due to their incorporation into (low-level) management decision-making channels (Clarke and Clements, 1977: 357–82). Some would argue that if employers gain from a participative relationship, it is therefore impossible for employees or trade unions to gain as well, because to conceive of positive sum notions of control is to 'engage in physical legerdemain' (Ramsay, 1985: 61). Whilst accepting that a relationship built upon participation and consent is unlikely to change the principal features of capitalist relations within organizations, it is also probable that cooperation with employers may enable unions and their members to gain more than they would have done by using adversarial tactics. For example, shop stewards who sit on consultative committees are generally aware of the limitations to such bodies, but regularly comment on the value of the information which is acquired through this machinery (see Marchington, 1987, for example). Equally, during periods when employers mount an 'offensive', many union officials feel that the maintenance of representation is crucial (Rose and Jones, 1985), and it is hardly likely that they will resist attempts by employers to support their activities, no matter how aware they may be of the potential disadvantage; the closed shop situation provides a good example of this. Finally, especially in the case of well-developed internal labour markets, employees may receive sizeable substantive gains, particularly in the form of high

165

wage increases, from their continuing cooperative relations with employers.

Of course, it could be argued that all these tactics may ultimately weaken rather than strengthen unions, but that is a matter for empirical evaluation in specified circumstances, as opposed to theoretical generalizations based upon zero-sum and dualist conceptions of the nature of control. What the above discussion does demonstrate, however, is that the pressures for cooperation and consent can be just as strong as – if not stronger than – those for conflict and coercion.

Direct employee involvement and communications

We have already seen that most of the evidence indicates a strong element of stability and continuity in the nature of British industrial relations during the last decade. At the same time, there has been a growth in management-initiated schemes for involving and communicating directly with employees over the course of the decade. Although it is impossible to make strict comparisons with earlier surveys, Millward and Stevens state that during the first half of the 1980s there was a 'very substantial increase in the number of managers reporting that in their workplace there had been an increase in two-way communication' (1986: 165). The stewards in the sample were less convinced about the extent of this change, but they did agree that this had been the biggest development since 1980. Support for this view comes from the studies by Batstone (1988), Storey (1988) and Edwards (1987). In the case of the latter, Edwards notes that the factory managers in his survey made regular reference to consultation, communication and involvement in the personnel policies of their firms. He notes two things from these replies:

> one is the stress on communicating with workers and generating a sense of commitment to the goals of the organization. The other is the detail and the specificity of the replies. It is not just managers picking up the currently fashionable language, for they were able to point to concrete arrangements . . . which had been introduced or extended.
>
> (1987: 139–40)

There are several sets of reasons why employee involvement (EI) schemes of this sort should have become more prominent during the last decade. First, employing organizations have been confronted by more competitive and internationally-based product market circum-

166

stances which, in their view, have put a premium on quality goods, customer service, prompt delivery and worker flexibility. Accordingly, employers have placed increasing emphasis on ensuring that employees are made aware of the competitive environment in which the organization operates and are prepared to contribute more fully to the achievement of organizational goals. Second, 'pop' management texts (such as *In Search of Excellence* (Peters and Waterman)), have had a tremendous impact on senior managers; amongst other things companies have been exhorted to develop employee involvement. Despite, or perhaps because of, the simplicity of its messages, this appears to have influenced management philosophy in many organizations. In addition, some employers have realized the potential public relations value of EI, since it can promote an image of a company which makes high-quality products largely by virtue of the nature of its workforce. Third, labour market conditions in Britain throughout the 1980s provided management with greater room for manoeuvre in deciding how to handle employee relations issues, and made it harder for trade union negotiators to resist EI, should they so desire. Relatedly, and despite the comments in the previous section, some employers may well have been keen to introduce EI specifically in order to undermine and marginalize the influence of trade unions. Regardless of whether or not this was a first order objective,[4] one of the consequences of greater EI may well be a lessened role for unions in the future, especially if employers become more effective in communicating their ideas to staff. Finally, with the advent of the Single European Market and the pressures from the EC for harmonization of labour standards, British employers may soon be required to illustrate convincingly that their systems for communication and consultation are equal to those elsewhere in the Community. Even if there is no compulsion, it could be argued that progressive employers would wish to maintain standards equal to or better than those of their EC partners. Put together, therefore, this combination of factors has helped to produce a trend towards EI throughout British industry.

Because most publications on EI tend to assume that these techniques are successful in transmitting information and creating attitudinal change, the focus here is on the problems with EI in practice. This is not to argue that EI never works – far from it – but merely to illustrate the limits to these communications schemes as devices to increase commitment or encourage employees to work harder. Since team briefing was the technique which seemed to be most extensively utilized by managements at the end of the 1980s, the following will concentrate on this particular approach. The basic principles of team briefing are probably well known: information is cascaded down the organization from the senior management team to the shop/office floor; all individuals are briefed by their immediate supervisor, usually in small groups; briefing should take place at regular intervals, and should be kept to about thirty minutes; questions should only be allowed on the brief itself, and the session should not develop into a more general discussion about work; the system should allow scope for information to be fed up the hierarchy, and for monitoring of progress. The objectives of team briefing – according to its major proponent, the Industrial Society – are to increase workforce and supervisory commitment, to reduce misunderstandings, to reinforce the role of line managers, to help people to accept change, and ultimately to improve upward communication (Grummitt, 1983: 3–7).

These grand objectives are not always easy to achieve, and some of them seem to rest upon highly questionable unestablished assumptions; see Marchington et al. (1989) for a more detailed discussion.[5] There is often a range of practical problems in making the briefing system work in accordance with the prearranged guidelines for its operation. For example, it is often difficult to ensure that team briefs take place at the correct time, and there are examples whereby the system effectively breaks down at certain times of the year due to an overriding necessity to meet production targets or customer demands. The content of briefs, intended to make employees aware of organizational circumstances and how these relate to individual departments, often falls rather flat, and there are regular complaints that the information passed on to employees is either out of date or irrelevant. There are frequent reports that briefers (usually, though not exclusively, first-line supervisors) lack the skills and/or motivation to present information and deal with questions in a way which generates commitment from employees. There are also examples of employees who repeatedly fail to turn up for the briefs due to other more pressing commitments (for example, part-time workers with childcare arrangements), or of briefers who are called away to deal with other issues (for example, customer complaints in a supermarket) during the course of the brief. In short, on practical grounds alone, there are doubts about the effectiveness of team briefing as a device for securing the consent of employees.

It is also difficult to determine whether or not team briefing will achieve the objectives which are claimed for it as a technique, largely because, as yet, it has been the subject of so little research. There is a danger, as in other areas of labour relations in recent years (MacInnes, 1987), that rhetoric may run ahead of reality, and that typicality may be assumed on the basis of unestablished claims. Whilst it may not seem unreasonable to assume that team briefing may reinforce management as the 'natural' leader within the workplace, this claim is also highly dependent on managers briefing with commitment and ability, as well as on the support of senior management for the system as a whole. In the cases examined by Marchington *et al.* (1989), there were several examples of managers or supervisors not taking the system seriously, and showing little enthusiasm for the process. In one case the managers were initially highly sceptical about the briefing system, and their continued hositility meant that it stood little chance of promoting attitudinal change amongst staff.

Equally, there must be doubts about the claim that team briefing increases worker commitment; again, the theoretical foundations for this view rest upon shaky foundations. The argument relies upon the notion that informing employees of current activity and future plans necessarily develops consent and produces a greater commitment to the organization; that is, it leads to a behavioural change. Results from a detailed and multi-method research project by Ostell *et al.* (1980) found that a communication exercise in a manufacturing plant had little effect on the workers there. Whilst a majority of employees took part in the briefings, only a third could recall much of the material several weeks later, and no more than a few could remember any of the general economic factors relevant to the plant. The authors conclude that the exercise had little success in motivating workers, and in fact might have increased insecurity amongst the group. Marchington *et al.*'s study casts further doubt upon the claim that briefing increases commitment; many respondents in one of the organizations where briefing had been introduced regarded the major benefit of the system to be 'twenty minutes off work' (1989: 28). Greatest interest was expressed in each case for items of local information, that relating to the workers' own jobs and departments, a finding which reinforces most of the literature on employee attitudes towards participation (Wall and Lischeron, 1977). Part of the problem undoubtedly lies in the size and structure of many large organizations, and the difficulty which employees have in identifying with the corporate body as a whole. It is hard to correlate one's own effort and performance with that of the organization as a whole, or to find much of interest in the activities of other establishments, new board level appointments or the financial dealings of the company.

Similar points could also be made about the other claims, especially the view that employees will be more willing to accept change even if they do not agree with the reasons for it, but space does not allow it here. A more serious concern relates to the problem of establishing benchmarks against which to evaluate the impact of team briefing, as well as disentangling the independent effects of any single technique on employee attitudes and behaviour. Part of the problem is choosing an appropriate point at which to start measuring, and whether this should be at the time briefing is actually implemented, or when it is first mooted, or at a set time prior to its introduction. Additonally, there are difficulties in establishing whether changes are due to this technique, or others, or indeed factors which occur outside of the workplace. Indeed, it can be argued that team briefing (or any other technique, for that matter) has the greatest chance of success in those situations where it is least needed by managers, and the least chance of success in those where it is needed the most. It appears that these issues seem to have been overlooked by those who argue that team briefing is a technique for increasing commitment and consent at work.

In conclusion, therefore, we can see that management-initiated schemes for EI are not always capable of achieving their objectives, thus indicating yet again the limits to management omnipotence. However, it is also clear that some of the messages do get through to employees, especially in a climate where they are favourably inclined towards the organization, either for instrumental/calculative reasons or for notions of self-worth and a desire to make a positive contribution to their own work. Equally, the fact that employees traditionally complain about poor communications from management must mean that they have some interest in discovering more about events at work.

PRODUCT MARKETS AND THE PRODUCTION OF CONSENT

There have been a number of studies which illustrate the links between product markets and the management of employee relations; broadly, these take one of two separate forms. First, there have been in-depth analyses of specific establishments, companies or industries which describe the key features of the product market – amongst other factors – and explicitly or implicitly link this to employee relations. Not surprisingly, the most comprehensive accounts have been in situations where the organization operated in fiercely competitive conditions, and for which the product represented a critical uncertainty for management decision-making. Consequently, this is often seen to create circumstances which hinder the achievement of employee participation, because managers become obsessed with satisfying market needs, to the detriment of employee interests and issues.

One of the clearest accounts of competitive product market conditions can be found in the work of Goodman and his colleagues, on the footwear industry. The market is highly competitive, suffers from seasonal and cyclical variations in demand, and is generally (for the British companies) in a state of decline. Fashion is also a key feature of the market. This uncertain and volatile market environment has led to considerable worker flexibility and adaptability, as well as close and collaborative relations between the union and employer organization at industry level (1977: 38). A similar picture emerges from the study of a kitchen furniture firm by Marchington and Loveridge; they report on the fashion orientation, intense competition, and considerable variation in demand, not just on a seasonal basis but also with rather less predictability from one week to the next. The competitive environment led to a management obsession with the market and the need for flexibility, speed of response, change and survival – hardly the kind of climate in which employee involvement and consent can be easily developed. Management 'regretted' the lack of EI, but rationalized it with reference to the demands of the product market (1983: 73–82). Similar patterns emerge from the studies of Rainnie (1984) on the clothing industry and Purcell and Gray (1986) on one division of a food company whereby the competitive market climate bolstered a strong belief in the managerial prerogative and militated against consultation. In each of these cases, the product market is presented as a highly significant factor which appears beyond the control of senior managers; there is little doubt that it exercises a disproportionate influence over the way in which decisions were made.

Rather less has been written about the relationship between markets and employee relations in less competitive conditions, or in situations where individual companies have greater power over the market, largely because in such circumstances the market is a source of little uncertainty. Studies on the chemical industry illustrate a quite different environment, one where lead times are much higher, there are high barriers to entry, and in each market there are only a small number of major suppliers (Pettigrew, 1985). Thus, in contradistinction to the clothing market, for example, the producers are relatively powerful in relation to the consumers. Each of these features tend to facilitate the development of management styles which emphasize consultation and involvement and place greater stress on the contributions of individual employees.

The second type of research examines the way in which adjustments in market conditions may be associated with different management styles. Friedman's (1977) distinction between responsible autonomy (RA) and direct control (DC) is also relevant here, because he explicitly relates these strategies for the management of labour to product market circumstances over a period of time. RA, he argues, is more likely to occur during periods of growth and a lower intensity of competition, since 'top managers will be tempted to placate worker demands', whereas DC is likely to be associated with a declining market, overhung with the threat of redundancies (1984: 189). Whilst this association appears to fit well with the history of the car industry up until 1980, it seems less adequate for the period since then. Contrary to the expected development, given high levels of unemployment and more competitive conditions, there have been moves towards RA (especially in companies such as Ford). Because he locates the roots of RA in worker resistance and the power to force management to loosen control, Friedman tends to overlook the possibility that managements may find RA strategies attractive at times when labour is relatively weak, and that they may take a more proactive stance in their attempts to generate worker consent.

Other studies illustrate the impact of sudden or major changes in market conditions on the management of employee relations, generally following a move from relative stability to greater competition or uncertainty. For example, Batstone et al. (1984) note the change in management style at British Telecom following liberalization of the network in the early 1980s: a change from consensus between management and unions, and support for each other's position, to a situation in which management tried to communicate direct with employees. The unions accused managers of undermining their role, whilst management spoke of 'distortions' and 'mischievous and slanted information' emanating from the unions (ibid.: 145–6). Again, similar pictures emerge from the work of Kochan et al. (1984) on the

US tyre industry, from Cappelli (1985) on airlines, and from Purcell (1981) in various other industries.

It is clear that much of this material on product markets is rich in detail, and very useful in setting the context for the particular studies examined. What it tends to lack, however, is a precision which would allow for comparisons of product market circumstances between different companies or industries, and so enable a more adequate theorization of the links between product markets and the production of consent. Below, a framework will be presented for categorizing product markets according to their potential 'power' over the organization, as will a model for analysing the links between markets and employee involvement.[6] Drawing upon the literature discussed above, as well as that of Porter (1979), this range of different aspects of the product market can be collapsed into two separate components – competitive pressure (or degree of monopoly) and customer pressure (or degree of monopsony) – both of which contribute to the overall power of the market.

Competitive pressure; degree of monopoly power

This measures the degree to which the company is able to dictate terms to the customer due to a lack of suitable alternative suppliers, or conversely the extent to which the company feels constrained to follow the general trend within the market as a whole. Added to this is the ease with which other firms may enter the market, that is whether or not there are barriers to entry – such as high initial capital investment costs or markets protected by patent or other restriction. Competitive pressures are likely to be less in the case where demand is growing, because the company's share of the market is likely to be on the increase, and when other companies find it difficult to establish a presence in the market; in such circumstances, management should generally have considerable room for manoeuvre, both in terms of influencing the direction of the market and in choosing appropriate responses to market pressures. Conversely, if demand for the company's product is in decline, and this is exacerbated by the entry of new competitors, senior management is likely to feel under increasing pressure from the market. Within such a context, the 'power' of the market may be seen by management to decrease their opportunity for choice and make it appear that the market determines management action; in this instance, management may see its primary task as that of engineering the 'best fit' with external contingencies. However, it is not appropriate to generalize from this type of situation and to assume that management action is automatically dependent on product market circumstances in all cases.

Customer pressure; degree of monopsony power

This measures the degree to which companies come under pressure from customers. Demand for a company's products may fluctuate over time (year/month/week/day) or it may be relatively stable. The degree to which this is predictable in advance may also vary. Therefore, a pattern of demand which is regular, stable and predictable can provide management with rather more room for manoeuvre than one which is subject to considerable variability. In the latter case, managers are more likely to feel the pressure of the market, to be forced to continually adapt to changing circumstances, and to feel that actions are determined by the nature of the product market environment. In addition, customer profile structures can vary; a single customer who buys from a range of competing producers is able to exert more pressure on the company than an uncoordinated group of individual consumers who purchase from a monopoly producer. In the former instance, the market will appear to leave managers with little room for manoeuvre, whereas in the latter managerial action is clearly not determined by the market.

Having presented a framework for assessing the 'power' of the product market over the organization, it is now appropriate to outline the model which illustrates the relationship between markets, management, employees, trade unions and product quality. This is shown in Figure 1. Whilst it must be stressed that this graphic representation of the model inevitably oversimplifies the complexity of the relationship, it does at least have the value of clarifying the interaction between these different factors.

The product markets within which companies compete clearly influence the nature of employee relations in the enterprise, to some extent through the responses of management at different levels to these circumstances, but also via the direct effect of the market on employees. It has already been noted that the potential for management discretion in employee relations seems greater when market power is low, and in these circumstances EI is more likely to be pursued by managers. Conversely, when managers feel that market power is significant, they perceive little room for manoeuvre in how to handle employee relations, regarding their actions as contingent on

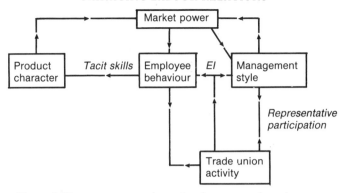

Figure 1 Management, employee involvement and market power

a market which appears beyond their control. But, there are many instances when the relationship is not solely one-way, and senior managers possess considerable power to influence the character of the markets within which the company operates; for example, in choosing the kind of products to be manufactured or sold, the location of facilities, the choice of geographical markets in which to compete, as well as the precise range of goods available to the customer. However, once the decision to compete in a certain range of markets has been made, management at establishment level are more often left with the task of responding to the market, and consequently choosing appropriate styles to manage employees in order to satisfy broader corporate objectives. Of course, market forces may also be 'blamed' by managers seeking to legitimize decisions which they would have made in any event, so closing down options for employee participation (Marchington and Loveridge, 1983).

Managers are not the only people to be influenced by the nature of the product market; employees also receive messages from this quarter as well, either directly or via management interpretations. Some of this will occur outside the workplace, via social contacts or media influences, but many of the pressures are apparent from the jobs on which employees are engaged; for example, the quantity of work which flows through a department can give employees some idea of the current state of the order book, as can informal conversations with colleagues or friends from other companies competing in the same product market. In some industries, such as those in the service sector, employees experience customer pressure through direct contact with consumers, whereas in others it is to a large extent mediated via management interpretations of the product market and

175

the results of decision-making at higher levels of the organization. In the former situation, especially if pressures are high, management may need to do little to reinforce the messages which are received from the market, since employees are already aware of the potential force of customer power. If employees are not generally in direct contact with the consumer, management may initiate EI schemes to increase their awareness of the market through exposure to key customers. In many companies, however, it may prove difficult to increase direct exposure, especially if the part the product plays in a finished article is hard to identify. In these circumstances, management's role is critical in interpreting customer and competitive pressures to employees, because of its superior access to such information.

In a non-union environment, it is unlikely that employees would challenge managerial interpretations of the product market, especially if they also lack direct contact with customers. Even in situations where they are personally exposed to the market, employees would find it difficult to contest management decisions, in the absence of collective organization. In a unionized environment, representative participation is likely to play an important role in the management of consent. Via their representatives, employees have greater opportunity to dispute managerial interpretations of market signals, and to put forward their own alternative perspective. Through an alternative information network, such as a combine committee or a trade union research department, union representatives can check the accuracy of the arguments used by management to justify decisions, and may attempt to discredit them if appropriate. Equally, shop stewards will also receive information from their presence on consultative bodies, and this too can be used to counter managerial interpretations of competitive pressures and the 'logic' of management decisions. Furthermore, it is clear that employee relations management does not develop in isolation from the influence of trade unions, and the willingness of management to make concessions to employees is also highly dependent upon the actual, potential, or anticipated power of trade unions. Even if trade unions lack centrality in many workplaces, as we have seen above, managements are both disinclined and unable to ignore their role altogether.

The final part of the model deals with the link between employees and the market, via the character of the product or service which their company provides, and focuses on the tacit skills of workers. A key feature of recent attempts to improve the competitive performance of

British companies has been the focus on customer care and product quality, both of which are substantially dependent upon employee actions. Whilst this link is at its most apparent in the service sector, where employees come into direct contact with customers, it has also become more central to the labour process in manufacturing companies. Techniques such as TQM (total quality management) have as their primary objective the improvement of quality within the company, and rest upon a philosophy which encourages all employees/departments to regard themselves as providers or customers of other employees/departments; the ultimate consequence of this is supposed to be a greater awareness of customer needs, thus leading to improvements in quality or reductions in the cost of finished products. But employees may just as readily use their tacit skills in order to thwart the objectives of employers as they may benefit the company as a whole. Since even the most unskilled of employees have at their disposal the ability to influence the character of the product (in either direction), some managements have seen the value of developing an investment-oriented style in an attempt to harness these capabilities and elicit worker commitment. Conversely, others have sought to minimize employee discretion through policies designed to standardize product character, and to further separate the execution of the task from its conception. Whatever the management approach, it is nevertheless clear that employees possess some capacity to influence the nature of the market.

CONCLUSION

It was stated at the outset of this chapter that consent has tended to receive rather less attention in most analyses of the labour process than has the parallel and equally important notion of conflict. This provided the basic reason for the above analysis not, it should be recalled, any fundamental belief that consent was a more typical feature of employee relations than conflict and struggle. The major objective in this chapter has been to provide a framework which will allow for more comprehensive and less disjointed explorations of the characteristics of consent. Thus, three separate, though interrelated, factors were discussed: tacit skills, which emanate from the actions of workers, although management often attempts to appropriate these and bind them into formal schemes such as quality circles or customer care committees; representative participation which emerges from jointly-consituted arrangements, especially and largely in unionized workplaces; and direct employee involvement and communications, which are managerially-instituted techniques for encouraging greater levels of commitment to the goals of the enterprise. Each of these is likely to be present to a greater or lesser extent in individual workplaces, depending on a variety of factors. In the final part of the chapter, we examined this in further detail, focusing on the links between the product market and the production of consent, and providing a model which should allow for further testing of these ideas.

The ideas which have informed this analysis come from a number of rather different sources, for example labour process studies, industrial relations theory, and even management consultants. Although the principal focus of this chapter has not been on my own empirical work, the frameworks and models have proved useful for analysing data in a number of British private sector companies researched during the late 1980s. It is hoped that these will also prove helpful to other students investigating organizations in Britain or elsewhere, and that further studies will demonstrate the utility of these ideas, or develop them rather more. As ever, concepts and theories require rigorous testing in empirical studies, if they are to add to our understanding of workplace labour relations.

NOTES

1 In addition to having doubts about the use of the word 'consent' in Burawoy's case, they also have doubts about the methodology and theoretical generalizability of his work. Methodologically, Knights and Collinson feel that Burawoy was unable to explore the symbolic meaning of actions because he concentrated too much on observable behaviour. In defence of Burawoy, the fact that he spent a period of time as a shopfloor worker at Allied should mean that he was able to substantiate his findings with other materials; incidentally, he spent rather longer than most researchers do in collecting his material. Knights and Collinson also feel that the situation at Allied was unusual, in that the company had the luxury of a secure product market, and that their own work at a company known as Slavs indicated the fragile nature of consent in less favourable market contexts.

2 This is a theme which has reappeared in a number of publications by Peters (1982, 1986) as well as in some of his videos.

3 The principal dissenter from this position has been MacInnes (1985: 106) who argues that 'the high birth rate and apparent renaissance of consultation is paralleled by an equally high but less visible death rate'. However, Daniel and Millward's finding (1983: 132) of an introduction to abandonment ratio of 9:1 between 1975 and 1980 seems to point to some expansion, even allowing for some fairly severe lapses of memory.

4 My own research in this area (Marchington and Parker, 1990) as well as that of Rose and Jones (1985) would support the idea that the undermining of trade unions is rarely a significant reason behind the introduction of EI schemes. Nevertheless, this is not to deny that EI can have a major impact on the position of workplace trade union organization.

5 For a more extensive discussion of team briefing, based upon studies in three organizations (drawn from manufacturing, retail, and the public service sector), see Marchington *et al.* 1989.

6 This model is developed in much more depth, and applied to four private sector companies examined by the author over a two-year period in the late 1980s. The full details can be found in Marchington and Parker (1990: 239–56).

REFERENCES

Analoui, F. (1987) 'An Investigation into Unconventional Behaviours within the Workplace', unpublished PhD thesis, Cranfield School of Management.

Armstrong, P., Goodman, J. and Hyman, J. (1981) *Ideology and Shop Floor Industrial Relations* (London: Croom Helm).

Batstone, E. (1984) *Working Order* (Oxford: Blackwell).

Batstone, E., Ferner, A. and Terry, M. (1984) *Consent and Efficiency* (Oxford: Blackwell).

Batstone, E. and Gourlay, S. (1986) *Unions, Unemployment and Innovation* (Oxford: Blackwell).

Batstone, E., Gourlay, S., Levie, H. and Moore, R. (1987) *New Techonology and the Process of Labour Regulation* (Oxford: Clarendon Press).

Beynon, H. (1973) *Working For Ford* (Harmondsworth: Penguin).

Black, J. and Ackers, P. (1988) 'The Japanisation of British Industry? A case of Quality Circles in the Carpet Industry', *Employee Relations*, 10 (6): 9–16.

Bradley, K. and Hill, S. (1983) 'After Japan; the Quality Circle Transplant and Productive Efficiency', *British Journal of Industrial Relations*, 21 (3): 291–311.

Braverman, H. (1974) *Labour and Monopoly Capital* (New York: Monthly Review Press).

Brewster, C., Gill, C. and Richbell, S. (1983) 'Industrial Relations Policy; a framework for analysis', in Thurley, K. and Wood, S. (eds) *Industrial Relations and Management Strategy* (Cambridge: Cambridge University Press): 62–72.

Brown, W. (1973) *Piecework Bargaining* (London: Heinemann).

Brown, W. (ed.) (1981) *The Changing Contours of British Industrial Relations* (Oxford: Blackwell).

Buchanan, D. (1986) 'Management Objectives in Technical Change', in Knights, D. and Willmott, H. (eds), *Managing the Labour Process* (Aldershot: Gower): 67–84.

Burawoy, M. (1979) *Manufacturing Consent: Changes in the Labour Process under Monopoly Capitalism* (Chicago: University of Chicago Press).

Burawoy, M. (1985) *The Politics of Production* (London: Verso Press).

Cappelli, P. (1985) 'Competitive Pressures and Labour Relations in the Airline Industry', *Industrial Relations* 22 (3): 316–38.

Child, J. (1985) 'Managerial Strategies, New Technology, and the Labour Process', in Knights, D., Willmott, H. and Collinson, D. (eds), *Job Redesign* (Aldershot: Gower): 107–41.

Clarke, T. (1977) 'Industrial Democracy: The Institutionalised Suppression of Industrial Conflict?', in Clarke, T. and Clements, L., *Trade Unions under Capitalism* (London: Penguin): 357–82.

Clarke, T. and Clements, L. (1977) *Trade Unions under Capitalism* (Glasgow: Fontana/Collins).

Claydon, T. (1989) 'Union Derecognition in Britain in the 1980s', *British Journal of Industrial Relations* 27 (2): 214–24.

Cressey, P. and MacInnes, J. (1980) 'Voting for Ford: Industrial Democracy and the Control of Labour', *Capital and Class* 11: 5–33.

Daniel, W. and Millward, N. (1983) *Workplace Industrial Relations in Britain* (London: Heinemann).

Edwardes, M. (1984) *Back from the Brink* (London: Pan).

Edwards, P. (1985) 'Managing Labour Relations through the Recession', *Employee Relations* 7 (2) 3–7.

Edwards, P. (1987) *Managing the Factory* (Oxford: Blackwell).

Edwards, P. (1990) 'Understanding Conflict in the Labour Process: The Logic and Autonomy of Struggle', in Knights, D. and Willmott, H. (eds) *Labour Process Theory* (London: Macmillan): 125–52.

Edwards, R. (1979) *Contested Terrain* (London: Heinemann).

Fidler, J. (1981) *The British Business Elite* (London: Routledge and Kegan Paul).

Friedman, A. (1977) *Industry and Labour* (London: Macmillan).

Friedman, A. (1984) 'Management Strategies, Market Conditions and the Labour Process', in Stephen, F. (ed.) *Firms, Organisation and Labour* (London: Macmillan): 176–200.

Friedman, A. (1990) 'Managerial Strategies, Activities, Techniques and Technology: Towards A Complex Theory of the Labour Process', in Knights and Willmott, op. cit.: 177–208.

Goodman, J., Armstrong, E., David, J. and Wagner, A. (1977) *Rule Making and Industrial Peace* (London: Croom Helm).

Gregory, M., Lobban, P. and Thomson, A. (1986) 'Bargaining Structure, Pay Settlements and Perceived Pressures in Manufacturing, 1979–84: Further Analysis from the CBI Databank', *British Journal of Industrial Relations*, 24 (2): 215–32.

Grummitt, J. (1983) *Team Briefing* (London: Industrial Society).

Incomes Data Services/Institute of Personnel Management (1989) *Customer Care: The Personnel Implications* (London: IDS/IPM).

Jones, B. (1989) 'When Certainty Fails: Inside the Factory of the Future', in Wood, S. (ed.), *The Transformation of Work?* (London: Unwin Hyman): 44–58.

Kelly, J. (1987) 'Trade Unions through the Recession', *British Journal of Industrial Relations* 25 (2): 275–82.

Knights, D. (1990) 'Subjectivity, Power and the Labour Process', in Knights and Willmott (eds) op. cit.: 297–335.

Knights, D. and Collinson, D. (1985), 'Redesigning Work on the Shop Floor:

A Question of Control or Consent?', in Knights, D. *et al*. (eds) op. cit.: 197–226.

Knights, D. and Willmott, H. (eds) (1986) *Managing the Labour Process* (Aldershot: Gower).

Knights, D. and Willmott, H. (eds) (1989) *New Technology and the Labour Process* (London: Macmillan).

Knights, D. and Willmott, H. (eds) (1990) *Labour Process Theory* (London: Macmillan).

Knights, D., Willmott, H. and Collinson, D. (eds) (1985) *Job Redesign* (Aldershot: Gower).

Kochan, T., McKersie, R. and Capelli, P. (1984) 'Strategic Choice and Industrial Relations Theory', *Industrial Relations* 23 (1): 16–39

Littler, C. (1990) 'The Labour Process Debate: A Theoretical Review', in Knights and Willmott, op. cit.: 46–94.

Littler, C. and Salaman, G. (1984) *Class at Work* (London: Batsford).

MacInnes, J. (1985) 'Conjuring up Consultation', *British Journal of Industrial Relations* 23 (1): 93–113.

MacInnes, J. (1987) *Thatcherism at Work*, (Milton Keynes: Open University Press).

Manwaring, T. and Wood, S. (1985) 'The Ghost in the Labour Process', in Knights, Willmott and Collinson, (eds) op. cit.

Marchington, M. (1982) *Managing Industrial Relations* (Maidenhead: McGraw Hill).

Marchington, M. (1987) 'A Review and Critique of Recent Research into Joint Consultation', *British Journal of Industrial Relations* 25 (3): 339–52.

Marchington, M. (1988) 'The Changing Nature of Industrial Relations in the UK and its Impact on Management Behaviour', in Dluglos, G., Dorow, W. and Weiermair, K. (eds), *Management under Different Labour Market and Employment Systems* (Berlin: de Gruyter): 207–20.

Marchington, M. (1990) 'Analysing the Links between Product Markets and the Management of Employee Relations', *Journal of Management Studies*, 27 (4).

Marchington, M.and Loveridge, R. (1983) 'Management Decision-making and Shop-floor Participation', in Thurley, K. and Wood, S. (eds), op. cit.

Marchington, M. and Parker, P. (1988) 'Japanisation: A Lack of Chemical Reaction?', *Industrial Relations Journal* 19 (4): 272–85.

Marchington, M. and Parker, P. (1990) *Changing Patterns of Employee Relations* (Hemel Hempstead: Wheatsheaf).

Marchington, M., Parker, P. and Prestwich, A. (1989) 'Problems with Team Briefing in Practice', *Employee Relations* 11 (4): 21–30.

Marsden, D., Morris, T., Willman, P. and Wood, S. (1985), *The Car Industry: Labour Relations and Industrial Adjustment* (London: Tavistock).

Millward, N. and Stevens, M. (1986) *British Workplace Industrial Relations, 1980-1984*, (Farnborough: Gower).

Mintzberg, H. (1973) *The Nature of Managerial Work* (New York: Harper and Row).

Nichols, T. and Armstrong, P. (1976) *Workers Divided* (London: Fontana).

Nichols, T. and Beynon, H. (1977) *Living With Capitalism* (London: Routledge and Kegan Paul).

Ostell, A., Macfarlane, I. and Jackson, A. (1980) 'Evaluating the Impact of a Communication Exercise in an Industrial Works', *Industrial Relations Journal* 11 (2): 37–48.

Parkin, F. (1972) *Class Inequality and Political Order*, (London: Paladin).

Peters, T. and Austin, N. (1986) *A Passion for Excellence* (New York: Warner Books).

Peters, T. and Waterman, R. (1982) *In Search of Excellence* (New York: Harper and Row).

Pettigrew, A. (1985) *The Awakening Giant: Continuity and Change in ICI* (Oxford: Blackwell).

Porter, M. (1979) 'How Competitive Forces Shape Strategy', *Harvard Business Review*, March – April.

Purcell, J. (1979), 'A Strategy for Management Control in Industrial Relations', in Purcell, J. and Smith, R. (eds), *The Control of Work* (London: Macmillan): 27–59.

Purcell, J. (1981) *Good Industrial Relations: Theory and Practice* (London: Macmillan).

Purcell, J. (1983) 'The Management of Industrial Relations in the Modern Corporation; agenda for research', *British Journal of Industrial Relations* 21 (1): 1–16.

Purcell, J. and Gray, A. (1986) 'Corporate Personnel Departments and the Management of Industrial Relations: Two Case Studies in Ambiguity', *Journal of Management Studies* 23 (2): 205–23.

Rainnie, A. (1984) 'Combined and Uneven Development in the Clothing Industry: the Effects of Competition on Accumulation', *Capital and Class* 22: 141–56.

Ramsay, J. (1985) 'What is Participation For? A Critical Evaluation of Labour Process Analyses of Job Reform', in Knights *et al.*, op. cit.: 52–80.

Roots, P. (1982) 'Industrial Relations, Involvement and Intervention?', *Employee Relations* 4 (2): 17–22.

Rose, M. and Jones, B. (1985) 'Managerial Strategy and Trade Union Responses in Work Reorganisation Schemes at Establishment Level', in Knights *et al.*, op. cit.: 81–106.

Rothwell, S. (1984) 'Company Employment Policies and New Technology in Manufacturing and Service Sectors', in Warner, M. (ed.), *Microprocessors, Manpower and Society* (Gower: Aldershot): 111–33.

Smith, S. (1989) 'How Much Change at the Store? The Impact of New Technologies and Labour Processes on Managers and Staff in Retail', in Knights, D. and Willmott, H. (eds), *New Technology and The Labour Process* (Macmillan: London): 143–62.

Stewart, R. (1976) *Contrasts in Management* (McGraw Hill: London).

Stewart, R. (1983) 'Managerial Behaviour; How Research has Changed the Traditional Picture', in Earl, M. (ed.), op. cit.: 82–98.

Stewart, R. (1984) 'The Nature of Management; A Problem for Management Education', *Journal of Management Studies* 21 (3): 323–30.

Storey, J. (1983) *Managerial Prerogative and the Question of Control* (Routledge and Kegan Paul: London).

Storey, J. (1985) 'The Means of Management Control', *Sociology* 19 (2): 193–211.

Storey, J. (1986) *The Phoney War? New Office Technology: Organisation and Control*, in Knights and Willmott (eds), op. cit.: 44–66.

Storey, J. (1988) 'The People Management Dimension in Programmes of Organisational Change', *Employee Relations* 10 (6): 17–25.

Terry, M. (1983) 'Shop Stewards Through Expansion and Recession', *Industrial Relations Journal* 14 (3): 49–58.

Terry, M. (1986) 'How do we Know if Shop Stewards are Getting Weaker?' *British Journal of Industrial Relations* 24 (2): 169–80.

Thompson, P. (1983) *The Nature of Work* (Macmillan: London).

Thompson, P. (1990) 'Crawling from the Wreckage; The Labour Process and the Politics of Production', in Knights and Willmott, op. cit.: 95–124.

Walker, R. (1989) 'Machinery, Labour and Location', in Wood, S., op. cit.: 59–90.

Wall, T. and Lischeron, J. (1977) *Worker Participation* (McGraw Hill: London).

Whitaker, A. (1986) 'Managerial Strategy and Industrial Relations: A Case Study of Plant Relocation', *Journal of Management Studies* 23 (6): 657–78.

Wickens, P. (1987) *The Road to Nissan: Flexibility, Quality, Teamwork* (Macmillan: London).

Willman, P. (1980) 'Leadership and Trade Union Principles; some Problems of Management Sponsorship and Independence', *Industrial Relations Journal*, 11 (4): 39–49.

Willmott, H. (1990) 'Subjectivity and the Dialectics of Praxis: Opening up the Core of Labour Process Analysis', in Knights and Willmott, op. cit.: 336–78.

Wood, S. (ed.) (1982) *The Degradation of Work?* (Hutchinson: London).

Wood, S. (ed.) (1989) *The Transformation of Work?* (Unwin Hyman: London).

Wood, S. and Kelly, J. (1982) 'Taylorism, Responsible Autonomy and Management Strategy', in Wood, S. (ed.) op. cit.: 74–89.

6

WATCHING THE DETECTIVES

Shop stewards' expectations of their managers in the age of human resource management

Peter Ackers and John Black

INTRODUCTION

After this brief introduction, the chapter begins by tracing the academic roots of a one-dimensional view of shop stewards' orientations back to the zero-sum conception of the employment relationship emanating from Marxist labour process theory. Various criticisms of this position are explored. The chapter then proceeds to empirical material from two case studies, breaking down shop steward's attitudes under a number of headings. First, their general 'frames of reference' are explored; then their conception of their own role within the workplace. Next, it focuses on attitudes towards management; initially as a general function, then on different levels of the management hierarchy. Third, it examines their responses to new management initiatives in the area of flexibility and communications. Finally, the conclusion suggests some tentative implications.

The shop steward has been a highly controversial figure throughout the post-war period. Academic industrial relations literature has attempted to convey a mundane if complex reality (MacCarthy, 1966; Terry, 1983). Official perceptions of the shop steward have swung between the 'lubricant' (HMSO, 1968), problem-solver, 'natural link' (HMSO, 1971) or go-between of the pluralist middle period, and the politically-motivated, unconstitutional (HMSO, 1957) wreckers (HMSO, 1951) and 'militants' (Edwardes, 1983) of before and afterwards. Popular depictions have never drifted far from the latter. The fictional Fred Kite of *I'm all right Jack*, and the real-life Jack Dash or 'Red Robbo' of Longbridge encompass a shared mythology which casts stewards as male, street-wise, working-class villains, who learn the rules only so that they can break them, and who run rings around their nonplussed managers. Their only aim is to make a quick buck, ensure that 'the lads' (women shop stewards are rarely considered) do as little as possible, and leave running the business to those it really concerns: management. The Left has lionized them as a cheeky, home-grown resistance movement of 'primitive rebels', while the Right has demonized them as obstacles to business efficiency and economic prosperity. But the essential stereotype has remained largely similar.

This chapter suggests that, in fact, many shop stewards have been watching their managers – the Detectives – at all levels, in a more informed and sympathetic, yet critical way than the Ealing comedy caricature might suggest. To support the claim that stewards are more industrially constructive than is widely understood, we have accumulated a body of comments from them, at two traditional, medium-sized (about 2,000 employees) West Midlands manufacturing firms – one producing locks, the other carpets – with high trade union densities and fairly strong, though not militant, shop stewards' organizations. The shop steward archetype is founded on British manufacturing industry, and these two firms are no more, yet no less, representative of it than a sample from, say, the car industry.

The orientations of our respondents are no doubt conditioned by the political and economic climate of the research, which can be broadly described as Thatcherism (Hall and Jacques, 1983; Ackers, 1988). This encompassed a major industrial shake-out at the start of the 1980s, a shift in the balance of workplace power towards management, and an unrelenting legal and ideological offensive against trade unions and collectivism. Three successive election defeats for the political arm of the labour movement, and falling trade union membership, encouraged the spread of a 'new realism', particularly in manufacturing trade unions. However, the manufacturing firms in this study had not experienced the more extreme rationalization – both companies had regained their pre-recession workforce size – nor was there any frontal assault on trade union representation. Institutionally, the firms are the very embodiment of the enduring stability of British workplace industrial relations (Millward and Stevens, 1986; Marchington in this volume).

The research was part of a study of changes in workplace industrial relations under Thatcherism (Ackers, 1988). The lock stewards were first interviewed in 1983, and then re-interviewed along with the carpet stewards in 1987. About ten interviews were tape-recorded at each firm, covering all the senior and more experienced representatives, across a wide range of loosely-structured industrial topics. The objective was to 'let them talk' and to gather some rich, qualitative, and largely unprompted oral material on the 'new' industrial relations. Our main aim here is to allow the stewards' complex and shifting 'social meanings' to challenge some theoretically informed expectations in the labour process literature, discussed below. The 'double-take' at the lock company – emerging from recession in 1983 and entering the consumer boom in 1987 – and other interviews with management, indicated that any changes in their opinions over this period had been gradual, and did not form a sudden break with an earlier pattern of entirely different attitudes.

Alongside the shift in workplace power occasioned by Thatcherism came a new stream of management thinking about employment relationships, sometimes described as Human Resources Management (HRM) (Freemantle 1985; Guest, 1987; Storey, 1988; Ackers, 1989). Before, mainstream management thought saw labour as a variable production cost, an extension of technology, to be deskilled, driven and controlled by stick and carrot and manipulation of the cash nexus. Today, it is a human resource to be nurtured and developed, thus engendering a wider commitment to the organization. From one perspective:

> Employers have been shifting from a primarily collective approach, in which they give most emphasis to dealing with and through trade unions, to a style that emphasises direct communication with employees and efforts to involve them as individuals in the operation of the business.
>
> (Edwards and Sisson, 1989: 3)

This takes in a variety of forms of employee involvement (EI), from financial participation, through direct communications by team briefing, to participation through quality circles.

To anticipate the argument below, it is too easily assumed that EI represents a threat or alternative to – a way of bypassing rather than complementing – established union-centred channels of communication. The relationship between shop stewards and the various manifestations of EI varies a great deal (Black and Ackers, 1987). EI can be either complementary to collective bargaining (Marchington, 1987), or actually union-centred (Black and Ackers, 1989; 1990). It is no foregone conclusion that management should want EI to leave shop stewards 'out in the cold'. Indeed, in the carpet firm discussed below, management would have welcomed a more active participation of stewards, as shopfloor figures of influence, in their quality circle programme (Black and Ackers, 1987).

As management begins to invite EI in many shapes and forms, a space is created and a challenge issued for workforce representatives to express more positive views about the ways work is organized and management manages. Some US unions have already wholeheartedly taken-up this invitation (Black and Ackers, 1989; 1990). Serious doubts remain about the true extent of HRM initiatives (Storey, 1988; Edwards and Sisson, 1989), but our concern is with how shop stewards regard such programmes, rather than in the extent to which management lives up to its rhetoric. In anticipation of this new industrial agenda, we look at the types of orientations and expectations some stewards already have.

RETHINKING THE CAPITALIST EMPLOYMENT RELATIONSHIP

It has been a sociological commonplace since Max Weber, that an understanding of actors' social meaning and interpretations of situations is crucial to understanding their behaviour. However, much of the debate over management control has often proceeded from the *a priori* structuralist assumption of a zero-sum power relationship between capital and labour. From this theory of capitalism, a permanently antagonistic and mutually suspicious encounter between 'real' managers and workers can be read-off. Hence the 'problem' in understanding shop stewards' industrial relations behaviour becomes one of explaining away forms of cooperation with management – over redundancy, new working practices, quality circles, team briefing or the introduction of new technology – as deviant, irrational, and the product of some form of 'false consciousness'.

Some researchers (e.g. Harris, 1988) have begun to criticize this caricature of the employment relationship, while continuing to recognize its assymetric character and potential for conflict. Among Marxist writers on the labour process, too, there has been a growing disenchantment with this simplistic model (Knights and Wilmott, 1990; Introduction), particularly associated with Braverman (1974). As Cressey and MacInnes (1980: 5) point out, it has 'failed to present a convincing analysis of the relationship between capital and labour' in the workplace, and spawned a one-dimensional trade union 'stategy of refusal' (ibid.: 21). This, through fear of 'incorporation', has locked labour into a negative position of permanent opposition. The authors trace this problem back to Braverman's assumption, after Marx, that the development from 'formal' to 'real' subordination of labour under capitalism, saw management wrest exclusive control and initiative over the production process. This ignores the 'two-fold' (ibid.: 13) character of the capital/labour relationship: the extent to which management continues to rely on the initiative, creativity and motivation of their workforce in the detailed performance of its various tasks, as a basis for social productivity; and labour's complementary dependence on the firm for its livelihood, creating 'an interest in the maintenance of that relationship and therefore the viability of the unit of capital which employs it' (Cressey and MacInnes, 1980: 13).

These considerations militate against the full-blooded pursuit of the basic antagonism between capital and labour by either party. They set limits on management's willingness forcibly to deskill labour and drive down its market price (Black and Neathey, 1989); as on labour's ability to respond militantly and intransigently to all the firm's proposals for change. Instead, both sides engage in a complex and constant 'effort bargain' (Baldamus, 1961), combining these contradictory elements of conflict and cooperation. According to this view, the legitimate concern of trade union strategy is the content of this bargain (and its putative reltionship to a wider socialist project); not the guardianship of some clear-cut 'frontier of control', chalked-out like a tug-of-war between Sisyphus and King Canute. This, in turn, supports Kelly's emphasis (Kelly, 1982; 1985; Ackers and Black, 1988) on the scope for organizational choice in areas like job design, and the opportunities this provides for negotiated solutions which both increase productivity and enhance job satisfaction. This point is underlined by evidence (Daniel, 1987) that workers and trade unions look much more favourably upon changes in work organization associated with new technology, than new working practices on the same technical base.

Thompson (1978) identifies the tendency of structuralist/functionalist Marxism to conflate the 'ideal type' economic model of the capitalist mode of production that is found in the pages of *Capital* with the complex and contradictory historical social formations in which real-life capital/labour relations have developed. This leads to industrial behaviour being extrapolated according to the 'logic of capital', reflecting:

> The reliance of most Marxist theories on an analysis of the bourgeois theories of capitalist organisation, rather than any direct study of its practitioners.
>
> (Cressey and MacInnes, 1980: 16)

Littler and Salaman (1982: 263) suggest that such a schematic and selective use of second-hand information to identify a single mode of labour control or a neat taxonomy is also 'vulnerable to empirically-based critiques, employing historical and current sources'. Equally, they challenge the characterization of work-place relations by some Marxist commentators as an all-out war across the 'frontier of control'. They point out that there are a wide variety of consituents to corporate profitability – not all centred on the labour process. Indeed, ratcheting-down control over the production process may seem less important at a particular moment than 'keeping the peace'. Such industrial settlements may be long-lasting: 'On the shopfloor a negotiated order may have been reached, a phase of accommodation, as in the British engineering industry between 1850 and 1880' (ibid.: 257).

Put simply, profit is the driving force of the capitalist enterprise, not labour control (Black and Neathy, 1989) and these two management objectives will not always coincide in a straightforward fashion. Storey (1988) extends this insight to more recent developments in HRM, challenging the assumption that such initiatives are necessarily driven by industrial relations labour control objectives, and not by other, more salient, aspects of management and business strategy.

Littler and Salaman (1982) point to those factors which cohere the employment relationship, as well as those which tear it apart. They suggest a complex and specific mix of 'forms of ideological relationships' (ibid.: 258) helping to cement the various degrees of consent among the workforce: active, passive, total and partial. These include: ideas about the inevitability of capitalism, 'ideologies of technocracy' (ibid.: 258) and cultural norms which assert the legitimacy of property rights in the enterprise. As important, however, are those ideologies which underpin managerial competence and expertise:

> The establishment of management as a separate function, distinct from shopfloor workers, with unique expertise and responsibilities, and with major and critical claims to authority over the shopfloor upon which the efficiency of the whole enterprise depends . . . is a crucial first step in the establishment of control over the workforce . . . they have accepted the normality of their subordination. Resistance, when and if it occurs will be largely about details, the important aspects – the hierarchical nature of the enterprise, the location of decisions,

capital investments etc., have effectively been removed from the agenda.

(Ibid.: 259)

On the other hand, an acceptance of the basic functional case for management may reflect a rational understanding of the realities of modern industrial systems – capitalist or socialist (Nove, 1983; Ackers and Black, 1988) – which does not preclude a critical stance on specific management objectives, styles and performances. The economic situation of the firm, at a particular historical conjuncture, such as the recession of the early 1980s, may also create a temporary and contingent harmony of interests in the employment relationship; even where the fundamental structural division between capital and labour remains.

> But at least in depths of recession, it is plausible to suggest that workers and management share a common interest in the immediate survival of their firm, and that both worker and management power and influence are directed along the same lines: not necessarily a 'new realism' but an awareness of at least temporarily convergent objectives.

(Terry, 1986: 177)

Once the need to explore actors' social meanings' is accepted, the evaluation of attitudinal material itself presents grave interpretative problems. While it is possible to refine and distinguish between concepts like 'consent', 'cooperation', 'commitment', 'legitimation' and 'compliance' at a theoretical level (Burawoy, 1979; Littler, 1982), at an empirical level such distinctions are very likely to be highly subjective, and possibly no more than semantic. In reality, where power relations are involved, active consent and dull compulsion are interwoven in such a highly complex way (Gramsci, 1971; Prior and Purdy, 1979), that it is difficult to impute one or other from observed behaviour or expressed attitudes. Just as it is problematic to distil the appropriate blend of objective and subjective causality from the complexity of actors' social meanings, so is it equally dangerous to erect elaborate theories of 'subjectivity' on an ambiguous empirical base.

Knights and Collinson's study, 'Slav' (1987), is a case in point. It deals with a strong, male, manual shopfloor union, similar to the traditional carpet weavers discussed here. In their analysis, shopfloor scepticism towards a soft EI initiative involving psychological forms of persuasion, is contrasted with their acquiescence to the 'hard' accountancy logic of a redundancy decision. The different responses are explained by the groups' distinctively 'macho' identity of independence, detachment and indifference. Such interpretations of evidence can be unpicked. The EI initiative, a new company newspaper, is one of the weakest and most peripheral of the techniques currently available; while the prospect of redundancy during a period of mass unemployment could hardly be more objectively overwhelming (Ackers, 1981; Terry, 1983). The general absence of serious resistance to redundancy in the 1980s suggests that, masculinity or not, 'take the money and run' was a rational surrender to inevitability. Moreover, comments supporting the macho sexist identity argument can be understood as arising from real status divisions between the working conditions of manual and white-collar workers. Similar comments, without the specific gender inflexion, are found among the large female manual workforces of piecework industries like carpets, locks, footwear and hosiery.

Significant issues of local cultural indentity were evident in the workplace organizations researched, most notably: a shared history of paternalism (Ackers and Black, 1989); marked sexual divisions of labour; a strong tradition of industrial collaboration in locks; and a male, craft culture of independence and autonomy (expressed in 'ownership' of looms) among the carpet weavers. These are partly reflected in the diversity of stewards' responses between and within the two firms. But at a more general level, stewards' more accommodating attitudes usually betrayed neither some 'false consciousness' nor a maverick 'subjectivity', but a realistic assessment of the alternatives available (Knights and Roberts, 1982) in a modern industrial society.

The foregoing criticisms need not invalidate Marx's distinction between labour purchased on the market and labour power realized in the workplace (Nolan, 1983; Edwards, 1990; Thompson, 1990), nor the crucial distinction between wage levels and unit labour costs (Roots, 1986) which flows from this. A structured antagonism that simultaneously unites and divides managers and workers (Edwards, 1990) does provide the dynamic behind the fluctuating wage and effort bargain. But numerous other internal and external factors (Ackers and Black, 1988) overlay and complicate the real life equation: the labour intensity of the workforce and the scope for increasing competitiveness through technological innovation; the traditional style of managing labour, including the density, depth, and character of trade union organization; the external pressures for change from product and labour market, the political and ideological environment, or arising from changes in ownership; political divisions within the capital and labour, etc. Policy decisions effecting workers will inevitably be the outcome of a complex and unpredictable political process of organizational struggle (Gramsci, 1971; Tomlinson, 1982), taking in all these factors.

Older companies, like the two in these case studies, are richer in cultural constraints, and inertias are embedded in every level of the organization (Ackers and Black, 1989). Like ocean liners, they cannot be turned around quickly, and except in a situation of extraordinary crisis (and not always then – some go down like the *Titanic*), they usually prefer to 'manage change' by developing tried and trusted strategies and relationships – 'what works now' – rather than by rethinking their whole approach in the white heat of abstract capitalist logic. Thus the labour process emphasis provides, at best, only a starting point, and perhaps a useful method or tradition of interpretation (Thompson, 1978), in understanding the development of workplace behaviour.

Both official trade union and shopfloor responses to management and HRM are important subjects of enquiry. Here, however, we have focused more narrowly on the attitudes of shop stewards, understanding that they will probably have a dinstinctive perspective of their own which arises from their role as mediators between the official union and its members, management and the workforce. It is argued here that shop stewards' attitudes to, and expectations of, management should not be conceptualized in the negative, defensive and one-dimensional way described above. Instead, it is suggested that many shop stewards have strong positive expectations of management: to 'modernize' the company as a profitable going concern (in terms of technology, working practices and industrial relations); to provide a strong, dynamic corporate leadership; and to manage in a consistent and open style at all levels. The outcome is more typically a complex and contradictory mixture of antagonistic and cooperative attitudes, focused on their particular management.

SHOP STEWARDS' ORIENTATIONS

Frames of Reference

To some extent individual shop stewards' attitudes will depend on their 'frames of reference' (Fox, 1966). This may reflect the ethos of their workplace or national trade union organization (though these are rarely transmitted in a straightforward, predictable way at workplace level) or wider political and religious influences. This research suggests that, apart from a small minority of 'radical' shop stewards who question the whole legitimacy of the management role (hardly represented in our sample), positive expectations are widespread and consistent with a 'pluralist' appreciation of what management's role is and what it should be. Most of the stewards interviewed adhered to a complex and shifting blend of consensus and conflict frames of reference.

Thus the Wilton carpet-weaving steward argued:

'Their main goal is to make theirs a profitable company . . . our job is to share more of that productivity.'

Though there is plenty of scope for cooperation, it has limitations:

'You can walk with management 99 per cent of the time . . . [but] when you start talking about X number of jobs going, then you've got to start thinking – "Well, to what extent do we go along with them?"'

However, when conflict did arise over new working practices which threatened job security, these sectional interests were articulated in universal terms which linked employer and employee:

'I don't think that it is in the best interest of the company and the people up there.'

The GMB carpet convenor made this case more openly:

'The trade unions should have some corporacy. We started to look at what affects the company's employees generally – rather than what affects the individual department – at the JWC [Joint Works Committee]'.

The GMB spinning steward described the relationship with management as:

'Very, very good, very good. We've never had a strike here; we've never had any arguments.'

The locksmith steward also sounded, on first hearing like a simple 'unitarist':

'I see it as a team really. There isn't any real conflict between shopfloor and management at all. . . . We don't get any aggro as regards any automation that comes in the company. We fully accept it on the view that it will benefit all the employees.'

However, on closer inspection, this 'close friendly relationship' belies a more ambiguous and contradictory consciousness. For instance, profits were a 'good thing' because they gave the union 'a great opportunity to go for rises for our members'. Nor was the trust in the goodwill of management absolute:

'Without unions [the workers] they'd be more or less slaves. . . . Undoubtably we have got good relationships with the management and with the directors, but without a union you wouldn't have that.'

The lock toolroom steward's more critical view contained similar nuances:

'The managing director's job is to produce locks as cheaply as he possibly can for the market and that includes keeping our wage rates as low as he can possibly keep them. . . . What they are interested in really is maintaining their share of the cake. They've done very well; they've got a whole lifestyle to maintain . . . they've got to make sure that the company floats because they've got that lifestyle out of it.'

Yet he still regarded the pressures for cost reduction as inescapable in 'the real world', and it was their distribution, in social amenities and reinvestment, which really mattered:

'I don't think that they can make too big a profit. It's what they do with it that's important. . . . In this economic environment . . . any company [must] . . . by every method that they can conspire to, either reduce what it costs to keep those people or reduce the number of those people . . . there has got to be a movement of labour.'

At the carpet firm, there was the added dimension of continuing family ownership, which played a part in employee perceptions. In the eyes of most stewards, for all the drawbacks of paternalism (Ackers and Black, 1989), it had ensured long-term investment, even when profits had been low, and had protected the firm from the high-interest loans, takeovers and asset-stripping which had caused the run-down and closure of many local firms. The carpet warehouse steward suggested that the family were 'very, very clever business people'. This outlook was shared with all levels of management, notwithstanding considerable scepticism about the family's 'steward-ship' from some stewards. As the GMB carpet convenor saw it:

'The end of paternalism came with the retirement of [the last chairman] who could actually hold a conversation with somebody on the shopfloor, on totally unrehearsed, unambiguous and level terms. They tend to trust the current generation . . . far less than they trusted the past generation. . . . You can imagine [the present chairman] running something else, somewhere else, because he's a different breed'.

The Joint Shop Stewards Committee (JSSC) Secretary had a grudging admiration for top management, and saw the demise of paternalism as a necessary exchange for the modernization of the company:

'It is more efficient; they know where they are going. We haven't yet got much . . . [of] the human touch, we always saw the gaffers . . . it has changed for the better. They realized they had to beat the world and they have done it.'

The AEU carpet convenor reiterated this muted corporate pride:

'With all the companies in the carpet industry, [this] is the only one who took the road up, expanding . . . coming up with new technology.'

The shop steward's role

The idea of the shop steward as a go-between or 'natural link' between management and the shopfloor commanded general support. The locksmith steward argued, after twenty-six years' experience:

'A shop steward's job is to keep peace between both employers and employees . . . you've got to be a bit fairer to keep the company running properly, smoothly; although you've got to be fairer with your members, to make sure that they get their rights.'

The more critical lock toolroom steward concurred:

'It's just as important for the shop steward to represent, to a certain extent, the management's point of view, as it is the individual worker's point of view.'

The Wilton carpet-weaving steward placed a heavier emphasis on defending his members' interests, but insisted:

'I haven't got a bad relationship with management . . . I see my role as a shop steward as trying to improve safety, improve the conditions in which we work, maintain people's earnings, and as a go-between [between] the shopfloor and management.'

The traditional Axminster carpet-weaving steward displayed the most resiliently traditional 'us and them' attitude:

'Now my manager . . . we have a good relationship, but he's the gaffer; we in the union know that . . . like all employers it's just how far they think they can go with you.'

There was little relish for industrial conflict, particularly at the lock firm. The locksmith steward expressed a widely-held viewpoint:

'A lot of the other places go bankrupt through strikes . . . we're fairly moderate.'

The lock convenor argued:

'We've had walkouts, but we're not a militant union . . . consultation is better than confrontation any time . . . you fight your battles from inside the factory.'

A woman executive member agreed:

'I think the management and the union should work together . . . I don't believe in strikes. I don't think it achieves anything.'

The GMB and the AEU carpet convenors believed that their unions had been important influences on the introduction of a 'peace-keeping' 1970s procedure agreement. The latter argued, characteristically, that 'all problems' could be solved by 'management talking':

'I have a problem; can you help me out? And we are here to help them. We have got individual managers who are not prepared to do these things. . . . If they would only talk to the shop stewards and try to solve it before making an explosion on the shopfloor. . . . The procedure and the national agreement is there to solve the problem.'

Only among the traditional carpet weavers was conflict regarded as a common feature of relations with management; and their senior steward resisted strongly the insinuation that they were 'militant'.

Shop stewards orientations towards the management function

Many of the stewards expressed frustration that their management was archaic, unwilling to introduce new technology (even when in the short term this could have been labour-displacing), poorly trained and therefore inconsistent in the application of policy (Knights and Collinson, 1987). The GMB carpet convenor was an authoritative figure, a Fabian Society member who has now become a full-time official. He had seven years' experience of national bargaining, access to all levels of management, and a wider strategic view of trade unionism at the the company and in the country. In his view:

'The level of training that's being offered to managers has been negligible . . . the spread of application across the company of the disciplinary procedure was something to behold in its variations.'

This vitiated talk of management having an 'actual, emergent, overall style'. Instead, management style was seen as being dependent on the way the wind blew when the managing director changes. At corporate level, this absence of consistent style meant: 'you rule your own kingdom either with a stick of toffee or a rod of iron'. Managers were also regarded as weak on 'man-management', and these characteristics combined to produce a 'conservatism that allowed things to remain basically the same'.

In 1983, the veteran, former lock convenor despaired of his firm's stagnation, in similar terms:

'There doesn't seem to be a lot of progress here at all . . . it's very flat . . . I can't see where we're going . . . there hasn't been a dramatic decline comparable to outside . . . we're just on a plateau and nothing happens.'

Five years later, this impression remained:

'You can't feel there's any drive coming from the top to get things changed; there's no sense of change at this company.'

The lock toolroom shop steward, who in 1983 had described himself as a Benn supporter, linked the weakness of management at his firm to a wider absence of industrial commitment:

'The biggest drawback of British industry as a whole is that everyone from a labourer to managing director . . . does his utmost to make sure that his stay at work is as comfortable and as easy as he can make it. . . . The alternative to that is to motivate people to give of their best. From our point of view, I think it's got to be profit sharing . . . and it's got to be an example set from the top . . . I think management in British industry has a lot to answer for. They put themselves on a pedestal and they don't live up to it. I've got a great respect for the Japanese and Germans and the way they work . . . With the British way of life, there's too much class distinction and it rubs off into industry. In Germany you don't get that, or Japan. You get the workplace, the unit people work in and they will work together.'

The AEU carpet convenor faced the threat of sub-contracting, and put the blame squarely on the weakness of his local manager:

'He is not strong enough . . . if he was strong there could be more jobs provided.'

Other stewards welcomed signs of the emergence of more professional and dynamic managers, even when they proved 'tougher', in positions as disparate as marketing, personnel and managing director. Nor were the more politically radical stewards, in terms of adherence to socialist ideology, necessarily the least sympathetically disposed to management problems within their firm. The GMB spinning steward said:

'I'm a socialist, I believe that we can work together – it'll make things a lot better.'

The lock toolroom steward was similarly positive about his new managing director:

'He's very much in favour of introducing new lines . . . I should say that's pretty high on the agenda . . . the criticism again is reinvestment in new plants and machinery and equipment. That's another reason why I think we're behind the leading industrial names, we don't plough enough back.'

The lock convenor concurred:

'He's improved a lot of areas of production by bringing out new lines . . . under the old system we were content to sit back on our laurels.'

The right to manage was widely acknowledged. As the locksmith's steward saw it:

'They're here to manage the factory or department . . . to manage us as best they can.'

Such general consent to being effectively managed was often framed by criticism of the style and competence of managements. The lock toolroom steward combined both elements eloquently:

'The workpeople should be consulted and . . . involved in the organization of their particular area a lot more. . . . We have no control over a lot of things to which I think we could effectively contribute. It's all left to the supervisor. Obviously a management decision has always got to be final, but it's just him and his two foremen. Now surely by averages there are other people. If their intelligence and brains were contributed to the organization of the department, and their opinions were sought, then that would be for the better and that would be another way of motivating people to give of their best.'

Among craft workers, like the carpet weavers, there was the complaint that management lacked knowledge and experience, and therefore respect. As the Wilton carpet weaving steward put it:

'In my day the manager was older than the people he managed . . . the manager before . . . was a Wilton weaver . . . you couldn't pull the wool over his eyes . . . now we are being managed by people who really and truly are not conversant with what they are managing.'

At both firms, such criticisms were linked to a more general suspicion of managers who came from 'outside', like the new graduate intake, and were unfamiliar with the distinctive company culture and labour process. The AEU carpet convenor had enjoyed a good relationship with management so long as they were 'people what has been a worker, gone up, you've got to know him'. But 'when management come from another company, then that's when you start to have a problem'. The female carpet preparatory steward found:

'A lot of the managers are younger today . . . they've been knighted and they can shout and bawl at you as much as they like. They haven't got the respect of the workers, and the workers haven't got the respect of them.'

In some cases this reflected a raw class resentment, as much as any doubts about competence. The carpet JSSC secretary criticized managers:

'Who have never actually worked on the shopfloor . . . who deal with problems of working on nights . . . who have never worked nights in their lives, who go home at four o'clock. They don't understand what it is like to be mentally and physically at your wits end at two o'clock in the morning.'

On the other hand, there was a widely-held presumption that a good line-manager had to be 'a bit of a bastard'. The GMB spinning steward's immediate boss was 'almost too nice to be a manager . . . he's a chap that you could go and talk to'. And, in partial contradiction of the plea for shopfloor experience, several stewards criticized, like the toolroom steward, the lack of technical qualifications of those promoted.

There was a widespread view that management and shopfloor should ideally work together, even where this was not the current situation. The lock toolroom steward described 'a shopfloor and management with different objectives', adding, 'I don't think they work together at all'. But he put this down to poor and authoritarian management, not some fundamental clash of interests. And often, as elsewhere, such problems involved the day-to-day petty and personal conflicts which constitute the micro-politics of workplace relations:

'All the line management I've come across . . . seem to magnify trivialties all the time . . . they don't consult people on the shopfloor.'

There was also the sense among stewards, expressed by the GMB spinning steward, of the trade union and management as joint custodians of the firm who:

'Share the same goals . . . [whereas] a lot of shopfloor blokes are quite happy just to come and get their money, and couldn't care less until the crunch comes.'

In this spirit of mutual dependency and responsibility, the AEU carpet convenor paraphrased his general secretary:

'If the companies don't work with the union they are finished, but if the members don't work with the company, they are out of a job.'

Different levels of management

Shopfloor orientations towards management are conditioned by the level of management involved and the personal characteristics of individual managers, in complex and unpredictable ways (Harris, 1988). The carpet stewards felt that, in general, top management was much more anti-union than middle management, but they vaccilated in this judgement according to individual circumstances. Their lock counterparts tended towards the opposite conclusion. The lock deputy convenor observed that since 1982 and the significant changes in industrial relations legislation, 'we've found that middle management have become anti-trade'. Top management, however, had not, because:

'[They] realize that they've got to live in harmony with the trade union . . . [which is] not going to go away. . . . In the dark days of 1983/84. . .we were really up against the wall . . . [Today] we have a mutual respect for both sides of the table, at senior level.'

At the carpet firm, top management had vetoed proposals drafted by the unions and the industrial relations manager, in 1981, to establish a formal closed shop agreement. Stewards believed this reflected the influence of 'Thatcherism' on a senior management with wide political and industrial contacts at the CBI and the Institute of Directors. They certainly expressed a more hostile attitude to trade unions than either their lock equivalents, or the line and personnel management at the same company, whose main reference point was the stewards they came across and knew well on their own shopfloor.

Again, personal relationships were always unpredictable, and familiarity can breed either contempt or understanding. Some stewards, like the carpet JSSC secretary, made quite contradictory statements motivated by local, personal resentment and a grudging respect for the dynamism of top management:

'The shopfloor and top management are both thinking the same thing, but unfortunately you've got the go-betweens, who are trying to hide their own shortcomings, and impress higher management with their efficiency.'

The carpet warehouse steward said:

'Middle management here, in my opinion are the trouble . . . [especially] the young ones trying to prove something.'

The GMB spinning steward felt 'the bigger boys do take more notice'. The carpet JSSC secretary squared the circle, by pointing to the pragmatism of top management:

'The managing director doesn't like trade unions full-stop, but he sees them as a useful means of communicating.'

For more rank-and-file stewards, the charge against top management of remoteness was inevitably a common one, especially as both firms had some tradition of personal contact paternalism. The Wilton carpet weaving steward only met top management at JWC meetings, or 'when they are having walks around the factory'. A steward of twenty years' standing, he held the widespread belief that the old paternalist management style:

'Seemed a lot more humane than the people you have today. But, having said that, the management now are probably under a lot more pressure.'

Nonetheless, today 'they seem to think you are a chattel', or "just a clock number" – an image repeated by several older stewards. The locksmith steward's management contact was largely restricted to the superintendant level, and he likewise regretted the decline in higher-level contact:

'We used to have a number of directors who used to make trips round. We hardly see any of these now, apart from the managing director . . . there used to be a vast interest by the directors in the company.'

By contrast, the lock convenor and his deputy, and the GMB carpet convenor and the carpet JSSC secretuary, all had fairly regular and easy access to top management. But the EEPTU carpet steward expressed a common feeling among ordinary stewards and middle management:

'The higher management don't seem to know what the attitude is on the shopfloor.'

The lock firm had recently been taken over by a south-east based electronics multinational, and the consequent remoteness from the centre of decision-making power was felt, even by leading stewards involved in the industry's industrial relations structures. The object of anxiety, which was often shared with local management, had become the distant, anonymous parent, who pulled the strings behind wages negotiations and controlled the whole future of the lock workforce. The former lock convenor commented:

'A lot of us can never understand where we fit in the group scheme of things.'

The deputy convenor felt the same concern:

'We can never pin management down to talk about future development . . . we worry about this . . . unfortunately we head up to a multinational group. If the time came when we were less profitable that we are now, they'd have no compunction about closing the place down.'

New management initiatives: flexibility and communications

The 1980s presented shop stewards with a new agenda, both in the negative terms of legislative and management pressure on union organization, and in the potentially more positive terms of a raft of new EI initiatives, which some commentators have also seen as a threat to stewards' representative role. A direct comparison of stewards' responses was impossible here because, while the carpet firm had introduced a wide range of HRM-style initiatives (flexibility, quality circles, employee financial reports with cascade briefings, profit-sharing, and a reintegration of personnel and industrial relations functions), the lock firm had stuck to their well-established, union-centred style of manpower management, even to the point of resisting pressure from the new parent company for team briefing. What follows is a combination of employees' aspirations at each company, together with the actual experiences at the carpet firm. Despite fairly hostile responses to specific techniques such as quality circles and profit-sharing from the carpet weavers, we suggest that EI in general was often greeted positively, as evidence of modernization and dynamism at the top, providing it was linked to a secure and central union role.

The lock toolroom steward was a strong advocate of consultation, participation and profit sharing. In 1983, he had admired Benn and Scargill, but had abhorred restrictive practices, and he had supported the ideals of the social contract and the Bullock Report against sectional union interests:

'I'm a believer that worker-directors possibly could work, if they had a worker sitting on the board, a worker deciding on the objectives and the products they're going to have.'

However, the experience of concrete EI initiatives may of itself breed cynicism. At the sharp end of a range of HRM initiatives, the Wilton carpet weaving steward was far more sceptical:

'They are definitely communicating a lot more with us than they ever did . . . [but] they are only communicating things to you that they really want you to know. You see they are very Victorian. . .they really believe. . .Margaret Thatcher's idea. . .to get back to Victorian values. This company has never got rid of them.'

Over the last five years, management had become 'very devious':

'I don't think there is the trust that there used to be . . . they are much more Bolshie now than what they ever was . . . you can get through negotiations and they'll get to the stage where they will say, "That's it, we are talking no more, we are implementing that, from such and such a day". That's not negotiations . . . agreements have been – I don't know who said it, Marx or Lenin I think it was, and I ain't a communist anyway – bits of paper. And that's exactly what they are to management here. They will break agreements by saying, "Well, the management's job is to manage".'

From this viewpoint, the new 'open' approach was no more than sugar-coated unilateralism.

The Profit Participation Scheme (PPS), which was introduced unilaterally and awarded as a lump sum just before Christmas, during national negotiations, with its industrial action penalty clause, was seen as 'a carrot on a stick'. Virtually all carpet stewards regarded the penalty clause, caustically, as a 'sword of Damocles'; a threat factor to complement the industry's shaky state. The traditional Axminister weaving steward admitted:

'I don't think I could get these people on strike down here again, even if I wanted to; there is too much to lose.'

While the AEU convenor despaired: 'I have lost all my negotiating rights.'

It was the penalty clause, not the idea of profit-sharing, which most stewards objected to. Only a few carpet stewards, mainly in the traditional weaving area, regarded direct communications *per se* as a threat. In 1987, the JSSC secretary publically 'welcomed the decision to post the PPS letters to employees' homes and hoped it would become normal practice'.

Scepticism about the efficacy of some EI techniques was more common. The GMB carpet convenor doubted whether the PPS had

'Any real value in terms of communicating to people, because if you read your PPS letter and then go and ask somebody, it hasn't come off the paper into their mind.'

He believed the attempt at communications had been a failure.

'I was naive enough to believe that management would tell us everything. But they won't tell us, you've got to dig for it . . . they are a waste of time, they are only talking, being fobbed off, and they could be a useful thing. Management don't really want to bother, that is the feeling we all get.'

The EEPTU steward was particularly scathing about the tone of the managing director's employee financial report and its accompanying video presentation:

'The way his attitude comes across to me on the video, is that you should work for this company for the love of it. . . . There's only one reason I came here, that's for money. While I'm here I work for it, but

I don't live and breath this place. As soon as I walk out of the gates, as far as I'm concerned, this place doesn't exist.'

Quality circles aroused similar feelings. For the Wilton carpet weaving steward they were 'a waste of time, I think they are doing management's job for them'. The failure of quality circles to thrive in weaving was largely due to union opposition or indifference, caused by fears of bypassing and other industrial relations tensions. The traditional weavers were the most strongly opposed, insisting that the weavers' 'body' should collectively control their circle, by electing delegates to it, in an attempt to preserve existing industrial relations channels, thus undermining the whole voluntary, individual ethos of the quality circle idea. As their steward put it, circle members were

'Responsible to us, on the shopfloor. They were elected. The "body" told them that they hadn't got to do so and so . . . but management ignored that and went above our heads to them as individuals . . . so we dropped out.'

The EEPTU steward saw quality circles as 'a very good way of getting ideas without paying for them'.

Quality circles met with some initial success among the automatic weavers, but they eventually fell victim to low trust relations in other industrial relations spheres. Elsewhere in the company, in spinning and preparatory, they continued on a modest scale and were not a bone of contention. Overall, the quality circles experience at the carpet firm illustrated the diversity of union responses to the same management technique, within a single workplace and between parts of the same union. It also revealed the ambiguous and fickle character of steward responses to this type of collaboration with management. The JSSC secretary had originally been a union advocate of quality circles, but he would have nothing to do with them now. On the other side, the AEU convenor was 'all for quality circles', while the spinning steward sat on the quality circles steering committee and was

'A strong believer [because] as a union man. . .anything that can make a working man's job easier, it's got to be a good thing. Also anything that will make the firm profitable and keeps men employed, has got to be a good thing.'

The traditional carpet weavers, with their strong craft tradition, resented most of all the pressures for changes in working practices:

'Management . . . keep telling us we are archaic . . . reluctant to accept change. But one of the reasons we are reluctant to accept change is because invariably that change . . . costs somebody their job . . . it don't matter how much you talk to management, if they decide they are going to do it, they'll do it. . . . If that's on the bottom of the letter – that it's going to enhance job security – then watch your back, because somebody is going to be nailed to the wall.'

He was concerned with management's unilateral style and imposition of change, as with its substance. In the build-up to the 1978 weavers' strike, they had begun to:

'Give dates when *this* would happen . . . you get it in your letter. . . "the date of commencement is so and so", when no date has been agreed.'

More recently, management had stopped 'using the stick' and returned to resolving problems 'mutually'.

The traditional Axminster weavers' grievances were not always viewed sympathetically by other stewards, and their own unilateral strike action in 1978 had turned the rest of the workforce against them and left lasting divisions. The carpet warehouse steward described them as 'miserable sods', while the JSSC secretary said, pointedly: 'flexibility is a dirty word to some people, but flexibility has saved jobs'. The former had seen his workforce halved by natural wastage, through a combination of new machinery and flexible working practices. But he commented, 'it's been wanted really, I mean Christ, before it used to be Charles Dickens days'. The AEU convenor was unhappy about job losses, but he had no time for slackers.

'There is a lot who is quite prepared to sit on the wall and draw the average wage. That's one of the problems of this company. . . . If he don't get rid of those bad apples, they all go – all those jobs go. . .if you don't cooperate you are out of a job.'

Most lock stewards had a less critical attitude to management communications, perhaps because they had hardly experienced it and anything seemed better than nothing. In practice, the convenor and a few key stewards were regularly briefed by management, while other stewards and the workforce were dependent on the grapevine. The demise of joint consultation was widely lamented and was attributed to lack of management commitment. The former convenor said in 1983:

'It is a washout . . . about vending machines. . .a works committee should be a real discussion [forum], but over the years it's never materialized. A lot of it because management didn't want it to.'

Five years later, the works committee had become 'dramatically worse', and never met. Yet it had once been a useful body which discussed 'where the company was going'. A woman steward remembered it as an opportunity to speak directly to the managing director, 'the only time some people can get close to the top'.

The prospect of team briefing being introduced via the new parent generally found more favour among stewards than with the firm's industrial relations management. The senior woman steward thought 'We'll probably have that, because it's good', while the former convenor welcomed any evidence of improved communications. However, he felt (quite correctly) that management did not seem interested in the group's ideas about team briefing, employee share ownership or communications in general. Their short-sighted attitude was: 'Well, the company's running all right, why have any problems?' For most lock stewards the prospect of EI was perceived not as a devious threat to collective bargaining, but as evidence of a more open management style (Marchington, 1987).

CONCLUSIONS

The interviews conducted between 1983 and 1987 reflected the impact of a changed economic and political environment on shopfloor orientations; one in which the survival and future of both companies *per se* had become more problematic (though neither looked like going out of business) (Terry, 1986). Perhaps the experience of Thatcherism and recession had conditioned a more favourable long-term attitude to management and HRM, beyond just waiting for the pendulum to swing back? The attitudes described must be set against the ideological traditions of these industries, the specific product and labour market pressures, and resultant management strategies motivating change (or non-change) in workplace industrial relations (Ackers and Black, 1988).

We have neither charted attitudinal development, nor uncovered precisely the mechanisms through which shopfloor ideologies emerge, beyond suggesting a combination of factors which might lead shop stewards to welcome certain management strategies. Though exogenous pressures vary across time and space – and in extreme cases render cooperation virtually either inevitable or impossible – we have tried to present, in stewards' own words, their general consciousness of interdependence and its implications for their role and expectations of management. This should serve as an antidote to a simplistic view of workplace industrial relations as structurally-driven conflict, in which every management initiative – be it new technology, new working practices, or EI – is perceived by stewards as a Machiavellian ploy to bypass or break the union, and intensify and deskill the labour process. A necessary complement to this analysis, would look at management's orientations, to consider how far they are influenced by the aforementioned labour control concerns, as against other pressures in the 'circuit of capital' (Kelly, 1985; Ackers and Black, 1988) to do with quality, customer service or labour turnover.

Shop steward postures will, inevitably, be conditioned by the times in which they are expressed. Nonetheless, we did not sense that the element of external economic and political compulsion was so overbearing as to vitiate any reasonable generalization from our research. Those reflections by stewards on the link between context and consciousness suggested both the compulsions of Thatcherism, and a more active reassessment of their trade union attitudes. But no one at either firm believe there had been a sea change in the latter, as a result of the former. Nor did it seem likely that some conditions associated with Thatcherism – a reduced national role for trade unions, increased global competition, or management's interest in HRM – would disappear with its political demise. In this respect, the 'Chinese walls' around stewards' expectations might have hardened into a more permanent structure: industry has moved on, there will be no return to the 1970s. As one businessman put it:

> When Fordist/Taylorist ideas were at their height, and mass production of standard product was the norm, poor industrial relations were inefficient. Today they can be lethal. That is why a new bargain has to be struck.
>
> (Sainsbury, 1990)

The straitened circumstances of the past decade and the horizon ahead have themselves generated a degree of consent. Put in another language, it probably reinforces a legitimacy already afforded to management authority, while bringing into the open the expectations associated with this. Other comments no doubt reflect dull compulsion: the traditional weavers still stoutly resist quality circles, and only recently ran a damaging overtime ban in support of a wages demand. The economic and political conditions have continued to fluctuate. Since then, we have passed through the consumer boom and Thatcherite ascendancy, emerging to the contradictory pressures of labour shortages and high interest rates of the early 1990s, and the beginnings of a new recession.

Comments from the two longest-serving stewards illustrate this complex mix, and the more 'passive, spontaneous side of consent formation' (Prior and Purdy, 1979) moulded partly by force of circumstance. In 1983, the former lock convenor pointed to the very low labour mobility, particularly among young workers with mortgages, who frightened to move, were 'far more docile', and took the view 'thank God I've got a job'. He went on:

'With the labour conditions outside over the last few years there's been a dramatic falling-off in the morale of the labour force . . . as far as industrial relations is concerned . . . most of it is to keep your head down and hope for something optimistic in the future, that it will pick up.'

In 1987, another veteran, the traditional weaving steward, supported this prognosis, with a concern about the long-term future of his department:

'We've got a realization that we're in a different era than ten years ago . . . unions haven't got the power they had. I've got to work within the law and we resent it. As for the shopfloor, they don't realize what's been done to trade unions. They've been wrapped up . . . we are not as effective now . . . we are not a force in this country now like we used to be. . . . The miners' strike proves that. . .we have got to be affected by what is going on in the country.'

The stereotype of the militant, obstructive shop steward gained currency partly due to an over-emphasis of post-war industrial relations research on large engineering firms, particularly car factories. While this chapter is based on research in strongly unionized, traditional manufacturing industry, the industries concerned have had more collaborative industrial relations traditions. We have explored shop stewards' perceptions of management in general, and of its various modernizing strategies. We suggest that, alongside natural caution and defensiveness concerning their members' rights, coexist more positive expectations of effective and dynamic leadership, which can ensure the growth, prosperity and expansion of the company – a recognition of management's distinctive role, and a belief that management should live up to these expectations. Such views may be comforting news for British management in their much-publicized war against restrictive practices and destructive attitudes, but they may also pose a wider challenge to the old-style autocracies which have run so many British manufacturing firms, and to the often superficial and disappointing promises of leadership, openness, consultation and employee involvement which have flowered in their wake. As the immediate threat of closure and redundancy recedes, and the new HRM culture fails to deliver, a new crisis of rising expectations may emerge among these opinion-formers.

REFERENCES

Ackers, P. (1981) 'Redundancy and Collective Bargaining', Warwick MA dissertation.

Ackers, P. (1988) 'Changes in workplace industrial relations in West Midlands manufacturing industry in the 1980s', Warwick M Phil thesis.

Ackers, P. (1989) 'Workplace benefits? Human Resources Management – coming to a workplace near you soon?', *New Socialist*, April/May.

Ackers, P. and Black, J. (1988) 'Managing organized labour in the 1980s: a tale of two companies', Paper to 1988 Aston/UMIST Labour Process Conference, in *Journal of Industrial Affairs*, 1 Jan, 1982.

Ackers, P. and Black, J. (1989) 'Paternalist Capitalism: an organizational culture in transition', Paper to 1989 BSA Conference in Cross, M. and Payne, G. (1991) *Work and the Enterprise Culture* (London: Falmer/BSA).

Armstrong, R. and Marchington, M. (1982) 'Shop Stewards and Employee Participation: a variety of views', *Employee Relations* 4 (4).

Baldamus, W. (1961) *Efficiency and Effort* (London: Tavistock).

Black, J. and Ackers, P. (1987) 'The Japanization of British industry: a case study of the carpet industry', Paper to 1987 UWIST Conference in *Employee Relations*, 10 June 1988.

Black, J. and Ackers, P. (1989) 'Between Adversarial Relations and Incorporation: Direction and Dilemmas in the US Auto Industry', Paper to 1989 UWIST Conference.

Black, J. and Ackers, P. (1990) 'Voting for Employee Involvement at General Motors: a case study from the United States', Paper to 1990 Aston/UMIST Labour Process Conference.

Black, J. and Neathey, F. (1989) 'Labour and deskilling: critique of managerial control in the glass industry', in Fong Chua *et al.* (eds) *Critical perspectives in Management Control* (London: Macmillan).

Braverman, H. (1974) *Labour and Monopoly Capital* (Monthly Review Press: New York).

Burawoy, M. (1979) *Manufacturing Consent* (Chicago: University of Chicago Press).

Cressey, P. and MacInnes, J. (1980) 'Voting for Ford: Industrial Democracy and Control of Labour', *Capital and Class* 11.

Daniel, W. W. (1987) *Workplace industrial relations and technical change* (London: Frances Pinter).

Edwardes, M. (1983) *Back from the Brink* (London: Pan).

Edwards, P. K. and Sisson, K. (1989) 'Industrial Relations in the United Kingdom: Change in the 1980s', ESRC Review Paper.

Edwards, P. K. (1990) 'Understanding Conflict in the Labour Process: The Logic and Autonomy of Struggle', in Knights, D. and Wilmott, H. (eds) *Labour Process Theory* (London: Macmillan).

Fox, A. (1966) 'Sociology and Industrial Relations' Research Paper 3, Royal

Commission on Trade Unions and Employers Associations (London: HMSO).

Freemantle, D. (1985) 'An end to the art of compromise', *Personnel Management*, May.

Gramsci, A. (1971) *Prison Notebooks* (London: Lawrence & Wishart).

Guest, D. (1987) 'Human Resources of Management and Industrial Relations', *Journal of Management Studies* 24 (5).

Hall, S. and Jacques, M. (1983) *The Politics of Thatcherism* (London: Lawrence & Wishart).

Harris, R. (1988) 'The analysis of perceptions of conflict in a chemical works', Paper to 1988 Aston/UMIST Labour Process Concerence.

HMSO (1951) 'Unofficial Stoppages in the London Docks. Report of a Committee of Inquiry' (Cmnd 8236).

HMSO (1957) 'Report of a Court of Inquiry into the causes and circumstances of a Dispute at Briggs Motor Bodies Ltd Dagenham' (Cmnd 131).

HMSO (1968) 'Royal Commission on Trade Unions and Employers Associations 1965–68 (Cmnd 3623).

HMSO (1971) 'Commission on Industrial Relations report No. 17., Facilities afforded to Shop-Stewards' (Cmnd 4668).

Jones, N. (1986) 'Decline and fall of the British Shop Steward', *The Listener*, 20 November.

Kelly, J. (1982) 'Useful work and useless toil', *Marxism Today*, August.

Kelly, J. (1985) 'Management Redesign of Work: Labour Process, Labour Markets and Products', in Knights, D. *et al.* (eds) *Job Redesign* (Aldershot: Gower).

Knights, D. (1987) 'Subjectivity and the labour process', Paper presented to 5th Annual Labour Process Conference, Manchester, April.

Knights, D. and Collinson, D. (1985) 'Redesigning work on the shopfloor: a question of control or consent?', in Knights, D *et al.* (eds) *Job Redesign* (Aldershot: Gower).

Knights, D. and Collinson, D. (1987) 'Discipling the shopfloor: a comparison of the disciplinary effects of managerial psychology and financial accounting', *Accounting Organization and Society* 12 (5): 457–77.

Knights, D. and Roberts, J. (1982) 'The Power of Organization or the Organization of Power', *Organizational Studies* 3 (1).

Knights, D. and Wilmott, H. (1990) *Labour Process Theory* (London: Macmillan).

Knights, D. Wilmott, H. and Collinson, D. (eds) (1985) *Job Redesign* (Aldershot: Gower).

Littler, C. and Salaman, G. (1982) 'Bravermania and beyond: recent theories of the Labour Process', *Sociology* 16 (2).

MacCarthy, B. (1966) 'The role of shop stewards in British industrial relations' Royal Commission on Trade Unions and Employers Associations, Research Paper No 1.

Marchington, M. (1987) 'A review and critique of research on developments in Joint Consultation', *British Journal of Industrial Relations* 25 (3).

Marchington, M. and Parker, P. (1990) *Changing Patterns of Employee Relations* (Hemel Hempstead: Harvester Wheatsheaf).

Millward, N. and Stevens, M. (1986) *British Workplace Industrial Relations,*

1980-1984 (Aldershot: Gower).

Nolan, P. (1983) 'The Firm and Labour Market Behaviour,' in Bain, G. (ed.) *Industrial Relations in Britain* (London: Macmillan).

Nove, A. (1983) *The Economics of Feasible Socialism* (London: Allen & Unwin).

Prior, M. and Purdy, D. (1979) *Out of the Ghetto. A Path to Socialist Rewards* (London: Spokesman).

Roots, P. (1986) 'Collective bargaining: opportunities for a new approach', Warwick Paper in Industrial Relations.

Sainbury, D. (1990) 'Industry needs new attitudes', *New Socialist*, February/March.

Storey, J. (1988) 'The People-Management Dimension in current programmes of Organisational Change', *Employee Relations*, 10 June.

Terry, M. (1986) 'How do we know if shop stewards are getting weaker?', *British Journal of Industrial Relations* 24 (2), July.

Terry, M. (1983) 'Shop Steward Development and Managerial Strategies', in Bains, G. S. (ed.) *Industrial Relations in Britain* (Oxford: Blackwell).

Thompson, E. P. (1978) *The Poverty of Theory* (London: Merlin).

Thompson, P. (1989) *The nature of work: An Introduction to Debates on the Labour Process* (London: Macmillan, Second Edition).

Thompson, P. (1990) 'Crawling from the Wreckage: The Labour process and the Politics of Production', in Knights, D. and Wilmott, H. (eds) *Labour Process Theory* (London: Macmillan).

Tomlinson, J. (1982) *The Unequal Struggle: British Socialism and the Capitalist Enterprise* (London: Methuen).

7

COMPUTER-BASED TECHNOLOGY AND THE EMERGENCE OF NEW FORMS OF MANAGERIAL CONTROL*

Michael Rosen and Jack Baroudi

INTRODUCTION

Computer-based information technology is a dominant form of production technology in today's post-industrial society. The 'typical' American worker is no longer the man on the assembly line turning out automobiles, but is the person working in an office processing information using a computer terminal or micro-computer. The computer has become synonymous with the workplace, and with this integration have come profound changes in the control of labour.

Although the computerization of the workplace is largely a recent phenomenon, it is historically tied to the development of earlier forms of industrial production technology. To understand fully the place of computer-based labour control it is critical to examine the relationship between technology, control and organizational form as this has developed in the modern era.

In the second section of this chapter we discuss the importance of labour process control and the ways in which technology can be used as a tool for enforcing control. The changes in organizational form and control are placed in historical context in the third secion. Here, we discuss the evolution of organizations from the early craft-based forms to today's post-bureaucratic forms, and describe how the mechanisms of labour process control have become less tangible and visible. In the following section, we focus on computer-based information technology and how this technology has created possibilities

* We are grateful to David Knights (UMIST), Andrew Sturdy (UMIST), Margi Olson (New York University) and Wanda Orlikowski (MIT) for their comments on earlier drafts of this chapter.

for labour control never before possible. In particular, we will examine the ability of the computer to foster hegemonic control – control based on eliciting consent towards the labour process, through the use of largely unobtrusive and invisible means. Finally, we outline the outcomes of control enabled by information technology. We focus on nine potential impacts, including changes to organization structure, job tasks, and job skill.

TECHNOLOGY AND ORGANIZATIONAL CONTROL

Control over the labour process is the primary problem of bureaucratic (or advanced administrative) organizations (Van Maanen and Barley, 1984). Output in such organizations, and hence productivity and profitability, is determined by the control of behaviour through a formalized rules system, rather than basing reward on output alone. As Edwards (1979) notes, the logic underlying bureaucratic control is structural, where control is embedded within the formalized rule system of the organization. By following the rules of an organization, its members will come to produce 'a fair day's' output.

However, given that most organization members do not share directly in any profit resulting from their individual labour (even if such a reward system were possible to calculate, in complex systems of production) and are thus not directly and selfishly motivated to produce for reasons of individual remuneration (as is the case in output-based control, such as piece-rate labour), labour's consent to the process of production, that is, labour's acceptance of the system of belief giving legitimacy to such production, becomes paramount. Labour power is more readily translated into useful labour, and hence productivity and profitability, when the relations of production are perceived as legitimate by all parties to the labour process; that is, when they are given consent.

Relatedly, the potential for resistance to the process of production is mediated to the extent that power and control can be made invisible in the structure of work itself. When that which is fundamentally political comes to be perceived as natural and neutral, an existential necessity in the order of things, it is likely to be resisted no longer. For example, while labour history indicates that an extensive division of labour and the separation of the conception of work (by management) from its execution (by labour) has political origins and was initially violently contested (Edwards 1979; Clawson 1980), such organization

214

is today perceived as natural and neutral, and thus is rarely contested.

Technology has proved to be an unusually powerful tool in exercising bureaucratic control, largely because the social element of technology tends to be overlooked in favour of its perceived 'pure' technical characteristics. The technical advantages of machinery are frequently obvious, or perceived as such, while the advantages of mechanization and automation for social control are less blatant. For example, work can be organized requiring a certain pattern of social interaction among the workers, necessitated by the physical requirements of the technology. Clawson (1980) argues that technological innovations were adopted into the production process *not only* on the basis of technical productivity, but largely as a means to impose control over the work process. Interaction with machine technologies necessitates standardized behaviour on the part of workers. Machines delimit the form, quality, and pace of both labour and material inputs and outputs (Perrow, 1973:23). The more thoroughly automated the production process, the more extensive are the possibilities for control of the labour process. Any machine, therefore, is a 'complex bundle of rules that are built into the machine itself' (Perrow, 1973:23). Interacting satisfactorily with the machine necessitates complying with the rules of the organization, though the rules are not visible and compliance may be totally unconscious.

The control structure characterizing these labour relations is bureaucratic, while the mode of control is hegemonic, based not on coercion *per se* of the labour force but on eliciting their consent towards the relations of production. Put differently, consent towards the relations of production characterizing bureaucracy is obtained by embedding control within the logic which governs the relationship between the worker and the material systems of production (Edwards, 1979). This relationship is constituted by the social relations of production – the system of rules and statuses underlying any social group – and the technological forces of production – the material means and technical knowledge of productive activity.

The development of any technology, therefore is tied critically to the social relations enabled through such technology. Any production work can usually be performed in a variety of ways, thus empowering different participants in the labour process. Consequently, because technology has tended to be developed for management it has frequently enabled the social relations and structuring of work favouring managerial interests, and thus increasing management's control over the labour process.

BUREAUCRACY AND BEYOND -
A HISTORICAL VIEW

Placed in its socio-historic context, bureaucracy is the first organizational form in which control is primarily indirect, embedded in 'objective' structural mechanisms. These include a formal rules orientation, a specialization and division of labour, an institutionalized hierarchy, and a career orientation. The formal rules orientation of bureaucracy is the most unique characteristic defining this form, differentiating it from earlier organizational types (Clawson, 1980).[1] In earlier organizational structures, such as craft-based production, hierarchically controlled organizations and internal contracting organizations, labour possessed greater skill and autonomy and, as a result, exercised greater control over the labour process (Edwards, 1979; Montgomery, 1979). Decisions over their own behaviour – decisions over task pace, task sequence, and so on – were within labour's domain, management being primarily concerned with output, and not with formalizing the behaviours through which it was produced.

The subsequent effort to standardize behaviour – and thus to control output – through a system of rules covering a broad range of task and non-task behaviours was dissimilar to the simple and hierarchical organizational forms preceeding this effort. In those earlier organizational forms, control was exercised directly, either through an owner or a foreman having the power of an owner: to hire or fire without due process, to pay differential salaries for performing the same task, and so on (Edwards, 1979). Control was also directed singularly towards achieving output. Task pace, and the sequencing of task steps, for example, were not standardized, but were left to the discretion of the producer. Further, owners/managers/foremen did not systematically possess task working knowledge, *per se*. Such knowledge, concomitant with the pace and sequencing of tasks, was primarily the property of labour (Clawson, 1980), hence empowering labour through their possession of a set of critical contingencies necessary in the production process (Hickson *et al.*, 1971).

A primary ramification of establishing the explicit and formal rules of bureaucracy, therefore, was the disempowering of labour through the transfer of working knowledge from labour to capital/management. As work is standardized via a rules system which defines a set of relatively specialized, simplified, and hence unskilled (or more correctly, deskilled) task structures, labour loses its strategic working knowledge, and is thus disempowered, and management is conse-

216

quently able to shift the distribution of power and remuneration more in its own favour.

From a power perspective, therefore, the chracteristics defining the structure of bureaucracy may be understood as mechanisms enabling the behavioural control of the labour process. These mechanisms include not only the formal rules orientation of bureaucracy, but the specialization of task, division of labour, separation of task conception from execution, strict hierarchy, differential reward according to level, and so on found in this organizational form (Weber, 1946). With the emergence of bureaucracy, control becomes less direct, and hence more invisible, embedded in the mechanisms of the organizational structure which channel behaviour. It is also frequently embedded in the role-distancing accommodations labour makes to the production process (see Sturdy, in this volume). Burawoy (1979) describes this as 'gaming', or approaching the labour process as a game. To the extent that labour creates a game out of work, potential and actual conflict is diffused, opposition diminished, and labour process consent engendered (Burawoy, 1979:80).

In this sense, bureaucracy may be identified as the first organizational arena in which hegemony emerges as the primary locus of control (Herman, 1982). Here control is based more immediately on mechanisms eliciting the consent of members towards the labour process, rather than on mechanisms more immediately based on coercion. Members agree to follow the predetermined rules of production, resulting in an acceptable level of production.

This is a second-order level of control, where output itself is not the direct focus of attention. Instead, behaviour is controlled, with the full expectation that 'correctly' enacted behaviour will result in suitable output.

While behavioural control is a dominant characteristic of bureaucracy, post-bureaucratic organizations depend on an even less direct, unobtrusive form of control to ensure productive activity. This is ideational control, a third-order level of control. Roughly put, the control of ideas, beliefs, values, attitudes, and their underlying rationality – all comprising the ideational realm – is the focus of control. To the extent that ideational control is realized, organization members will enact behaviour which will result in suitable output.

As Habermas notes, however, even here there is a dialectical boundedness to the hegemony of ideational control, a realm of limitation because, at least for Habermas:

217

traditions important for legitimation cannot be regenerated administratively. Furthermore, administrative manipulation of cultural matters has the unintended side effect of causing meanings and norms previously fixed by tradition and belonging to the boundary conditions of the political system to be publicly thematized. In this way, the scope of discursive will-formation expands – a process that shakes the structures of the depoliticized public realm so important for the continued existence of the system.

(Habermas, 1973:47–8)

Ideational control is theorized here as ultimately a genesis for crisis, but is an increasingly central form of late-twentieth century organizational control.

The existence of this ideational form of control is found in Ouchi's statement that:

the basic mechanism of control in a Japanese company is embodied in a philosophy of management. This philosophy, and implicit theory of the firm, describes the objectives and the procedures to move towards them. These objectives represent the values of the owners, employees, customers, and government regulators. . . . Those who grasp the essence of this philosophy of values and beliefs (or ends and means) can deduce from the general statement an almost limitless number of specific rules or targets to suit changing conditions. Moreover, these specific rules or targets will be consistent between individuals. . . . This theory, implicit rather than explicit, cannot be set down completely in so many sentences. Rather, the theory is communicated through a common culture shared by key managers and, to some extent, all employees.

(1981:34)

We have here evidence of an organizational structure in which an explicit system of specific rules governing behaviour is superceded by a more encompassing ideational structure, channelling organizational responsibilities, expectations, behaviours, and output (see Table 1). A shared meaning system obviates the need for an explicit rules orientation, which is the conspicuous means for control in the classic bureaucracy.

If a shared meaning system becomes the fulcrum for control – in this manner achieving consent towards the labour process – the fixed

Table 1 Modes and forms of organizational control

Forms of control	Modes of control	Bases of control
Simple control Hierarchical control	Dominative	Direct supervision Immediate discretion of owner/foreman/manager Task fragmentation – division of labour Separation of conception from execution
Bureaucratic control	Hegemonic	Explicit rules orientation Technological systems enabling behavioural conformity and rule invisibility Extensive and strict hierarchical stratification Task fragmentation – division of labour Separation of conception from execution
Post-bureaucratic control	Hegemonic (expanded)	Ideational focus Technological systems – extensively IT based – structuring task conception and execution Matrix formations Loose-coupling Boundary-spanning roles Multi-disciplinary teams

division of labour characteristic of bureaucracy may be transcended, as may the Taylorist deskilling of labour via a strict specialization of task, the separation of staff versus line personnel, the strict hierarchy of single reporting relationships, and so on (see Table 2). As noted, these characteristics of bureaucracy form a particular structure fitting a formalized rules system, all geared towards standardizing behaviour. To the extent that an explicit rules system becomes redundant – as rules are internalized within the culture system of the members of the

Table 2 Structural outcomes of expanded managerial hegemony

De-bureaucratization

A. Disappearance of explicit rules orientation
B. Disappearance of extensive and strict hierarchy
C. De-Taylorization of tasks
D. Appearance of decentralization through centralization
E. Routinization of 'expert' tasks
F. Restructuring of complex tasks at times of crisis to reduce collective bargaining ability of organized labour
G. Deprofessionalization
H. Expanded invisible control
I. Transcendence of the time and space limitations of bureaucratic production

---

organization and /or are written into the interaction of members with the materials systems of production – these structural characteristics of the rational-legal bureaucracy also become redundant. As the infrastructural and morphological characteristics of the rational-legal bureacracy do not fit an ideationally-based form of hegemonic control, they are giving way to organizational characteristics fitting post-bureaucratic forms. De-bureaucratization and new organizational arrangements are the result. Many of these new arrangements are supported or enabled by computer-based technologies.

All this talk of differing modes of control in pre-to-post forms of bureaucratic organization is not to ignore the larger mode of capitalist production and consumption as the Petri dish within which organizational control proliferates. And a *sine qua non* of capitalism, as it trudges on through the increasing commodification of seemingly all aspects of social existence, is control of the individual, merely through the 'dull compulsion of economic relations'. Consent lies simply in rearing children who clamour after the T-shirts, entire sets of plastic toys, lunch boxes, Hallowe'en costumes, Saturday morning cartoons, comic books, videos and tickets to the full-length feature film memorializing the adventures of the Teenage Mutant Hero Turtles. That is, one needs to sell one's own or appropriate the labour of another to secure the funds to participate in society.

INFORMATION TECHNOLOGY AND ORGANIZATIONAL CONTROL

As information technology reaches throughout an organization, becoming pervasive to the extent that numerous tasks and decisions are controlled by this form of automation, technical rationality may similarly become pervasive, reducing discretion beyond that realized with previous technologies. To the extent that managers are dependent on, and accepting of, computer decision support systems, the technical rationality underlying such systems is likely to be overlooked. Herein, members are little aware of the limitations and premises inherent to the system (Orlikowski, 1986:20).

Thus, as Orlikowski (ibid.:9) notes, information systems increase rationalization and control through the limiting of available choices and the reduction of discretion, while at the same time increasing the perception of discretion through the utilization of self-selection facilities and pre-planned menus. Similar to earlier technologies, information technology requires the use of predefined and standardized responses, where 'much of the variance in possible outcomes will already have been eliminated' (Pfeffer, quoted in Heydebrand, 1985:106).

It is in this very basic sense that information technology cannot be a neutral tool, for such technology is an objectification of the intentions and expectations of its creators and managerial sponsors.

Information systems are commissioned, designed and implemented by individuals and groups with certain parochial interests, predilections, resources and goals [explicit and implicit] . . . They are human artifacts, constructed essentially and entirely by the interaction and action of individuals. Much like writing a book, writing software bears the indelible stamp of the author's intentions and/or their mandate. Once developed, the information systems are then maintained over their lifetimes and the frequency, manner and nature of such activity (or its lack thereof) too reflects current exigencies and political agendas.

(Orlikowski, 1986:19)

The shared ideational system surrounding computers and information technology by members of the organization also increases the technology's ability to penetrate numerous aspects of organizational process, and thus enables new control structures. Many members of an organization will agree to the purported benefits to be achieved from computerization. In many cases workers have grown up with computers. They have been exposed to them since school, and consider interacting with them as a normal part of everyday life, from banking, shopping, cooking, to engaging in numerous forms of entertainment. Such is the case with 'cash machines', which have been in widespread existence sufficiently long for nearly an entire generation to have been weaned into the banking system on them. Indeed, this technology has become so extensive as to link entire networks of nominally independent and distinct financial institutions into cooperating entities, thus enabling the realization of an electronic financial system at the individual level and a centralized tracking system at the social level. This is to say nothing of the increased potential for national and international banking, the emergence of electronic money, governmental and corporate surveillance of the individual, and so on. Again, the realization of ease and convenience for the individual travels concomitantly with increased hegemony.

Computers have become such an accepted part of our culture that to oppose their use is 'irrational'. While resistance to the introduction of automation is still experienced in many companies, we believe that this will lessen greatly as more and more of the workforce grows up with the computer, accepting it as easily as our parents accepted the telephone as a natural part of the work setting. Consequently, we believe the ability of workers to recognize and resist the control facilitated by computerization is greatly reduced as the technology is accepted as a not only natural, but also necessary part of the workplace. The implicit and explicit cultural assumptions holding the computer as an efficient and effective tool, whose deployment in many cases can be seen as necessary to the very survival of the organization, facilitate this control. Additionally, managers who share the same general cultural orientation as their workers are probably not consciously deploying computer-based technologies to specifically increase their control over the labour process. Instead, they are instituting computer use with the intention of achieving the reputed efficiencies arising from such use. Increased managerial control is as much a product of such deployment as its impetus.

Accordingly, we argue that increased domination, on one hand, and hegemony, on the other, are each facilitated through the use of computer-based technologies. In the remainder of this chapter, therefore, we will explore the role of information technology in facilitating the expansion of hegemony – and to a more limited extent, domination – as a mode of organizational control. However, we do not propose that an organization employing information technology will exhibit all or even a portion of the structural outcomes we identify as characteristics of post-bureaucratic control; nor that information technology in and of itself determines organizational development in a hegemonic manner. Instead, as we indicate below, information technology may be understood as a tool facilitating the development of post-bureaucratic organizational characteristics if it is so deployed, whether consciously or unconsciously. Computer-based information technology allows a great diversity and dispersion of control structures to emerge, many of which are not possible with simple machine technology.

Finally, we do not propose a unilinear, causal relationship between the emergence of post-bureaucratic, ideational control and that control enabled through the use of computer-based technologies. One is not the requisite of the other, nor its logical outcome. Instead, there is a not coincidental confluence of technology and ideology drawn from the same cultural waters which, when once again merged, have significant forces as to result in their own particular sets of eddies, undertows, sinkholes and backwashes. These are deserving of study on their own, without the need to presume that they have come from nowhere and are on their way nowhere else.

STRUCTURAL OUTCOMES ENABLED BY COMPUTER-BASED TECHNOLOGY

Disappearance of explicit rules orientation

As described earlier, a formal rules orientation forms the essence of bureaucratic control. As also noted, however, mechanization obviates the need for such explicit organizational rules, insofar as it standardizes behaviour in the place of explicit rules. While machine technology has primarily enabled this form of explicit rules replacement at the immediate point of production, that is, 'on the shop floor', information technology readily expands this capability to also include administrative and supervisory tasks as well. For example, a major New York City investment banking firm tracked the monthly number of hours worked by each data processing (DP) employee. DP personnel filled out elaborate time sheets each week, which were then handed to the secretary, whose responsibilities included compiling this information into one overall report. The secretary had difficulty preparing the report, however, because programmers and analysts often failed to follow the rules for report preparation. Some would annotate the sheet with a note such a 'see George for project number'. Others would use the wrong descriptors for various categories, or simply fail to provide the information in the required, usable format.

Rather than attempting to enforce the reporting rules, however, management decided to develop a computerized system. Instead of filling out paper time-sheets, the new system 'allowed' DP personnel to directly enter their information into the computer. The system did not allow for annotation, and if incorrect or incomplete descriptors – i.e. non-standardized information – were entered, the system prompted the user and listed the possible categories. While the system did not guarantee information accuracy, it did force personnel to enter data in a standardized format, thus making obsolete the previous system of rules for reporting. Management was able to acquire the desired information (which was needed to bill user departments for project development) in the format required without having to issue new rules or enforce old ones. Instead, the information system was used as a form of procedural control, which Ginzberg (1980) defines as those systems which increase control over the tasks they support by reducing the discretion of the person(s) performing the tasks. These systems may also increase control by increasing the number of those to whom the standard operating procedures may be applied.

Disappearance of extensive and strict hierarchy

Crozier (1986:87) notes that hierarchy is a key element of bureaucratic organization, providing a basis to subordinate possible means and alternative goals to the authority of management. 'Hierarchical structures seem to be indispensable to establish the necessary authority patterns to get things done', he writes.

Hierarchical stratification is necessary, however, only insofar as managerial control is not otherwise realized over the labour process. To the extent that technologies embed control within the production process, making redundant the direct control responsibilities of supervisors, hierarchical stratification may be modified and/or replaced. With such control, flat organizational structures are possible. An American retail company, Mrs Field's Cookies (*INC*, 1987:65; *Information Week*, 1989:46) provides an example of this type of organization. Through the extensive use of micro-computer and telecommunications technology they were able to eliminate entire layers of middle management. Mrs Field's requires very few headquarters staff to monitor and control the over 635 outlets and over 5,700 employees. Using this technology Mrs Fields is able to monitor daily sales and worker productivity at all outlets. Any exceptional situations, such as employee theft, are quickly spotted and corrected. Buchanan and Boddy (1983:249) note that the implementation of computer-aided production technologies made managerial supervision redundant in several factories they observed. Moreover, the dramatic ability of corporations to reduce, and ultimately largely eliminate, the need for production workers is evident with the emergence of robotics and 'workerless' factories.

De-Taylorization of tasks

Information technology may facilitate the de-Taylorization of work – a shrinking of the extensive specialization and division of labour characteristic of bureaucracy – while at the same time maintaining managerial control. De-Taylorization may be achieved by enabling employees to reframe their jobs, in essence to design them, in accordance with the philosophy of sociotechnical systems (STS) theory (e.g. Bostrom and Heinen, 1977; Mumford, 1981; Mumford *et al.*, 1983). As Mumford (1981) demonstrates, the STS strategy may be used to make automated jobs more interesting and satisfying by using job enrichment approaches (Hackman, Oldham, and Purdy, 1975). Labour is motivated by fitting what employees 'want' in terms of variety, feedback, and so on, with what the job provides, that is, by satisfying what Mumford (1981) calls the job satisfaction 'fit' of the job to the person.

Employees are thus performing tasks which appear more autonomous, transcending the Taylorist strict specialization of task. Consent towards the labour process is more readily elicited in such STS-designed jobs, as the employee perceives his or her participation in designing the task, and the job now is more likely to contain individually relevant satisfying dimensions. Substantial control by employees over their own work is absent, however, because the overarching task parameters have been predetermined by management. The options from which employees can choose have been set forth in the strategic design phase of the STS process over which management exerts substantial control (Bostrom and Heinen, 1977).

Illusions of decentralization

Somewhat relatedly, information technology facilitates a decentralization of task and decision making, while at the same time maintaining or increasing the centralization of control. Accordingly, as Heydebrand (1985:105) notes, centralization and decentralization 'are no longer opposites or alternatives, but they are mutually dependent and operate simultaneously' (see also Orlikowski, 1986:12). Because information technology may reach directly from the bottom to the top of a hierarchy – from the shop floor to the corporate office – it may facilitate the centralization of control through the standardization of information, more complete record-keeping, and faster information processing (Robey, 1981). 'Thus, what appears to be greater decentralization may simply entail the delegation of more routine decisions whose outcomes are more closely controlled' (ibid.: 681). By increasing the formalization of the task and by monitoring lower-level decision outcomes, if not prescribing the outcomes altogether, management may be able to achieve the appearance of decentralizing decision-making, while centralizing control over outcomes.

Another example of information technology facilitating centralization through decentralization may also be seen in the case of Mrs Field's Cookies. Even though individual stores may be thousands of miles from the corporate headquarters, with very few headquarters staff to supervise them, the appearance of decentralization and decentralized control is an illusion. In fact, Mrs Field's is an organization with highly centralized control. All decisions regarding local production of baked goods, hourly sales quotas, labour scheduling, etc., are made by computer, leaving little autonomy or discretion to the local workforce. Centralized surveillance of hourly sales and the missing or exceeding of sales quotas is now possible, this data being communicated to headquarters staff each night, where any exceptional conditions can be immediately noted. A fundamental aspect of this is the knowledge on the part of the employee that such detailed information on their performance is collected as a matter of course. In this sense, domination is extended as control becomes routinized. Yet the perception of centralized control has been obscured to the extent that it has been built into the technology system and the system of administration.

Routinization of 'expertise'

Whereas machine technology readily enabled the routinization and standardization of many production tasks, administrative and decision-making tasks were not at all readily controlled through technology. Instead, they were subject to control through the explicit rules system of bureaucracy. Information technology, on the other hand, facilitates the effort to routinize many previously non-routinizable 'expert' tasks, thus enabling the creation of less skilled, less powerful, and less well-paid positions. Such was the case with the introduction of automated material requirement planning (MRP) systems. At one time MRP was considered a difficult problem, requiring highly skilled individuals to plan the flow of materials. The introduction of MRP systems, however, enabled this task to be routinely structured, allowing top management to reduce their dependence on such uniquely skilled labourers/employees and to replace them with others, performing a relatively less skilled task.

As will be explored below, this deskilling of expert tasks through the application of information technology is closely related to the process of deprofessionalization.

Reducing the power of collective bargaining

Related to the above, information technology may be used at times of crisis to restructure complex tasks, thus largely eliminating the collective bargaining power of the organized labour performing expert tasks. An example of this process is provided by the 1981 American air traffic controllers' (PATCO) strike. A newly instituted computer system was able to reduce and simplify the flow of air traffic, such that supervisory level personnel could maintain the system while new recruits were trained. This ability to reorganize the system during a labour crisis drastically undercut the collective bargaining ability of the PATCO workers (Sterling, 1982).

Deprofessionalization

Individuals performing tasks traditionally identified as professional are increasingly faced with the deprofessionalization of their labour, which Haug (1973:197) defines as 'a loss to professional occupations of their unique qualities, particularly their monopoly over knowledge, public belief in their service ethos, and expectations of work autonomy and authority over the client'. Instead, there is an increasing 'convergence of professional and bureaucratic functions' as the distinction between professionals and bureaucrats gives way to a new systematic division of labour in which technical workers perform both managerial and service functions.

Haug (1977:215) proposes that the storage and data processing capabilities of information systems provide access to knowledge previously the preserve of professionals, thus facilitating the erosion of professional autonomy and authority. 'Almost by definition', she notes (1973:201),'*academic* knowledge, upon which the diploma credentials validating professionals' expertise are largely based, is codifiable and therefore amenable to computer input.'

An extreme example of such deprofessionalization may be seen in the case of knowledge engineering and artificial intelligence techniques (Barr and Feigenbaum, 1981). Here the possibility exists for the automation of task areas that formerly required highly skilled, professionalized workers, and the routinization of problems that were previously considered too unstructured for automation. Expert systems (Shortliffe, 1976) allow less skilled workers to have access to the knowledge and skills of the professional, as described above. If a worker is empowered by the knowledge and skill they possess, then expert systems, by codifying this knowledge, may facilitate the disempowering of workers even at the highest levels of the organization, including those perceived to do professional work, such as doctors, lawyers, accountants, actuaries, and computer specialists, as well as strategic managers.

This discussion of expert systems is not to presume that the tacit skills of professionalized workers are easily automated; such is not the case. The more clearly a task is understood – operating a manual elevator, for example – the more readily it can be automated – replacing the worker with a panel of buttons. A more highly complex and possibly intuitive system – medical diagnosis, master chess, or ballet choreography – provides more difficulty for routinization and automation, and greater opportunity for resistance (Edwards, 1979). This possibility for resistance is also increased where the countervailing power of professional licensure – as was earlier the case with unionization – collides with the forces of capital. The relationship between computerized automation of expert skills and resistance is thus again dialectical, while the tendency towards increased automation and deprofessionalization cannot be denied.

Orlikowski, expanding upon Herman (1982), indicates that deprofessionalization may be conceived according to whether the professional loses either the technical or the ideological basis of his or her work. In the latter instance the professional maintains technical authority and the specialized set of skills particular to his or her work, but loses control over the *ends* of this work.

Technical deprofessionalization, on the other hand, involves a loss by the professional over the *means* of his or her work, that is 'their technical authority is diminished through task fragmentation, deskilling and increased rationalization' (Orlikowski, 1986:17). This process of technical deskilling is further evident in the rise of para-professionals and semi-professionals, where less skilled and cheaper individuals are hired to perform 'professional labour', frequently with the aid of sophisticated information technologies. Orlikowski provides an example of architectural firms hiring non-professional workers to operate computer-aided design equipment, replacing the need for skilled draughtsmen and architects. She points out that professionals already do the specialized, fragmented work of drafting while client contact and creative tasks are largely left to the organization elite. As a result, the employment of non-professionals, combined with the use of computer-aided design technologies, downgrades 'the already tenuous skills of these [architecture] professionals' (ibid.)

Invisible control

To a large extent, hegemonic control denotes 'invisible' control, that is, the operation of control systems which are not readily perceived. As we have discussed, such systems may be embedded in the rules systems of organizations and in their technologies. Information technology facilitates the use of invisible control systems, as may be seen in the case of a particular New York City financial institution. This organization was concerned with security at its various facilities, and thus installed computerized locks on each door and issued magnetized cards to each employee. To enter a room an individual placed the card in the card reader on the door, which transmitted the information to the central computer, where the information was recorded. If the person was authorized access to that area, the door was electronically unlocked.

Beyond the obvious restriction of movement provided by the system, however, it also provided an additional control benefit, one not advertised to the employees. Management was given the means to track where each employee had been in any day, and how much time had been spent in each location. In effect, management could now monitor employees' movements throughout the bank's facilities without their being aware of such surveillance. While similar information is possible via video monitoring, this is not as easily processable into reports on individual employees, and in other ways is less pervasive and more obvious. On the other hand – and as is the case throughout – new forms of resistance emerge. For example, an employee could play with the computerized tracking system, and possibly undermine it, by borrowing or stealing another employee's card and going from here to there for fun or profit.

Transcendance of time and space limitations

The traditional time and space limitations characteristic of bureaucracy – the official work hours and office space discussed by Weber (1946) – can in certain instances be transcended with the use of information technologies. An example of this is the increasing possibility of working at home (Olson, 1983). This phenomenon, which appears as an opposite of the 'factory' and 'office' concepts central respectively to the industrial and post-industrial forms of organization, has the potential to return much of the control of a job's pace and performance to the worker. Conversely, work at home has the potential to extend monitoring and control from the workplace into the home.

For example, several data entry clerks from a large insurance firm chose to work at home because they had family obligations which made commuting to a central workplace difficult. These individuals (all women) would receive batches of insurance claim forms by messenger, and would then keypunch them into a terminal with local storage capabilities. When they had finished the batch they would dial up the central computer system and transmit the batch via the phone lines. The workers were paid on a piece-rate basis, and had control over the hours they chose to work and the pace of their job. Management, however, did have expectations that a certain number of forms would be keyed each week, and set the piece rate accordingly. Beyond this guideline, however, management did not direct the work process. The women, who were classified as part-time workers, received none of the usual health or retirement benefits from the company.

While the above is an example of a 'loosely controlled' work-at-home strategy, a more controlled approach is also possible. In one case, somewhat replicating the office relationship, the company required all at-home-workers to be available by phone from nine in the morning until five in the afternoon in case a supervisor or colleague should need information. A more extreme case used the terminal at home linked to a central office computer to keep track of the number of hours the individual was logged into the system and working, which is very similar to the case of the finance workers explored above. Usually the expectation was that the individual would be on the system during regular working hours, but additional work time was also encouraged. The computer also made it possible for the supervisor to log into the system and check the employee's work and progress.

In each of these variations on the work-at-home theme, the basic aspects of bureaucratic power, control, and domination are in transition. First, the traditional middle manager's degree of control over the labour process was historically seen as deriving from managing individuals in the workplace. As work is decentralized in the home, eliminating the centralized workplace *per se*, the power of this middle manager is largely reduced, if not erased altogether. Further, the very definition of employment is called into question. Such workers, who may previously have worked in a centralized office, being paid on a salary basis and receiving many of the welfare remunerations of bureaucracy (such as health and unemployment insurance and a retirement plan), are now classified as part-time workers. At-home workers are not entitled to such forms of remuneration, though they may produce as much as centralized full-time workers. The control ramifications of this work-at-home design are unclear, and will emerge as this form develops more fully. However, the failure of this option to grow more rapidly may be due to middle management's recognition that it erodes their power (Olson, 1985).

CONCLUSION

Many of the advanced societies are moving from an industrial economy to an information and service-based economy. With this movement we are witnessing many structural changes, enabled by the rapid penetration of computer-based technologies into the workplace. These changes, however, are usefully viewed as an extension of the organizational developments begun with industrialization and the penetration of mechanical technologies into the workplace.

We believe that we are entering a period of greater managerial control over the labour process, a control which is increasingly hegemonic in nature. This hegemony is enabled by cultural values which facilitate ideational control and the rapid advancement in computer-based technologies. The post-industrial organization will not have the obvious machine control of the shop floor or the assembly line, but will possibly have the increasingly unobtrusive control enabled by computer-based technology.

This chapter has given several examples of the types of structural change that we see occurring, and how the computer plays a role in these changes. We must be careful to state, however, that we do not see these changes as a dictate of the technology. Computer-based technology is extremely flexible, and has as much potential to liberate as to constrict the labour process. Computer-based technology is, however, a social product carrying with it the norms, values, history and thus the form of its creators and sponsors, who have primarily been either managerial workers or aligned with the managerial classes. The socio-historic struggle between management and labour for control over the labour process is thus also currently being enacted, perhaps largely unconsciously, in the development and deployment of computer-based technologies and the emergence of post-bureaucratic forms of hegemonic control.

NOTES

1 Embedded within this rules orientation are the assumptions of deskilling and the specialized division of labour. Hierarchy emerges as a 'necessity' for control when these conditions come into being.

REFERENCES

Barr, A. and Feigenbaum, E. (eds) (1981) *The Handbook of Artificial Intelligence* (Los Altos: William Kaufman, Inc.).

Bostrom, R. and Heinen, J. S. (1977) 'MIS Problems and Failures: A Socio-Technical Perspective', Parts I & II. *MIS Quarterly*, 1, 3 and 4: 17–31, 11–28.

Buchanan D. A. and Boddy, D. (1983) *Organizations in the Computer Age: Technological Imperatives and Strategic Choice* (Aldershot: Gower).

Burawoy, M. (1979) *Manufacturing Consent* (Chicago: University of Chicago Press).

Clawson, D. (1980) *Bureaucracy and the Labour Process* (New York: Monthly Review Press).

Crozier, M. (1986) 'Implications for the Organization', in Otway, J. and Peltu, M. (eds) *New Office Technology* (Ablex): 86–101.

Edwards, R. (1979) *Contested Terrain* (New York: Basic).

Ginzberg M. (1980) 'An Organizational Contingencies View of Accounting and Information Systems Implementation', *Accounting, Organizations and Society*, 5 (4): 369–82.

Habermas, J. (1973) *Legitimation Crisis* (Trans.: T. McCarthy) (Boston: Beacon Press).

Hackman, J. R., Oldham, R. and Purdy, K. (1975) 'A New Strategy for Job Enrichment', *California Management Review*, 17 (4): 57–71.

Haug, M. (1973) 'Deprofessionalization: An Alternative Hypothesis for the Future', *Sociological Review Mongraph*, 20.

Haug, M. (1977) 'Computer Technology and the Obsolescence of the Concept of Profession', in Haug, R. and Dofny, J. (eds) *Work and Technology* (Beverly Hills, CA: Sage): 215–28.

Herman, A. (1982) 'Conceptualizing Control: Dominance and Hegemony in the Capitalist Labor Process', *The Insurgent Sociologist*, 11 (3): 7–22.

Heydebrand, W. (1983) 'Technocratic Corporatism', in Hall, R. and Quinn, R. (eds) *Organizational Theory and Public Policy* (Beverly Hills: Sage).

Heydebrand, W. (1985) 'Technarchy and Neo-Corporatism: Toward a Theory of Organizational Change under Advanced Capitalism and Early State Socialism', *Current Perspectives in Social Theory*, 6: 71–128.

Hickson, D. J., Hinings, C. R., Lee, C. A., Schneck, R. E. and Pennings, J. M. (1971) 'A Strategic Contingencies Theory of Intra-Organizational Power', *Administration Science Quarterly*, 16 (2): 216–29.

Hirschhorn, L. (1984) *Beyond Mechanization: Work and Technology in a Postindustrial Age* (Cambridge, Mass: MIT Press).

INC (1987) 'Mrs Fields' Secret Ingredient', 65 (October).

Information Week (1989) 'MIS Holds Together A Crumbling Cookie', 46 (13 March).

Montgomery, D. (1979) *Workers' Control in America: Studies in the History of Work, Technology, and Labour Strugges* (New York: Cambridge University Press).

Mumford, E. (1981) 'Participative Systems Design: Structure and Method', *Systems, Objectives, Solutions*, 1: 5–19.

Mumford, E., Bancroft, N., and Sontag, B, (1983) 'Participative Design – Successes and Problems', *Systems, Objectives, Solutions*, 3 (3): 133–41.

Olson, M. (1983) 'Remote Office Work: Changing Work Patterns in Space and Time', *Communications of the ACM*, 20 (3): 182–7.

Olson, M. (1985) 'Potential of Remote Work for Professional Workers', *National Executive Forum: Office Workstations in the Home* (National Academy Press).

Olson, M. H. and Turner, J. A. (1985) 'Rethinking Office Automation', *Proceedings of the Sixth International Conference on Information Systems*, Indianapolis, Indiana.

Orlikowski, W. (1986) 'Computer Technology in Organizations: Some Critical Notes', Paper presented at the UMIST/Aston 4th Annual Conference on Organization and Control of the Labour Process.

Ouchi, W. G. (1981) *Theory Z* (New York: Avon).

Perrow, C. (1973) 'The Organizational Context of Human Factors Engineering', *Administrative Science Quarterly*, 28 (4): 521–41.

Robey, D. (1981) 'Computer Information Systems and Organization Structure', *Commucations of the ACM*, 24 (10): 679–87.

Shaiken, H. (1984) *Work Transformed: Automation and Labor in the Computer Age* (New York: Holt, Rinehart, Winston).

Shortliffe, E. H. (1976) *Computer-Based Medical Consultations: MYCIN* (New York: North-Holland).

Sterling, T. (1982) 'Unionization of Professionals in Data Processing: An

Assessment of Recent Trends', *Communications of the ACM*, 25 (11): 807–16.

Van Maanen, J. and Barley, S. R. (1984) 'Occupational Communities: Culture and Control in Organizations' in Staw, B. M. and Cummings, L. L. (eds), *Research in Organizational Behaviour*, 6. (JAI Press) (Used here in manuscript form, November, 1982).

Weber, M. (1946) *From Max Weber: Essays in Sociology*. Translated and edited by H. H. Gerth and C. Wright Mills (New York: Oxford University Press).

8

'DISCIPLINARY POWER' AND THE LABOUR PROCESS

Ron Sakolosky

INTRODUCTION

My purpose here in applying Foucault's theory of 'disciplinary power' to the labour process is not to discount the value of Marxist research on a subject which has traditionally been squarely within their domain. As Foucault himself said, 'I am neither an adversary nor a partisan of Marxism' (Fourcault in Rabinow, 1984: 355). Rather, my intent is to offer what I trust will be a complementary analyis, building on both the insights of Neo-Marxism and offering a Foucauldian critique of society and its institutions, which questions and expands upon those insights. In so doing, the intention is to create a more nuanced analytical framework for viewing the labour prcess, which points toward new directions not encompassed by previous frames of reference.

In approaching this task, I begin by delineating the points of convergence and divergence in Foucauldian and Marxist scholarship in relation to the concept of power. From there, I turn to an explanation of Foucault's theory of 'disciplinary power', focusing on its relation to the constitution of both the labour process and the body and psyche of the labouring subject. In order to ground these theoretical abstractions in the constructed reality of the contemporary workplace, I examine management discourse as a power/knowledge discourse in relation to such disciplinary techniques as computer surveillance and quality circles. Finally, I point to the areas of conviviality between Foucauldian and Neo-Marxist conceptions, so that future researchers might fruitfully construct new theoretical paradigms based upon the insights of both approaches.

FOUCAULT, MARXISM AND POWER

If one is to apply Foucault's concept of discipline to the labour process, 'discipline' must be understood in Foucauldian terms as constitutive of that process in the first place. As Foucault conceptualizes it:

> Discipline may be indentified neither with an institution nor with an apparatus; it is a type of power, a modality for its exercise, comprising a whole set of instruments, techniques, procedures, levels of application, targets; it is a 'physics' or an 'anatomy' of power, a technology.
>
> (1979: 215)

His theory of 'disciplinary power', unlike Marxist theories of power, concerns itself with 'capillary' forms of power. By focusing on the extremities of power, Foucault's approach is in contrast to the orthodox Marxist 'descending' emphasis, where the state and its characteristic mode of production shape the labour process from the top down.

In Foucault's complex cosmology, power is never monolithic, rather it is polyvalent and dispersed: it circulates. While criticized by some for creating an ontological circle and deducing power from power, Foucault maintains that '. . .there is no Power, but power relationships which are being born incessantly as both effect and condition of other processes' (1989: 187). Everyone both exercises power and is subject to it, although the degree of exercise *vis-à-vis* subjection may differ, depending on such factors as class, gender, and race.

While Foucault sees knowledge and power as being intrinsically related, they are not one and the same to him. Rather, his project is to study their relationship. In Foucault's view, there cannot be a power relation without the constitution of a field of knowledge/discourse as a corollary, nor can there by any knowledge that does not at the same time imply power relations. 'Discourses' and 'disciplinary practices' are entwined in social formations in ways that make for relations of dominance and subjugation. In this sense, capitalism can be analysed in Foucauldian terms as a 'power/knowledge regime' which, in the words of Marike Finlay, is 'the site but not the source of power' (1987: 203). Foucault's approach while realizing that capitalism can and does play an active role, is not narrowly causalist.

Accordingly, he focuses his analysis on specific localized practices. Moreover, for Faucault, power is not merely 'repressive', as not only orthodox but even Frankfurt School Marxists tend to characterize it, but 'productive' (conducive) as well. Using Foucault's approach, one can both study the creation of a 'science' of management as a knowledge/power discourse, and analyse the capitalist labour process in terms of the compelling techniques of 'disciplinary power' at the micro level of the workplace.

In this regard, Foucault's approach is not necessarily at odds with Marxism. Moreover, in explaining his relationship to the Frankfurt School in particular, Foucault has noted,

> It is a strange case of non-penetration between two very similar types of thinking which is explained, perhaps, by that very similarity. Nothing hides the fact of a problem in common better than two similar ways of approaching it.
>
> (Foucault in Raulet, *Telos*, Spring 1983: 200)

It is the object of this present discussion to explore both the differences and areas of confluence between Foucault's Nietzschean genealogical approach and various Marxist, as well as anarchist, perspectives in relation to the labour process. Foucault did not choose to write much about the labour process *per se*, perhaps because that process is traditionally a Marxist concern, which he did not see, as do some Marxists, as being central to an understanding of all power. Yet Foucault's approach not only has relevance to an understanding of the capitalist labour process, but it can also offer a critique of actually existing socialist states in which the labour process closely resembles that of capitalism.

Rather than focusing on orthodox Marxist 'power as property' questions, Foucault's 'strategic' concept of power is concerned with how power is exercised and the effects of that exercise on individuals. In analysing control, he focuses his analysis somewhat in the same vein as Max Weber's earlier work on discipline as 'automatic obedience' (Weber, 1947), concentrating on the 'disciplinary power relations' which are actually constitutive of the labouring subject in the first place, rather than on questions of the relative independence of power relations to production or the effect of the capitalist mode of production on the labouring subject. Foucault concerns himself with constructing a genealogy of the modern subject by analysing the inscription of forms of power on the body and psyche of individuals ('political anatomy'), and the correspondening forms of administration, governmentalization, and regulation that pertain to that objectivized subject. For Foucault, then, the shape of the labour process is not secondary and subordinate to the mode of production, and does not exist merely to maintain and reproduce that mode of production.

While orthodox Marxists tend to perceive the mode of production as the fundamental power which determines the labour process, Foucault's concept of 'disciplinary power' offers a new tool for understanding the labour process through an analysis that can range from the 'disciplinary techniques' of the early factories, to bureaucratic computerized workplace monitoring or the 'debureaucratized control' (Grenier, 1988) of the quality circle. His emphasis on discipline as a form of domination linked to science and the development of the 'disciplinary society' can be better understood in reference to the discipline mechanism which he terms 'panopticism'.

THE INFORMATION PANOPTICON

The 'disciplinary gaze' which characterizes Jeremy Bentham's 'Panopticon' was indeed inspired by his brother's factory in Russia, but was nevertheless rooted in models of the military camp, the hospital, the asylum, the school, and the monastery. Only later was it used to enhance the particular form of domination known as capitalism. As Foucault has noted in this regard,

> The system of imprisonment was invented as a generalized penal system during the eighteenth century and consolidated in the nineteenth century in connection with the development of capitalist societies and states.
>
> (Foucault, 1989)

It entailed a system of constant surveillance or, more precisely, the possibility of constant surveillance. Bentham's system was originally designed for prisons, but he posited that it would be appropriate for factories as well. In fact, many facets of the techniques of disciplinary power were already in evidence in workshops by the time of the industrial revolution.

The Panopticon, the 'Enlightenment' solution to the disciplinary problem that prisons posed, is explained by Foucault in terms of 'disciplinary power'. He sees it as a mechanism for assuring the automatic functioning of power in which

> . . .the perfection of power should tend to render its actual exercise unnecessary; that this architectural apparatus should be a machine for creating and sustaining a power relation indepen-

dent of the person who exercises it; in short, that the inmates should be caught up in a power situation of which they are themselves the bearers.

(1979: 201)

In the system of the Panopticon, power is made both visible and unverifiable.

The inmates are constantly aware of the tall tower from which they might be spied upon, but are never sure at any given moment that they are being watched. In workplace disciplinary institutions, the exercise of power by top management is automatized and dis-individualized through 'disciplinary mechanisms' based on 'subtle coercion' which, in turn, act to individualize the subjected worker, often rendering even resistance as an individual matter rather than a collective action by class subjects. The worker, like the inmate, is subject to being seen without ever seeing; correspondingly, manage-ment (whose gaze emanates from the 'central tower') can see without being seen (and with the computerization of the workplace, even middle management increasingly has no place to hide). The extreme case, the Panopticon, then, reveals the essence of the 'disciplinary society' by concentrating on the point at which power is applied in direct relation to the subject. It is this phenomenon of a whole society internalizing surveillance that Finlay (1987), building on Foucault, terms 'social panopticism'.

According to Foucault, in 'disciplinary institutions' the application of power produces varying degrees of docility in three ways: 'hier-archical observation', 'normalizing judgement', and their combination in 'examination' (1979: 170–94). While Foucault's primary concern in *Discipline and Punish* is to diagram the disciplinary power grid of panopticism in relation to the prison, he also connects it to the contemporaneous rise of the factory system. In reference to the industrial revolution and the rise of the managerial profession and its power/knowledge discourse, Foucault notes:

What was now needed was an intense, continuous supervision; it ran right through the labour process; it did not bear – or not only – on production (the nature and quantity of raw materials, the type of instruments used, the dimensions and quality of the products), it also took into account the activity of the men, their promptness, their zeal, their behaviour. But it was also different from the domestic supervision of the master present beside his workers and supervisors and foremen . Supervision. . .became a special function which had, nevertheless, to form an integral part of the production process, to run parallel to it through its entire length. A specialized personnel became indispensable, constantly present and distinct from the workers.

(1979: 174)

Surveillance (the all-seeing eye of the Panopticon) became a managerial function which both constituted and objectified the labouring subject. While more impersonal than the old apprenticeship system which it replaced, close supervision still retained the human element of the supervisor looking over one's shoulder or even the efficiency expert hovering nearby with stop-watch in hand. Currently, computer technology makes the monitoring of the labour process ever more anonymous and automatic, and power relations more entrenched in what Shoshana Zuboff (1988) has called an 'information panopticon'.

In discussing the panoptic power of information technology, Zuboff says;

> Systems can become information panopticons that, freed from the constraints of space and time, do not depend upon the physical arrangement of buildings or the laborious record keeping of industrial administration. They do not require the mutual presence of observation. They do not even require the presence of an observer. . . . The counterpart of the central tower is the video screen.
>
> (1988: 322)

In this regard, it is no coincidence that in my home state of Illinois, the Department of Corrections (read Prisons) has recently opted for a system of 'electronic monitoring' of offenders, using electronic ankle bracelets hooked up to video screens as part of its work release programme. At the same time that prisoners are being 'released' to work under surveillance, the workplace itself becomes more like a prison – using the same terms of discourse, 'electronic monitoring' or 'electronic supervision', and a similar computer-video based technology, in both instances.

Since there is no escaping the 'intense illumination' of the 'information panopticon' and there is no egalitarian access to the electronic text, workers must increasingly adopt tactics of 'anticipatory conformity' and appearance management at each level of the organization in order to reduce the risk of 'involuntary display' in the presence of 'universal transparency' and an environment 'saturated with measurement' (Zuboff, 1988). Such is the current interlocking configuration of power in telematic systems.

Using what Giles Deleuze (1988) sees as Foucault's cartographic approach, one can map out the blueprints of disciplinary power in a decentred way and thereby facilitate an understanding of the dynamics of a wide variety of diffused systems of domination, with the computerized workplace being one of them. Foucault then

> does not deny the existence of class and class struggle, but illustrates it in a totally different way. . .[in which] power is not homogeneous but can be defined only by the particular points through which it passes. Modern societies can be defined as 'disciplinarian'; but 'discipline' cannot be identified with any one institution or apparatus precisely because it is a type of power, a technology, that traverses every kind of apparatus or institution, linking them, prolonging them, and making them converge and function in a new way.
>
> (Deleuze, 1988: 25–6).

Foucault's emphasis is not on workplace supervision *per se*, but on surveillance itself as a 'disciplinary mechanism', and this is what Zuboff builds upon in her theory of the 'information panopticon'. In the capitalist workplace as a consolidated site of disciplinary power, faced with a desire to eliminate 'downtime', computerized management systems are increasingly designed to act as technological watchdogs, while at the same time masking class conflict in claims to objectivity associated with the assumed truth value of hard data. While management has always been preoccupied with meeting output quotas, in the past, output increases might be achieved through the use of close supervision on the shopfloor or by hiring outside time/ study experts to make Taylorist recommendations for speeding up the labour process and directing the bodily motions of the workers.

Today, however, computers allow top management to retrieve information on production operations as they happen, twenty-four hours per day. This information then enables them to make minute and precise time-study analyses of individual workers and to do comparative evaluations of different shifts or even of geographically dispersed plants. Aside from its effect on production workers, this greater degree of vertical visibility has increased that segment of management that can be similarly monitored by those higher up the ladder of hierarchy. Computerized manipulation of what Mark Poster

(1984) terms 'the mode of information' greatly extends the scope of hierarchical surveillance throughout the entire workplace.

The abundance of shopfloor data now available to top management for examination is presently quite formidable. For example, in terms of the factory, CAM (computer-aided manufacturing) as a 'disciplinary mechanism' works in the following way:

> The system links a large central computer to a micro-processor on a machine. When the machine cycles it is recorded in a large central computer. When the machine doesn't produce a part within the allotted time, it is immediately obvious to more than the computer: that information is displayed on a video screen in the foreman's office and recorded on a computer printout. The video screen instructs the foreman to go to the machine and investigate the problem. The printout is also forwarded to higher management for analysis. Every minute of the workers' time is accounted for. The record shows how many minutes he was back from lunch or break, how many minutes the machine was down without explanation and how many breakdown minutes were recorded. Under this system, the foreman no longer decides to discipline the workers. He merely carries out the 'automatic' decisions of the system.
>
> (Moberg, 1979: 13)

As one top-level manager at another workplace has put it:

> From my desk I can look at any plant. They all know what I am looking at. They can see it, too, and how they stack up. . . . A worker under these conditions does not need to be controlled – you simply expect him to respond to the information the same way you do.
>
> (Zuboff, 1986: 35)

In the age of the multinational corporation, it is in this manner that managerial norms of performance evaluation are internalized by the worker, through a surveillance apparatus that extends beyond the individual plant and even beyond national boundaries.

Similarly, in the computerized 'office factory' disciplinary power has been designed into the labour process. Picture if you will the office worker who spends her/his working hours looking at a VDU screen all day long. Upon arrival, she/he finds that his/her schedule for the day has already been typed into the computer, listing specific jobs and time expectations for the completion of each one. In essence then we have 'Taylorism' in a new form, adding potentially harmful microwaves to the heightened level of physical and psychological stress.

Yet it would surely come as no surprise to Foucault to realize that resistance is not eliminated, even under the above conditions. This is not because there is an ontological opposition between power and resistance, but because any power situation includes resistance as part of the relationships that define it. Not only do production workers constantly attempt to counter computer surveillance, but foremen and middle managers do so as well. In relation to the former, Zuboff finds both 'passive resistance' and 'wheeling and dealing' in her case studies of panoptic power (Zuboff, 1988). In fact, surveillance is often seen as a challenge by workers. As one shopfloor operator put it,

'There are only a few standard operating procedures we can cheat on because it can't be traced. When they can't trace it, we feel more freedom' (Zuboff, 1988: 352).

In this regard Zuboff found that workers often claim to be working on a trouble spot, when in fact they might actually be sleeping or reading a book during the hour or so the system is recording them as problem-solving.

In relation to management resistance to surveillance by those above them in the chain of command, one foreman confided to Zuboff,

'If we let the computer run us, we look bad, so we manipulate the computer. We are not trying to cheat anybody or steal. We are trying to deal with the human element involved' (1988: 354).

As another foreman noted,

'It is a vicious cycle. If my boss sees that he did not meet his boss's productivity, can't he change the data too? He wants everybody's printout to look good. How much cheating is going on? Who knows?' (Zuboff, 1988: 354).

In contrast to Harry Braverman's orthodox Marxist analysis of the 'degradation' of the labour process (Braverman, 1974), 'Taylorism' can be alternately read in Foucauldian terms as just another 'chapter in the history of the political technology of the body' (Morris and Patton, 1979: 123). One dimension of capitalism's emphasis on the controlling of human rhythm and motions is the imprinting of power on the body through automation's combination of numerical control and the time and body management of 'robotization' (Noble, 1984).

In relation to the latter, on the car assembly line at General Motors, the technology is designed not simply so that robots and humans can work together, but in order that human work can be subject to machine-pacing in a new way which makes robots and people more interchangeable. As Harley Shaiken notes:

> The pace of the line is determined by the mechanical arms. The worker loses even the limited autonomy of working up or down the line that is present on a conventional system. The robots will be programmed to do their jobs by engineers off the floor, following the example set by numerical control, where machine tools are effectively controlled by the engineering office. The recorded program will then be transferred from the methods laboratory to the floor where authorized personnel can make minor corrections if necessary . . . . If there is a malfunction of the robot, the system is designed so that the mechanical arm can be pulled off the line and a human worker inserted in its place. The human would then be doing a job designed and paced for a robot while the robot itself was being repaired.
>
> (Shaiken, 1984: 173)

These PUMA (Programmable Universal Machine for Assembly) robots described by Shaiken are specifically constructed so as not to be programmable by an operator on the shopfloor. In this way, only the *managerially*-defined work rhythm is embedded in the machinery and, in turn, in the bodies of the workers on the line, through a 'micro-physics of power'. Aside from degrading the labour process à la Braverman, robotization when fully realized ensures surveillance, by seeking to eliminate entirely the human element. Moreover, for those human beings still on the line, one can only speculate on the alarming implications of the increasing use of mandatory urine analysis and drug testing as future forms of organizational surveillance which are based on bodily activities engaged in outside the workplace itself.

NORMALIZING JUDGEMENT

Disciplinary mechanisms for shaping work rhythms have always been contested by workers seeking self-management. Even 'disciplinary society' is never *fully* disciplined. However, building on both Marx and Foucault, David Knights (1987) contends that the subjective dimension of the labour process cannot be merely reduced to an analysis of the 'contested terrain' of labour resistance, à la Richard Edwards (1979), but must come to terms with non-repressive forms of power. Management and labour are not simply pitted against one another in shaping the labour process, but also have a reciprocal relationship of cooperation and mutual dependence that complicates the picture.

Rather than concentrating on the orthodox Marxist focus upon the system of capitalism and how it seeks to subordinate labour, in another study, Knights' Foucauldian approach directs analysis towards the specific disciplinary mechanisms of the labour process. As Knights has put it:

> Whilst not discounting the system of domination within which the labour process is embedded, the approach allows for an analysis of the everyday, immediate practices of production and control, and how workers and managers become positioned as subjects within them. It thereby escapes the dualism of the creative, autonomous subject who, seized upon by capitalist power, is denied the expressive essence of his or her essential being. It also involves a different understanding of control and resistance and how they are frequently implicated in one another, and not just as a result of colonization in more global systems of power.
>
> (1987: 27)

For Knights, it is by an analysis of such commonplace 'normalizing' disciplinary practices as 'managerial accounting' (Knights and Collinson, 1987) that the play of power is revealed, and it is just such 'normalizing judgement' which Foucault has identified with disciplinary institutions. In this sense, 'normalization' involves a variety of 'consent games' (Burawoy, 1979). One could examine 'participatory management' schemes such as quality control circles as 'normalizing' devices which are designed to manufacture consent by gaining the commitment and loyalty of workers to the labour process. As Dwight Hansen of United Auto Workers Local 600 described the Employee Involvement programme at Ford's Dearborn Stamping Plant,

'My first impression was that this was either an introductory psychology class or a football coach's pep talk room. . . . Each session reminded me of an encounter group, with the circle manager being the shrink'. (Hansen, 1981: 8).

In Theory Y management terms, this can be done through what Guillermo Grenier terms 'debureaucratizing control', in which the participation process as it manifests itself in quality circles becomes itself a form of control.

245

Depending more on the managers' skills than on bureaucratic regulations, more on the call to volunteerism than on the appeal of authority, the trick is to make the workers feel that their ideas count and their originality is valued while disguising the expansion of managerial prerogatives into the manipulation area of pop psychology. By depending less on impersonal rules and more on personality characteristics, today's manager effectively debureaucratizes the control mechanism of the firm.

(Grenier, 1988: 131)

In this sense, the human relations approach of 'debureaucratized control' is not, as is typically assumed in the management literature, a departure from Taylorism. Rather it is the extension of Taylor's concern with disrupting class solidarity at the workplace, albeit moving from control over physical movements, into the realm of manipulation of human interaction and consciousness (see also Rosen and Baroudi, in this volume).

The goal here, as far as management is concerned, is not worker self-management, but what Donald Wells terms 'worker self-regulation'. As one supervisor revealed to Wells,

'Even without realizing it, the guys themselves are thinking quality and good housekeeping and meaning it. Their concerns are slowly but ever so surely paralleling our own as managers' (Wells, 1988: 23).

With the concurrent blurring of the lines between worker and management and the supplanting of work group solidarity and union loyalty with the management ideology of productivity that governs the quality circle; control is embedded not just in the machinery of production or surveillance, but in the workers' psyche.

HEGEMONY, TRUTH AND REBELLION

It is in this regard that Andrew Herman (1982) brings Antonio Gramsci's (1971) theory of hegemony to bear on the labour process, detecting a new mode of control which is intertwined with human relations ideology which he terms 'hegemonic control'. However, Foucault's approach would explain hegemonic control somewhat differently: not linking it in orthodox Marxist fashion to ideologies imposed from above on the autonomous worker, but to the relationship between power, knowledge and the body/psyche at the micro-level in constituting that labouring subject in the first place. The two approaches, however, can be viewed as complementary in relation to an analysis of specific practices of the capitalist workplace.

Perhaps at this historical juncture, the charateristics of what Herman terms 'hegemonic control' are becoming a more visible part of the labour process than previously was the case. As the body and increasingly the mind of the worker become disciplined through computerized automation/surveillance and quality control circles, not surprisingly in terms of Foucault's analysis, resistance appears as part of the power equation. Whether in the form of a reflexive 'bad attitude', or a more decidely active attempt to subvert both the physical and mental colonization of the workplace, or even to revolt against work itself and call for its abolition; resistance reveals the dynamics of power in the current ensemble of relations.

Moreover, for Foucault, resistance is not only to be expected, but is desirable. As Rebecca Comay has noted, 'Foucault . . . speaks of *seizing the rules*, wresting them from their guardians and converting them from instruments of oppression into instruments of release' (1986: 114–15). Foucault is no pessimistic prophet of doom and gloom, although orthodox Marxists wedded to a facile 'Enlightenment' notion of progress have often dismissed him (occasionally with hostility) as despairing and nihilistic. Rather, his approach may ultimately be conceived of as being even more materialist than that of Marx. He clearly does not understand power and truth as being external to one another, and so is suspicious of those intellectuals who claim to speak truth to power. Instead, in his analysis he seeks to point to the specific dangers that each particular type of power/ knowledge configuration produces, including Marxism, which he views as an 'Enlightenment' discourse with a reverence for Reason as an emancipatory force. His is, as he puts it, 'a rational critique of rationality' (Foucault in Raulet, 1983: 201). In this sense, Foucault's genealogical approach is not merely critical of *instrumental* reason à la Marxist analysis, but concerns itself with the not always salutary role of Reason itself in relation to the interplay of forces of domination and resistance.

Yet, by this point, it should be clear that the insights gleaned from the Neo-Marxist approach and that of Foucault, when taken together, reveal different dimensions of the labour process, and so offer a deeper analysis than either does separately. In fact, Foucault does not contend that class has no explanatory role to play. A more congenial point of view would be to perceive his investigations into the 'microphysics of power' as unveiling the detailed material /power dimensions of any form of domination, including class. But as Paul Patton puts it, 'that should not be taken to exclude, however, the possibility of an eventual reformulation of the notion of "class domination" itself' (Patton in Morris and Patton, 1979: 127).

Rather than blaming a lack of class consciousness on ideological hegemony, 'disciplinary power', as Foucault conceptualizes it, may be understood as being taken over by capitalist institutions for use as a 'normalizing' instrument towards a particular end or as a means of reinforcing internal power mechanisms through surveillance. In a larger sense, one can speak of a 'disciplinary society' characterized by the 'panoptic' modality of power. However, Foucault's thesis is that the 'technologies of power' are multiple, and must be studied separately rather than thinking of them as reducible to one another, as is the case in the orthodox Marxist emphasis on the mode of production as the root of all domination. As Mark Poster has remarked:

> Once the pretensions of Marxism to serve as a totalizing historical theory are put to rest, it is then possible to assess the value of class analysis for particular historical objects. At this level, Foucault's position does not at all exclude Marxist historical analysis. . . . Each position will be able to illuminate certain aspects of the historical field, and the merits of each position *vis-à-vis* the others are relative, not *absolute*.
>
> (Poster, 1984: 9)

Each, in their unique manifestation, reveals something about the nature of the 'totally administered society'. Even Nicos Poulantzas, whose emphasis was on constructing a Marxist theory of power quite different from Foucault's genealogical approach, conceded that 'Foucault . . . furnishes a materialist analysis of certain institutions of power' (Poulantzas, 1980: 67).

While only a detotalized Marxist analysis of capitalist domination would be compatible with Foucault's approach, it is my contention that the labour process might be the nexus for beginning to explore the creation of such an analysis through an application of Foucault's theory of 'disciplinary power'. In that the labour process is an area of study neglected by Foucault, and perhaps overemphasized by Marxists (particularly those prone to economism), perhaps it can offer a handle on integrating Foucault and Marxism in a new and fruitful way.

For Foucault, to focus on the labour process as constitutive of the subject/producer would be useful but limited, and to inflate this process into a global first cause of all other processes of domination would not be acceptable at all. In Foucault's cosmology, it is the relationship between 'discursive systems' and 'disciplinary mechanisms' of power which leads to the formation of labouring subjects at the workplace. Rather than focusing on ruling-class ideology as leading to 'false consciousness' and consent, instead of class consciousness and proletarian revolution, Foucault's analysis is posited on the premise that the 'technologies of power' by which human beings are made into subjects provide the precondition for consent. Discourses, then, are not ideological representations of class positions as orthodox Marxists would have it, but are themselves loci of power which involve structural power practices, in the form of 'disciplinary technologies'.

For Foucault, it is the relations of 'truth' and 'power' that are constitutive of hegemony, while for the Marxists it is vice versa (Smart in Hoy, 1986: 161). Knowledge, then, is not merely ideological (i.e., repressive), it is also, for Foucault, 'true'. In this regard, Foucault shifts the debate to the micro-level of 'disciplinary power', characterized by normalization and surveillance, thereby rejecting both reductionist base/superstructure assumptions about political economy and the more sophisticated theoretical emphasis on ideological hegemony. Foucault's 'nominalistic' approach conceives of knowledge as always being intertwined with power. In his conception, power is not a substance to be possessed and exerted upon human subjects, but is a complex disciplinary grid which not only constitutes those subjects but is one of the constituent elements of the mode of production in the first place. Moreover, with Foucault's approach, there is no reliance on the Marxist dialectic of progress or the millennial concept of a non-ideological knowledge existing in a classless society where domination disappears and 'true consciousness' emerges. Resistance to domination need not be predicated on a revolutionary outcome.

In offering a simultaneously Foucauldian and anarchist-feminist critique of the Marxist notion of 'false consciousness'. Kathy Ferguson explains:

> Consciousness is not an object, but a process, an ongoing interaction with others, with nature, and with the world in which the individual both creates herself and is created through these connections. Once this is understood, atttempts to judge the contents of consciousness to be true or false must necessarily result in standoffs between liberalism and Marxism. . . . Instead

of judging the content of consciousness, feminist discourse looks to judge its context, distinguishing between situations that are relatively autonomous and those that are relatively manipulative.

(Ferguson, 1984: 178)

Moreover, her approach offers not simply a critique of bourgeois ideology, but also an analysis of bureaucratic discourse as a 'discourse of truth', which is intimately related to the mechanisms of 'disciplinary power'.

Ferguson's embracing of the subversive potential of radical feminism as an example of a Foucauldian 'insurrection of subjugated knowledge' follows from her analysis of bureaucratic discourse. Since gender can be seen both as a 'conditioning' and 'conditioned' relation, one can appropriately speak of the gendered subjectivity of bureaucratic discourse as a 'normalizing' aspect of the labour process which has particular unequal power effects at the workplace. Moreover, the fact that 'insurrection' is not the only female response to gendered inequality has been documented in Aihwa Ong's analysis (1987) of the 'normalization' of peasant women who work in the electronic industry in the Malaysian free trade zones, where management-sponsored beauty contests and cosmetic consumerism workshops are actually situated at the workplace itself.

In these factories, in a very blatant manner, power produces not only the reality of the capitalist workplace, with surveillance taking the form of close supervision, but the constitution of the labouring subject is expanded by capitalist applications of 'normalizing' disciplinary power to include the sexuality and the gender identities of the overwhelmingly female labour force. In response, these Malay factory women alternate between compliance, self-regulation and daily acts of defiance. This mixture of responses can be perceived in what Ong terms the 'ritualized rebellion' of spirit possession on the shopfloor, which evidences both resistance to dehumanization and accommodation to it through the safety-valve function of individual and mass hysteria. In their moments of resistance, these group possessions at the point of production are more akin to what Rick Fantasia has termed in another context, 'cultures of solidarity' (Fantasia, 1988), than, strictly speaking, class or gender consciousness. Though both are Foucauldians, unlike Ong, in her analysis of resistance, Ferguson claims Foucault for anarchism. In this regard, she is not alone. Though Foucault never referrred to himself as an anarchist, and was even a member of the French Communist Party for a few months, theorists as politically diverse as Jameson (1982), Meroquior (1985), Baudrillard (1987), and Deleuze (1988), have detected a strong strain of anti-statism, libertarianism or anarchism in his writings. Foucault's theories simultaneously challenge the centrality of the State and the vanguard party (with its misguided emphasis on conquering State power). As Foucault's English translator, Alan Sheridan contends, 'The Foucauldian geneology is an unmasking of power for the use of those who suffer from it. It is also directed against those who would seize power in their name' (Sheridan, 1980: 221).

CONCLUSION

As Foucault conceives of it, knowledge is always subject to distortion, and the 'will to power' does not cease to exist when vanguardists claim to be acting altruistically on behalf of the working class. Marxist analyses of how capitalism in particular distorts knowledge in relation to the labour process are not invalid as such, but an examination of the 'micro-physics' of power can add some welcome detail and depth to those analyses while, at the same time, placing them in the context of 'disciplinary power'. As Foucault himself notes:

> The important thing is not to attempt some kind of deduction of power starting from its centre and aimed at the discovery of the extent to which it permeates into the base, or the degree to which it reproduces itself down to and including the most molecular elements of society. One must rather conduct an *ascending* analysis of power, starting, that is, from its infinitesimal mechanisms, which each have their own history, their own trajectory, their own techniques and tactics, and then see how these mechanisms of power have been – and continue to be – invested, colonized, utilized, involuted, transformed, displaced, extended, etc., by ever more general mechanisms and by forms of global domination.
>
> (Foucault in Gordon, 1980: 99)

In conclusion, power for Foucault is evidenced in the micro-technologies of such disciplinary mechanisms as 'surveillance' and 'normalization', but this does not mean that more systemic forms of control such as capitalism are merely the projection of individual discipline. Rather, in focusing on the labour process as a disciplinary process, one must be concerned with their interdependence, both with one another and within the discourse of disciplinary power.

REFERENCES

Andrew (1981) *Closing the Iron Cage: The Scientific Management of Work and Leisure* (Montreal: Black Rose).

Arac, J. (1988) *After Foucault: Humanistic Knowledge, Post-modern Challenges* (New Brunswick: Rutgers University Press).

Arney, W. R. (1982) 'What Do You Do With Foucault?' *Dialogue*, Spring.

Baudrillard, J. (1987) *Forget Foucault* (New York: Semiotext(e)).

Black, B. (1987) *The Abolition of Work* (Port Townsend, WA: Loompanics Unlimited).

Bookchin, M. (1978) 'Beyond Neo-Marxism', *Telos*, Summer.

Bouchard, D. (ed.) (1977) *Language, Counter-Memory, Practice: Selected Essays and Interviews* (Ithaca, NY: Cornell University Press).

Bourdieu, P. (1977) *Outline of a Theory of Practice* (Cambridge, MA: Cambridge University Press).

Braverman, H. (1974) *Labour and Monopoly Capital* (New York: Monthly Review Press).

Burawoy, M. (1978) 'Towards a Marxist Theory of the Labour Process: Braverman and Beyond', *Politics and Society*, vol. 8.

Burawoy, M. (1979) *Manufacturing Consent* (Chicago: University of Chicago Press).

Clark, G. and Dear, M. (1984) *State Apparatus* (Winchester, MA: Allen and Unwin).

Clawson, D. (1980) *Bureaucracy and the Labor Process* (New York: Monthly Review Press).

Comay, R. (1986) '. . . Foucault . . .' *Telos*, Spring.

D'Amico, R. (1986) 'Going Relativist', *Telos*, Spring.

Daraki, M. (1986) 'Foucault's Journey to Greece', *Telos*, Spring.

Deleuze, G. (1988) *Foucault* (Minneapolis: University of Minnesota Press).

Dews, P. (1985) *Foucault and the Frankfurt School* (New York: Institute of Contemporary Arts).

Dreyfus, H. and Rabinow, P. (1982) *Michael Foucault: Beyond Structuralism and Hermeneutics* (Chicago: University of Chicago Press).

Edwards, R. (1979) *Contested Terrain* (New York: Basic Books).

Fantasia, R. (1988) *Cultures of Solidarity* (Berkeley, CA: University of California Press).

Ferguson, K. (1983) 'Feminism and Bureaucratic Discourse', *New Political Science*, Spring.

Ferguson, K. (1984) *The Feminist Case Against Bureaucracy* (Philadelphia: Temple University Press).

Finlay, M. (1987) *Powermatics* (New York: Routledge and Kegan Paul).

Fischer, F. and Sirianni, C. (eds) (1984) *Critical Studies in Organization and Bureaucracy* (Philadelphia: Temple University Press).

Foucault, M. (1972) *The Archeology of Knowledge* (New York: Pantheon Books).

Foucault, M. (1973) *Madness and Civilization* (New York: Vintage Books).
Foucault, M. (1975) *The Birth of the Clinic* (New York: Vintage Books).
Foucault, M. (1978) 'Politics and the Study of Discourse', *Ideology and Consciousness*, Spring.
Foucault, M. (1979) *Discipline and Punish* (New York: Vintage Books).
Foucault, M. (1980) *The History of Sexuality*, vol. 1. (New York: Vintage Books).
Foucault, M. (1988) 'Is It Useless To Revolt?', *Philosophy and Social Criticism*, 8, (1).
Foucault, M. (1989) *Foucault Live* (New York: Semiotext(e)).
Foucault, M. (1991) *Remarks on Marx* (New York: Semiotextes).
Freund, P. (1982) *The Civilized Body* (Philadelphia: Temple University press).
Fuentes, A. and Ehrenreich, B. (1983) *Women in the Global Factory* (Boston, MA: South End Press).
Gandal, K. (1986) 'Foucault: Intellectual Work and Politics', *Telos*, Spring.
Garson, B. (1988) *The Electronic Sweatshop*, (New York: Simon and Schuster).
Goldhaber, M. (1980) 'Politics and Technology: Microprocessors and the Prospect of a New Industrial Revolution', *Socialist Review*, July–August.
Gordon, C. (ed.) (1980) *Power/Knowledge; Selected Interviews and Other Writings of Michel Foucault* (New York: Pantheon Books).
Gorz, A. (1985) *Paths to Paradise; On the Liberation from Work* (London: Pluto Press).
Gramsci, A. (1971) *Prison Notebooks*, (New York: International Publishers).
Grenier, G. (1988) *Inhuman Relations: Quality Circles and Anti-Unionism in American Industry* (Philadelphia: Temple University Press).
Habermas, J. (1970) *Toward a Rational Society* (Boston, MA: Beacon Press).
Habermas, J. (1975) *Legitimation Crisis*, (Boston, MA: Beacon Press).
Habermas, J. (1979) *Communication and the Evolution of Society* (Boston, MA: Beacon Press).
Habermas, J. (1981) *The Theory of Communicative Interaction*, vol. 1, (Boston, MA: Beacon Press).
Herman, A. (1982) 'Conceptualizing Control: Domination and Hegemony in the Capitalist Labor Process', *Insurgent Sociologist*, Fall.
Hirschhorn, L. (1983) *Beyond Mechanization* (Boston, MA: MIT Press).
Howard, R. (1981) 'Microshock in the Information Society', *In These Times*, January 21–27.
Howard, R. (1986) *Brave New Workplace* (New York: Viking).
Hoy, D. C. (ed.) (1986) *Foucault: A Critical Reader* (New York: Basil Blackwell).
Jameson, F. (1982) *The Political Unconscious* (Ithaca, NY: Cornell University Press).
Jay, M. (1984) *Marxism and Totality* (Berkeley, CA: University of California Press).
Knights, D. (1987) 'Subjectivity and the Labour Process', Labour Process Conference paper, published in Knights, D. and Willmott, H. (eds) (1990) *Labour Process Theory* (London: Macmillan).
Knights, D. and Collinson, D. (1987) 'Disciplining the Shopfloor', *Accounting Organisations and Society*, 12, (5): 457–77.

Lacláu, E. and Mouffe, C. (1985) *Hegemony and Socialist Strategy*, (New York: Verso).

Macdonald, V. (1985) 'Bureaucracy and Culture: A Conference Report', *Telos*, Summer.

Makower, J. (1981) *Office Hazards: How Your Job Can Make You Sick* (Washington, D. C.: Tilden Press).

Markoff, J. and Stewart, J. (1979) 'An Office on the Head of a Pin', *In These Times*, March 7–13.

Merquior, J. G. (1985) *Foucault*, (Berkeley, CA: University of California Press).

Moberg, D. (1979) 'The Computer Factory and the Robot Worker', *In These Times*, September 19–25.

Morris, M. and Patton, P.(eds) (1979) *Michel Foucault: Power, Truth and Strategy* (Sydney: Ferel Publications).

Noble, D. (1984) *Forces of Production* (New York: Knopf).

Ong, A. (1987) *Spirits of Resistance and Capitalist Discipline: Factory Women in Malaysia* (Albany, NY: State Univ. of New York Press).

Parker, M. (1985) *Inside the Circle: A Union Guide to Quality of Work Life* (Boston, MA: South End Press).

Pasquinelli, C. (1986) 'Power Without the State', *Telos*, Summer.

Poster, M. (1984) *Foucault Reader* (New York: Pantheon Books).

Poulantzas, N. (1980) *State, Power, Socialism* (New York: Verso Press).

Rabinow, P. (ed.) (1984) *The Foucault Reader* (New York: Pantheon Books).

Rajachman, J. (1985) *Michel Foucault: The Freedom of Philosophy* (New York: Columbia University Press).

Raulet, G. (1983) 'Structuralism and Post-Structuralism: An Interview with Michel Foucault', *Telos*, Spring.

Reinecke, I. (1982) *Electronic Illusions* (New York: Penguin Press).

Shaiken, H. (1984) *Work Transformed: Automation and Labor in the Computer Age* (New York: Holt, Rinehart and Winston).

Sheridan, A. (1980) *Michel Foucault: The Will to Truth* (London: Tavistock Publishers).

Smart, B. (1983) *Foucault, Marxism and Critique* (New York: Routledge, Kegan and Paul).

Taylor, C. (1984) 'Foucault on Freedom and Truth', *Political Theory*, 2.

Taylor, C. (1985) *Michel Foucault* (New York: Methuen).

Weber, M. (1947) *The Theory of Social and Economic Organization*, ed. and intro. by Talcolt Parsons (New York: Free Press).

Wells, D. (1987) *Empty Promises: Quality of Working Life Programs and the Labor Movement* (New York: Monthly Review Press).

West, C. (1989) *The American Evasion of Philosophy: A Geneology of Pragmatism* (Madison, Wisconsin: University of Wisconsin Press).

White, S. (1986) 'Foucault's Challenge to Critical Theory', *American Political Science Review*, 80 (2).

Wolin, R. (1986) 'Foucault's Aesthetic Decisionism', *Telos*, Spring.

Zimbalist, A. (ed.) (1979) *Case Studies in the Labor Process* (New York: Monthly Review Press).

Zuboff, S. (1988) *In the Age of the Smart Machine: The Future of Work and Power* (New York: Basic Books).

INDEX

US: foreign policy 52;
  protectionism 50, 52
wage relation 99–100
wages *see* pay
Warde, A. 97–113
Weber, M. 116, 141, 217, 230, 237
welfare provision 99–100, 103, 109,
  112
white-collar *see* clerical
wildcat strikes by Appalachian
  miners 34, 57
will to power 251
Willis, P. 7, 10, 26, 28, 55, 58, 72,
  117
Willmott, H. 1–18, 115, 116, 119,
  120, 140, 142, 143, 149, 150, 188
women: Appalachian coal industry
  36; and class solidarity 56–7;
  endurance 80–1, 85; intellectual
  work 73; pay 70; physical
  inferiority 80–1; printing

industry 72–90; reproductive role
  of 68; resistance 70; ritualized
  rebellion 250; subordination 67;
  as tools in degrading work 70,
  75; typing skills 79
'women's work' 73, 77–9
Wood, S. 1, 2, 3, 4, 7, 9, 69, 118,
  149, 150, 151, 155
work avoidance 130, 131–2, 133,
  136, 137, 138, 141
work ethic 116
work measurement 132–3
working to rule 132, 154, 155
workload *see* pressure of work
workplace relations and external
  politics 98, 100, 103
works councils 206

Yarrow, M. 25–63

Zuboff, S. 240, 241, 242, 243